BENEATH
THE SEVEN
SEAS

Thames & Hudson

Edited by George F. Bass

BENEATH THE SEVEN SEAS

Adventures with the Institute
of Nautical Archaeology

With 433 illustrations, 410 in color

Half-title: *A Canaanite gold pectoral from the Uluburun shipwreck, Turkey.*

Title-page: *Anchor from the probable wreck of the* Glamis, *built in Dundee, Scotland, in 1876 and lost on Grand Cayman's East End in 1913.*

Contents pages: *Canaanite gold jewelry, including a fertility goddess, from the Uluburun shipwreck; replicas of iron javelin heads from the Kyrenia ship, Cyprus; Byzantine gold coins from the 7th-century Yassıada shipwreck, Turkey; bronze lion from the Shinan wreck, Korea; gold earring from the Pepper Wreck, Portugal; Chinese porcelain from the Sadana Island wreck in Egypt; door handle from* Cleopatra's Barge, *Hawaii; pewter tableware from Port Royal, Jamaica.*

First published in 2005 in hardcover in the United States of America by
Thames & Hudson Inc., 500 Fifth Avenue, New York, New York 10110

thamesandhudsonusa.com

Library of Congress Catalog Card Number 2005900862

ISBN-13: 978-0-500-05136-8
ISBN-10: 0-500-05136-4

Printed and bound by Tien Wah Press Pte Ltd, Singapore

Contents

THE OLDEST WRECKS

ANCIENT GREEK WRECKS

ROMAN AND BYZANTINE WRECKS

MEDIEVAL AND RENAISSANCE WRECKS

SEVENTEENTH-CENTURY WRECKS

EIGHTEENTH-CENTURY WRECKS

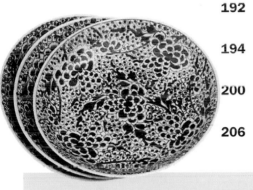

WRECKS OF MODERN TIMES

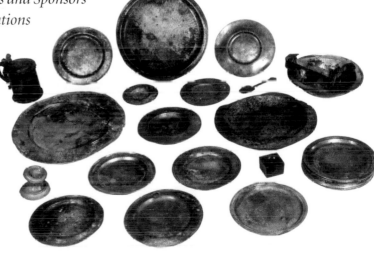

Contributors

GEORGE F. BASS was the first person to excavate an ancient shipwreck in its entirety on the sea bed. Since 1960 he has excavated Bronze Age, Classical Greek, and Byzantine wrecks. Founder of the Institute of Nautical Archaeology (INA), he is now Distinguished Professor Emeritus at Texas A&M University. He has been awarded the Archaeological Institute of America's Gold Medal for Distinguished Archaeological Achievement, an Explorers Club Lowell Thomas Award, a National Geographic Society La Gorce Gold Medal and the Society's Centennial Award, the J.C. Harrington Medal from The Society for Historical Archaeology, and honorary doctorates by Boğaziçi University in Istanbul and the University of Liverpool. In 2002 President George W. Bush presented him with the National Medal of Science. His books include *Archaeology Under Water*, *A History of Seafaring Based on Underwater Archaeology*, and *Ships and Shipwrecks of the Americas*, all published by Thames & Hudson.

J. BARTO ARNOLD III is the director of the Denbigh Shipwreck Project, and a staff member of the Institute of Nautical Archaeology at Texas A&M University. In over 20 years as Texas State Marine Archaeologist his work has included the Padre Island shipwrecks of 1554 and French Explorer La Salle's ship *La Belle*. He has served as secretary-treasurer of the Society of Professional Archeologists, chairman of the Advisory Council on Underwater Archaeology, and president of the Society for Historical Archaeology.

ROBERT D. BALLARD is a Professor of Oceanography and Director of the Institute for Archaeological Oceanography at the University of Rhode Island's Graduate School of Oceanography. His major research interests are archaeological oceanography, ocean exploration, educational outreach, and the development of tele-presence technologies needed to implement them. His archaeological research focuses on the deep-water trade routes of the Mediterranean and Black Seas. His publications in archaeological oceanography have appeared in *Deep-Sea Research* (2000), the *American Journal of Archaeology* (2001 and 2002), and the *International Journal of Nautical Archaeology* (2004).

JOHN D. BROADWATER is Program Manager for the Maritime Heritage Program at the National Oceanic and Atmospheric Administration. During the 1980s he directed the excavation of an 18th-century British merchant vessel in Virginia, and from 1998 to 2002 he was chief scientist for expeditions that mapped the Civil War ironclad USS *Monitor* and recovered its engine and gun turret. Dr Broadwater has written numerous book chapters and articles and is working on a book on the Yorktown Shipwreck Project.

DEBORAH CARLSON is Assistant Professor of Nautical Archaeology at Texas A&M University. As a classical archaeologist, she has participated in excavations on land and under water in Italy, Greece, and Turkey. Her research interests embrace all aspects of Greek and Roman seafaring, including transport amphoras, ancient harbors, and maritime ritual. Dr Carlson is currently preparing the final publication of the Tektaş Burnu shipwreck and co-authoring, with Elizabeth Greene, a book on shipwrecks and maritime trade in the ancient world.

FILIPE CASTRO, with degrees in Civil Engineering and Business Administration, first became involved in nautical archaeology as an amateur, and was part of the team that in 1997 created the Portuguese state agency for nautical archaeology. In 2001 he received a PhD in Anthropology from Texas A&M University, where he now teaches in the Nautical Archaeology Program. He has directed or participated in the excavation of shipwrecks from the period of European maritime expansion, and published *A Nau de Portugal* and *The Pepper Wreck*. Currently he is writing a book about 16th-century Iberian ships.

WILLIAM H. CHARLTON JR is a retired US Marine Corps officer who earned his Master of Arts degree in Nautical Archaeology at Texas A&M University in 1996. He has served as Divemaster for various INA shipwreck excavations in Turkey and Israel, and as the Diving Safety Officer for the Institute for over ten years. While working on the Kinneret Boat project, he hand-built the model that is now displayed alongside the ancient boat in the Yigal Allon Museum at Kibbutz Ginosar, Israel.

ARTHUR COHN is co-founder and Executive Director of the Lake Champlain Maritime Museum. After a short career in law, he became a professional diver. For three decades he has worked on the documentation, management and public policy issues of underwater cultural resources. Art, who served as a US State Department Delegate for the development of the UNESCO Treaty for the Protection of Underwater Cultural Heritage, has received honorary doctorates from the University of Vermont (1996) and Middlebury College (2004). He recently published *Lake Champlain's Sailing Canal Boats* (2003).

KEVIN CRISMAN is an Associate Professor in the Nautical Archaeology Graduate Program at Texas A&M University. He has specialized in ships, seafaring and the maritime world from 1400 to 1900, with a focus on the inland waters of North America. Since 1980 he has studied a wide variety of steam, sail, canal, and naval vessels. Dr Crisman's publications include books on the War of 1812 brig *Eagle* and horse-propelled ferryboats of the 19th century.

DONALD A. FREY, a former professor of physics, has been with INA from its beginning. Now its Vice President, he served as INA's second President. A director of past INA surveys, with a special interest in remote sensing, Dr Frey is also INA's photographer and videographer, with results seen in books, articles, and on television around the world. A resident of Turkey since 1974, he also has a special interest in foreign languages.

JEREMY GREEN has been Head of the Department of Maritime Archaeology at the Western Australian Maritime Museum since its establishment in 1971. In 1996 he was appointed head of the Australian National Centre for Excellence in Maritime Archaeology. He helped to found the Australasian Institute for Maritime Archaeology and has been editor of the Institute's *Bulletin* since 1977. He is a fellow of the Australian Academy of the Humanities, Research Associate with INA, advisory editor for the *International Journal of Nautical Archaeology*, and adjunct associate professor at Curtin University of Technology, Perth, and James Cook University, Townsville.

ELIZABETH GREENE is a Mellon Postdoctoral Fellow in the Department of Classical Studies at Wellesley College. Her primary research interests lie in Archaic Greek travel, transport, and exchange as viewed through material and literary culture. To this end, she has participated in and directed shipwreck excavations and surveys throughout the Mediterranean: in Greece, Albania, Egypt, and Turkey. Along with the publication of the Pabuç Burnu shipwreck, Dr Greene is co-authoring, with Deborah Carlson, a book on shipwrecks and maritime trade in the ancient world.

NERGİS GÜNSENİN is Professor at Istanbul University's Vocational School of Technical Sciences, and chair of its Underwater Technology Program. Her research interests concern late Byzantine amphoras, their kiln areas, and the monastic wine commerce in the Sea of Marmara, where she has conducted land and underwater surveys and excavated an 11th-century amphora kiln. She has participated in underwater excavations elsewhere in Europe, and published about forty articles. Dr Günsenin is currently working on the publication of her Çamaltı Burnu I wreck excavation.

JEROME LYNN HALL is Assistant Professor of Anthropology at the University of San Diego. He continues to excavate the Monte Cristi "Pipe Wreck" and is working on two books chronicling the story of the excavation and finds. Dr Hall earlier served as the Director of the Office for Underwater Archaeology in Puerto Rico, and then as INA President. His special interest is European – and specifically Dutch – expansion in the New World during the 17th century.

DONNY L. HAMILTON is Professor in the Nautical Archaeology Program at Texas A&M University where he holds the George T. & Gladys H. Abell Chair in Nautical Archaeology and the Yamini Family Chair in Liberal Arts. He is also the President of INA and the Director of the Conservation Research Laboratory. His research centers on artifact conservation and the underwater excavation of Port Royal, Jamaica. His publications include *Conservation of Metal Artifacts from Underwater Sites* (1976) and *Basic Methods of Conserving Underwater Archaeological Material Culture* (1996).

FRED HOCKER is the Director of *Vasa* Research for the National Maritime Museums of Sweden. He was formerly a research director at the National Museum of Denmark and Yamini Associate Professor of Nautical Archaeology at Texas A&M University. He has excavated, recorded and reconstructed shipwrecks in North America, Turkey, the Netherlands, and Scandinavia, on land, under water and under ice. His research interests concentrate on maritime economics and shipbuilding in the Middle Ages and Renaissance. Dr Hocker's publications include *The Philosophy of Shipbuilding* (2004) with Cheryl Ward.

PAUL F. JOHNSTON is Curator of Maritime History at the Smithsonian Institution's National Museum of American History in Washington, DC. He has worked on shipwrecks in the Mediterranean and Baltic Seas, the Atlantic, Pacific and Indian Oceans, the Great Lakes and some great little lakes, rivers and harbors. Dr Johnston has around 100 publications, including seven books, and is now completing a book on the Royal Yacht of Hawaiian King Kamehameha II. He also rides and writes about motorcycles.

SUSAN WOMER KATZEV, a graduate of Swarthmore College, trained as a sculptor. Starting in 1961 she was diving artist for excavations of the 7th- and 5th-century AD merchantmen off Yassıada, Turkey, where she mapped remains on the sea bed and made artifact drawings for publications. Her husband Michael L. Katzev directed the Kyrenia Ship's excavation and preservation. Since his death in 2001, Susan has headed the Kyrenia Ship Project, coordinating the work of ten scholars to complete publication of that excavation.

MARGARET LESHIKAR-DENTON is Archaeologist for the Cayman Islands National Museum. As a Research Associate with INA, she has worked in the Caribbean, Mexico, the United States, Spain and Turkey. Her publications focus upon Caribbean shipwrecks. She is a member of the ICOMOS International Committee on Underwater Cultural Heritage and the Advisory Council on Underwater Archaeology, and serves as Chair of the Society for Historical Archaeology UNESCO Committee. Her doctorate is from Texas A&M University.

ROBERT S. NEYLAND is the Head of the Underwater Archaeology Branch of the Department of the Navy. He is Project Director for raising and conserving the Confederate submarine *H.L. Hunley*, a project that has earned prestigious national awards. Dr Neyland has worked on shipwrecks in the Mediterranean, the Netherlands, the Caribbean and North America. Recent field projects include US Navy ships from the anti-slavery patrol, World War II wrecks from D-Day, and American Revolutionary War naval shipwrecks.

BRETT PHANEUF is a doctoral student in the Department of Oceanography at Texas A&M University, and a founding member of the program in Archaeological Oceanography, launched in the fall of 2005. He has directed numerous research projects for INA in Turkey, Morocco, Italy, France, and the United States, and also founded ProMare, Inc., a non-profit corporation dedicated to marine research in the deep ocean.

ROBIN PIERCY is an INA Field Staff Member in Bodrum, Turkey. He has participated in numerous excavations underwater in both the Mediterranean and North America. His research interests include waterlogged wood conservation, and wooden hull restoration and display. He is currently publishing the results of his excavation in Mombasa Harbor, Kenya, of the wrecked Portuguese frigate *Santo Antonio de Tanna*.

CEMAL PULAK is an Associate Professor in the Nautical Archaeology Program at Texas A&M University and INA's Vice President for Turkey, where he has excavated shipwrecks, directed underwater surveys, and currently is involved with the publication of the 14th-century BC Uluburun wreck. With post-graduate degrees in both mechanical engineering and archaeology, Dr Pulak's research interests include various aspects of nautical archeology, ancient ship construction, and Bronze Age maritime trade. He has published numerous scientific and popular articles.

DAVID C. SWITZER is Emeritus Professor of History and Distinguished Teacher at Plymouth State University, Plymouth, New Hampshire. Prior to excavating the *Defence*, he gained nautical archaeology experience in Turkey and Scotland. In addition to being the state nautical archaeologist, he has been an archaeologist and a director of the excavation and recovery of the bow section of a Maine-built clipper ship in the Falklands Islands, now on exhibit at the Maine Maritime Museum, and the subject of the award-winning book *Snow Squall: The Last American Clipper Ship* (2001), co-authored with Nicholas Dean.

FREDERICK VAN DOORNINCK is Emeritus Professor of Nautical Archaeology at Texas A&M University. In Turkey, he was assistant director of the Byzantine shipwreck excavations at Yassıada, co-director of the Byzantine shipwreck excavation at Serçe Limanı, and has been a major contributor to their publication. His research interests have included the manufacture, use and standardization of Byzantine amphoras and anchors, Byzantine ship construction, and the history of the waterline ram.

SHELLEY WACHSMANN is Meadows Professor of Biblical Archaeology in Texas A&M University's Nautical Archaeology Program. From 1976 to 1989 he served as Inspector of Underwater Antiquities in the Israel Department of Antiquities and Museums and in 1986 he excavated the Galilee (Kinneret) Boat. Dr Wachsmann has also worked in Portugal, Greece and Egypt, and has published numerous scholarly and popular articles and four books, the latest being *Seagoing Ships and Seamanship in the Bronze Age Levant* (1998). His main research interests are seafaring in biblical times, deep-submergence archaeology and Near Eastern archery.

CHERYL WARD teaches in the Department of Anthropology at Florida State University. Her research interests include maritime archaeology and archaeobotany in the Indian Ocean and eastern Mediterranean spheres, and she currently directs an underwater archaeological survey of harbors and anchorages used by the pirates of Roman Rough Cilicia. Among her publications are *Sacred and Secular: Ancient Egyptian Hull Construction* (2000) and *The Philosophy of Shipbuilding* (2004) with Fred Hocker.

Introduction: Reclaiming Lost History from Beneath the Seven Seas

GEORGE F. BASS

Before there were farmers or shepherds, there were seafarers. Before people could make pottery or work metals, before they even lived in houses, they could cross expanses of open water. As far back as 40,000 years ago they reached and populated the continent of Australia by watercraft. A new land cannot be peopled by just two or three individuals washed ashore by accident; a deliberate population movement is necessary.

In the Mediterranean 11,000 years ago, cave dwellers made round trips from the Greek mainland to the island of Melos, where they collected obsidian, the volcanic glass that they fashioned into blades and scrapers. Mariners colonized the large Mediterranean islands of Crete and Cyprus some 8,000 years ago.

Without seafarers, then, there would have been no Minoan civilization. Without river craft the great Egyptian pyramids could not have been built of the massive stones quarried far up the Nile. Without great merchant vessels, neither Greece nor Rome, dependent on grain from the Black Sea and North Africa, could have prospered. And without rowed warships, the Greeks could not have turned the tide against invading Persians in the famed sea battle at Salamis in 480 BC.

Try to imagine a history of the world without the ships, boats, and mariners that followed: Viking longboats, Chinese junks, Vasco da Gama, Columbus, Magellan, the Spanish Armada, kayaks, Arab dhows, the *Mayflower*, birch-bark canoes, East Indiamen, Trafalgar, steamboats, ironclads, clipper ships, *Titanic*, *Lusitania*, U-boats, aircraft carriers…the list goes on. Entire continents have been discovered, re-discovered, colonized, supplied, invaded, and defended by sea. D-Day and the Battle of Midway, turning points in the European and Pacific theaters of World War II, were both dependent on seagoing vessels designed for warfare. Even now, to fuel our cars and factories, we are dependent on oil shipped around the world in giant tankers.

There can be no meaningful study of the past, therefore, without some knowledge of the history of the watercraft that helped shape our globe as we know it.

There is another, equally important reason to study watercraft from the earliest times. Everything ever made by humans has been transported at one time or another by water, from tiny obsidian blades to the marble elements of great temples and churches. Further, when any vessel sinks, it takes with it to the bottom, except for those objects that float away, everything used or carried on that vessel during a finite moment of time. In freshwater rivers or lakes, or even on the ocean bed if quickly covered by protective sediment, all of this material, both organic and inorganic, is preserved – comparable to the preservation found in frozen northern lands or dry desert sands.

Above **The Bodrum Museum of Underwater Archaeology, which displays the results of INA research in the 15th-century Castle of the Knights of St John, is the most visited archaeological museum in Turkey. Bodrum sponge divers have guided INA archaeologists to more than a hundred ancient shipwrecks.**

Right **INA's Research Center in Bodrum comprises five buildings, including this central neo-Ottoman office building. The other buildings are a dormitory, a library, a conservation laboratory, and a computer center.**

If a shipwreck can be dated – by historical records, tree-rings, radiocarbon, or coins or inscriptions in the wreck – its contents, except for the rare antiquity or heirloom that might have been on board, can be dated. The century-by-century and even decade-by-decade study of shipwrecks, therefore, will ultimately provide the most accurate and complete story of material remains ranging from weapons and tools to ceramics and glass to games and musical instruments.

This book describes shipwreck excavations by an institute devoted to the archaeological study of the history of ships, the Institute of Nautical Archaeology, or INA. Not all of the excavations were sponsored by INA, but all were conducted by members of INA's extended family, who will be introduced, in turn, in the history that follows. Some of the projects were started under the aegis of the University of Pennsylvania Museum, but in each case were completed by INA. We must, however, start at the beginning:

Pioneers of Shipwreck Archaeology

The wealth of archaeological material to be found under water has long been known. For centuries after the Greek city of Helike sank into the Gulf of Corinth during an earthquake in the 4th century BC, visitors wrote of the large bronze statue and other relics they could still see beneath the waves. In the first half of the 16th century, a diver gazed in wonder through the crystal plate in his wooden helmet at a giant Roman pleasure barge lying on the bottom of Italy's Lake Nemi. That was only a hint of what was to follow. To date, for example, most extant Greek bronze statues in the world's museums have come from the sea, netted by fishermen or salvaged by helmeted sponge-divers in the 19th and 20th centuries, and found more recently by sport divers wearing scuba (self-contained underwater breathing apparatus). Statues that remained on land were mostly scrapped and melted down for other uses.

It was the development of reliable, easily maintained scuba by Jacques-Yves Cousteau and Emile Gagnan in France in the 1940s that gave divers the necessary mobility to do more than salvage artifacts. In the 1950s, serious studies of Roman shipwrecks were made by Italian and French teams off their own shores, and by the French off Tunisia. Their projects introduced some of the basic items of equipment still used in shipwreck excavations: metal or nylon grids to divide wreck sites into coherent squares to allow controlled excavation and to aid mapping; vertical pipes, called airlifts, that suck up and discharge sediment like underwater vacuum cleaners;

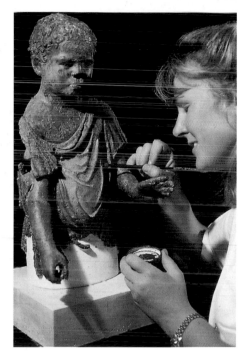

Above **Conservator Jane Pannell Haldane treats the bronze statue of a tunic-clad African youth netted by Bodrum sponge-dragger Mehmet Imbat near Yalıkavak, Turkey. The discovery led to pioneering uses of sonar and submersibles in the search for the ancient wreck that carried it and at least two other netted bronzes.**

Opposite **In his quest for ancient wrecks in 1958 and 1959, Peter Throckmorton dived with helmeted Turkish sponge divers who had stumbled on and remembered dozens of cargoes lost since antiquity.**

Right **By the mid-1960s, the University of Pennsylvania archaeologists who later founded INA were mapping sites with stereo photographs taken from the submersible *Asherah*, decompressing in a submerged chamber (upper right), and using an underwater telephone booth and various types of metal detectors, lifting balloons, and airlifts.**

large balloons that, once attached to a heavy object on the sea floor and inflated, can buoy the object to the surface; underwater cameras for recording sites; and underwater television to monitor the work from the surface.

These pioneering efforts culminated in 1960 in an explosion of underwater archaeological projects in Europe, Asia, and North America. Diving archaeologists were planning construction of a coffer dam around five Viking ships they had found in Roskilde Fjord, Denmark, so that the water could be pumped away from the vessels before excavation. Elsewhere in Scandinavia, divers were preparing to raise the almost perfectly preserved royal Swedish warship *Vasa*, which had heeled over and sunk in Stockholm Harbor almost immediately after being launched in 1628.

In North America, the Civil War ironclad *Cairo* was being raised from the Yazoo River in Mississippi, while farther north, in the state of New York, the first colonial bateaux seen in modern times were raised from Lake George. Still farther north, on the Canadian border, "white water" archaeologists began searching beneath dangerous rapids for artifacts spilled from overturned fur-traders' canoes.

In all but the last case, the goal was to study a vessel in open air, as in a terrestrial excavation, either by pumping the water away from it, as from the Roskilde cofferdam, or by taking it completely out of the water.

Archaeologists Take the Plunge

On the Asian side of Turkey, in 1960, the approach to a shipwreck was different. American photojournalist Peter Throckmorton had lived on Turkish sponge boats in 1958 and 1959, asking the divers to show him any ancient remains they had seen on the sea floor. Among the wrecks Peter recorded was the oldest then known, a Bronze Age wreck from about 1200 BC. It was Peter's idea that wrecks could and should be excavated as carefully on the seabed as terrestrial sites are excavated on land. He wrote to Professor Rodney Young at the University of Pennsylvania Museum, asking if the Museum would sponsor an excavation of the wreck. He knew that Young was already excavating in Turkey, at Gordion, capital of King Midas of the golden touch. By chance I had worked as a student assistant at Gordion in 1957. By chance I was one of Professor Young's doctoral students in 1959, freshly returned from being the officer in charge of a small US Army signal unit in post-war Korea. By chance my major interest was the Mediterranean Bronze Age. And by chance I had read everything on diving I could get my hands on since I was a child, although I never dreamed that I, myself, would dive.

In retrospect, it seems it was almost fated that Professor Young asked me if I would learn to dive to be the archaeologist for Peter's proposed excavation of the Bronze Age shipwreck. After six weeks of a ten-week YMCA diving course, I headed with Peter Throckmorton for Turkey, to begin working 28 m (92 ft) deep off Cape Gelidonya. Elsewhere in this book, I describe what followed, but it resulted in the first complete excavation of an ancient shipwreck on the seabed, and the first directed by a diving archaeologist.

This set the stage for much that went after. Professional divers, wanting to keep a monopoly on underwater work, even after 1960 wrote that archaeologists could never learn to dive well enough to accomplish anything useful at depth. That notion was put firmly to rest between 1984 and 1994, when archaeologists and archaeology

Below **One diver cleans freshly harvested sponges while another tends a companion searching for sponges far below the 10-m (33-ft)** *Mandalinçi,* **on which Peter Throckmorton lived during the summer of 1958, and which served as a diving platform during the 1960 excavation of the Cape Gelidonya shipwreck.**

students made the majority of 22,500 dives to between 44 m (145 ft) and 61 m (200 ft) in order to excavate another Bronze Age shipwreck, at Uluburun, Turkey. It was the deepest large-scale diving project ever conducted with normal scuba, made possible by extreme safety measures that could not be duplicated by weekend avocational divers, who should not dive to such depths.

The year 1960 was the only time I would ever work with Peter Throckmorton, who went on to find Bronze Age wrecks in Greece, excavate Roman and Byzantine wrecks in Italy, and pioneer the study of the last surviving clipper ships, in the Falkland Islands. He also saved from a shipyard in Greece the disintegrating 19th-century sailing ship *Elissa*, now restored as a major tourist attraction in Galveston, Texas.

I did not intend to continue diving. I was ready to return to dry land archaeology, *real* archaeology. At the end of the 1960 excavation, however, Claude Duthuit, a French diver brought to Cape Gelidonya by Peter, said that we had started something good together, and that I, with the archaeological credentials to make it possible, ought to continue this promising field of research just a bit longer.

So I returned to Turkey in 1961 with Claude and a group of mostly novice divers, including fellow University of Pennsylvania graduate Frederick van Doorninck, Boston University undergraduate David Owen, and Swarthmore College undergraduate Susan Womer who would draw our artifacts. For four summers at Yassıada we excavated a 7th-century Byzantine wreck about 39 m (129 ft) deep, also found by Peter Throckmorton, constantly improving techniques of mapping, airlifting, and conservation. During those years we were joined by another University of Pennsylvania archaeology student, Michael Katzev. More than a decade later, all of these people played pivotal roles in the creation of the Institute of Nautical Archaeology.

In the 1980s, several of the original excavators of the Cape Gelidonya shipwreck returned to the site annually and, with sophisticated metal detectors and motorized underwater scooters, located and uncovered many artifacts undetected during their 1960 excavation.

Fred van Doorninck, after his initial excavation campaign at Yassıada, asked if he could undertake a study of the broken bits of wood we were recording and raising. For the following three summers, and several years thereafter, he slowly made sense of what sometimes seemed little more than kindling, eventually writing his doctoral dissertation on a reconstruction of the ship and its anchors, the first reconstruction of a wrecked ship excavated on the seabed. Mediterranean hulls became as exciting as their contents.

In 1963, J. Richard (Dick) Steffy, an electrical engineer with a serious interest in ship modeling, read an article I wrote for *National Geographic* on the Byzantine wreck, and asked if he could build a series of research models of it. I put him in touch with van Doorninck, beginning a cooperation that continues to this day.

Meanwhile, I was spending perhaps more time on engineering than archaeology, developing a method of mapping seabed remains in three dimensions with stereo-photography, first suggested by Claude at Cape Gelidonya, and ordering construction of the first commercially built submersible for any field of research in the United States. Before launching the two-person *Asherah*, named for a Phoenician sea goddess, I obtained on loan from the US Navy a 20-m (66-ft) steel-hulled vessel, *Virazon*, to tend the little sub, and arranged for it to be shipped to the Mediterranean without charge as deck cargo. That year, 1964, I received my doctorate in Classical Archaeology and joined the faculty of the University of Pennsylvania, where I soon offered a graduate seminar on ancient seafaring. Annually I invited Dick Steffy to lecture on what he was learning from building research models of ancient hulls we were excavating.

Above **Donald Rosencrantz slides a camera, hanging vertically on gimbals, along a horizontal bar above the 7th-century Byzantine shipwreck at Yassıada, Turkey. He takes pictures at predetermined points marked on the bar, providing pairs of stereo photographs from which accurate three-dimensional plans can be made.**

Right **INA's *Virazon*, built in 1954 as a US Army T-boat, was first taken to Turkey for archaeological work in 1964. Now fitted out with a deeper keel and all necessary equipment for major underwater projects, including a double-lock recompression chamber, this 20-m (66-ft) vessel annually serves both excavations and surveys.**

Above **A treacherous reef running out from Yassıada, literally "Flat Island" in Turkish, has sunk nearly a dozen ships from Roman times until 1993, when a modern freighter went down. Excavating remains of these ships, some lying just below the wooden diving barge, the author spent seven summers in a camp established on the barren rock. The 20-m (66-ft) trawler *Kardeşler*, also anchored off shore, served INA's initial 1973 survey.**

New Tools for Undersea Archaeology

During our next excavation, in 1967 and 1969, a wreck from the late 4th or early 5th century AD at Yassıada, Fred and I were obsessed with improving seabed efficiency. Our greatest enemy was time. To understand why, one must understand decompression sickness, or the bends.

When a diver descends, the weight, or pressure, of the water on his or her body would soon crush the diver's lungs, ears, sinuses, or other air-filled cavity unless the diver is breathing air at a pressure equal to that of the surrounding water. Diving equipment provides such pressurized air, whether through a hose to an air compressor on the surface or through a regulator attached to a tank of compressed air on the diver's back. There is, however, a limit beyond which divers cannot descend while breathing compressed air. Nitrogen, which comprises 80 percent of air, produces an increasingly narcotic effect as pressure increases when the diver goes deeper. A rule of thumb is that every additional 15 m (50 ft) of depth is like drinking another gin martini, a major reason sport divers should not try to imitate the deep work mentioned above. In addition, oxygen, the other 20 percent of air, becomes increasingly toxic under pressure. Nevertheless, although slightly tipsy from narcosis, we regularly work between 30 m (99 ft) and 40 m (132 ft) deep.

While working at depth, our bodies absorb the compressed air we breathe. At reasonable depths, this does not present a problem – as long as we remain at depth, under pressure. If one ascends too rapidly at the end of a dive, however, the gas in the diver's body can come out of solution and form bubbles, just as the sudden release of pressure on champagne causes it to bubble. Nitrogen bubbles in one's blood can block its flow, leading to paralysis or death.

To avoid this diver's illness, called the bends, the diver must ascend in stages, pausing to breathe off the pressurized air. This is called decompressing. According to tables designed by diving physiologists, the deeper the dive, and the longer the dive, the longer must be the decompression. In the 1960s, we sometimes worked for 40 minutes at a depth of 40 m (132 ft), requiring extremely long, twice daily decompression stops. To avoid the cold and boredom (although we soon learned that paperback books can last for weeks under water without disintegrating), I designed a submersible decompression chamber into which the divers could swim and let themselves up 3 m (10 ft) at a time, while sitting in dry comfort. (Today, on the advice of specialists in hyperbaric medicine, we never work at depth for more than 20 minutes, decompressing with tables designed by Richard Vann of Duke University, which call for us to switch from air to pure oxygen during decompression to flush the nitrogen out of our bodies more quickly.)

To provide a safety refuge in case of equipment failure and a place from which to speak to the surface by telephone, Michael Katzev and Susan Womer, by now Mr and Mrs Katzev, designed what we call an "underwater telephone booth," an air-filled Plexiglas dome into which divers can swim and stand, dry above their shoulders, in case of equipment failure.

At this time we also experimented with methods of finding wrecks deeper than we could dive. The catalyst for building *Asherah* was a sponge-dragger's netting, in 1963, of the bronze statue of a tunic-clad African youth at a depth of 85 m (280 ft), beyond the limits of compressed-air diving. Limited visibility through our submersible's small ports, however, made her unsuitable for open water searches. Thus, although we knew the general area where the statue had been caught, we wanted to pinpoint the wreck before sending *Asherah* down. Volunteer engineer Donald Rosencrantz, who had helped design *Asherah* and who had perfected a method of accurately mapping the seabed from the sub by stereo-photography, organized a search with side-scan sonar, although no ancient shipwreck had been found by sonar. In just one morning a team from the Scripps Institution of Oceanography spotted a wreck in the area with its sonar, a target verified by *Asherah*.

During those early days we also used a towed, one-person submersible called a Towvane, shaped like an early Mercury space capsule. The pilot, by depressing or raising the leading edges of wings on the capsule's sides, could make it descend or ascend. After one of our team found himself being bounced upside down over the seabed at a depth of around 90 m (300 ft), we decided this was not the safest method for finding wrecks!

Another device tested in our research in Turkey in the 1960s was a magnetometer – an instrument capable of detecting iron – brought to us by Englishman Jeremy Green, who describes some of his own research in these pages.

Above right **The single occupant of the Towvane, seen being lowered over the side of a Turkish trawler, planed downward by angling the vanes or wings while being towed.**

Right **INA's underwater telephone booths, air-filled acrylic hemispheres, allow divers to remove their mouth pieces and, dry from their chests up, talk to one another or, via cable, to the surface, or to change their scuba in case of equipment failure.**

Left **Maurice McGehee of the Scripps Institute of Oceanography, examines the paper print-out of a sonar that in a single morning revealed the position of an ancient shipwreck, positively identified from the submersible *Asherah*, in the center of the area being searched for the wreck that yielded the African youth and two other statues.**

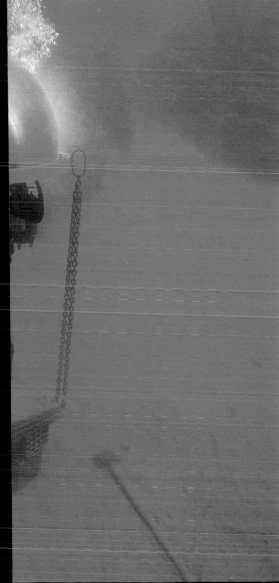

Nautical Archaeology Comes of Age

When invited to undertake a survey for ancient shipwrecks by the government of Cyprus, I asked the Katzevs to go in my stead. Their subsequent excavation and restoration of the 4th-century BC wreck off Kyrenia set a new standard for shipwreck archaeology in the Mediterranean. They had learned all they could at Yassıada, and then improved on it, not only raising the timbers, but conserving them. And then, working with Dick Steffy, who took leave of his electrical business, they began to actually put the hull back together both for study and for public display in the castle at Kyrenia.

This was another first for underwater archaeology in the Mediterranean. While by no means ignoring the cargoes that first attracted archaeologists to the seabed, our specific branch of underwater, marine, or maritime archaeology was now focused more than ever on the ship itself – the *naus* in ancient Greek. Publication of the *International Journal of Nautical Archaeology* began at about this time in the United Kingdom.

Burned out in 1969 from teaching a normal load of courses while directing and raising funds for what the head of US Navy salvage and diving told me was the largest diving operation in the world at the time – 25 divers working twice a day at 40 m (132 ft) for months on end – I decided to retire from underwater archaeology. We had already sold *Asherah*. In 1971 I started the excavation of a mainly Neolithic land-based site in southern Italy, trying to determine how and when certain animals were introduced into the region. But I never stopped wondering how much more knowledge of this period we might gain from just one Neolithic shipwreck in the Adriatic Sea.

An Institute Devoted to Shipwreck Archaeology: First Glimmerings

Fred van Doorninck and I, while spending a summer working on the final publication of the Yassıada 7th-century Byzantine ship, began vaguely discussing ideas of an institute devoted just to shipwreck archaeology. We naively dreamed aloud of building a compound and growing our own food outside Bodrum, Turkey, which had served as our annual base of operation. Remember, this was the early 1970s – as revealed by the size and lengths of our sideburns in photographs taken in those days!

In 1972, while driving back from inspecting a hull recently uncovered in the sands of a New Jersey beach, Dick Steffy pulled to the side of the highway and waved for me to stop my car behind his. He then told me that he had decided to sell his electrical business and become a professional ancient ship reconstructor. He had a wife and two sons to support. I told him he was crazy. Within months, however, I gave written notice to the University of Pennsylvania that I was resigning my tenured associate professorship to form an independent institute devoted to shipwreck archaeology. Professor Young wrote to a colleague that he thought I had gone a little crazy, but, although he had groomed me to head the department on his retirement, he told me that he understood why I had to leave: "You have the 40 fidgets."

Michael and Susan Katzev were living on Cyprus, on leave from Oberlin College where Michael was teaching, in order to reassemble the Kyrenia ship. They suggested that I base the new American Institute of Nautical Archaeology (AINA) there, where the cost of living was less, and where we would be centrally located in the eastern

Mediterranean, the area that interested us most. I would serve as president and Michael would resign his position at Oberlin to be AINA vice-president.

But who would pay for this new institute? I thought that all of the people and foundations that had supported my shipwreck excavations for the University of Pennsylvania would put even more money into an institute devoted to full-time underwater archaeology. An institute without even a business address, however, must not have been tempting. I was turned down by every foundation I approached.

Then I mailed a copy of my newly published *A History of Seafaring Based on Underwater Archaeology* to Tulsa, Oklahoma, businessman Jack W. Kelley, only an acquaintance, asking if he would like to sit on the Board of Directors of AINA. To my surprise, he called immediately, not only agreeing to serve, and making a three-year pledge of funding, but telling me that he had a friend who would probably join him, retired Cleveland, Ohio, businessman John H. Baird. They were soon joined by John Brown Cook, a generous supporter of the Katzevs' Kyrenia project.

An Institute for Nautical Archaeology

We held our first board meeting in Philadelphia in the spring of 1973. Melvin M. Payne, chairman of the board of the National Geographic Society, and another AINA founding director, arrived with a check to pay for our first field project, a search off the Turkish coast for another wreck to excavate.

Before the survey, however, I attended a week-long, federally sponsored conference at a retreat in Virginia to help write a national program projecting the role of humans in the sea. My roommate was a doctoral candidate in oceanography, about ten years my junior. We sat up late, talking of dreams. I dreamed of a successful Institute of Nautical Archaeology. He dreamed of exploring the seabed in the deep-diving submersible *Alvin*. A student later interviewed us independently and wrote a term paper entitled *And All Their Dreams Came True*. His name was Robert Ballard, who would go on to find the *Titanic*. In this book he describes the deep-water archaeological work he has done with the assistance of our institute's Cheryl Ward.

My wife, Ann, and I soon afterward sold everything we owned – house, car, furniture, pictures off the walls, even our two sons' toys – and moved to the island of Cyprus, where we were greeted by the Katzevs, Dick Steffy, and the rest of the Kyrenia team, including Robin Piercy.

There was, however, a serious problem. None of us knew of another wreck to excavate. Leaving Ann on Cyprus to find a house and locate schools for our boys, I returned to Turkey, where I had done all of my previous underwater excavations.

For the first six weeks I lived on the open deck of a 10-m (33-ft) fishing boat, *Günyel*, with seven companions. One was physics professor Donald Frey, who had been a volunteer diver my last summer at Yassıada. Another was sonar-operator John Broadwater, who had taken me on my first Atlantic dive, on a Civil War blockade-runner, not long before. John later abandoned his career as an electrical engineer, obtained a doctorate in maritime studies at the University of St Andrews, and fully excavated the wreck he describes in these pages.

There was no room in *Günyel*'s cabin for anything other than the sonar and underwater television gear. Unwilling to dive without a recompression chamber on hand to treat any possible case of the bends, we swept swaths of seabed hundreds of

For three months in 1973, during INA's initial survey for ancient shipwrecks, the author and five companions lived on Turkish fishing boats, first on the 10-m (33-ft) *Günyel* (*below*), its cabin so filled with sonar equipment that the team had to eat and sleep on the crowded open deck for six weeks. With the arrival from the United States of a two-person, double-lock recompression chamber, now bolted to the deck along with compressors and air bank, the survey team moved for six weeks onto the larger trawler *Kardeşler* (*right*), sleeping in its fish hold.

meters wide with the sonar. When a possible wreck appeared as a dark smudge on the sonar read-out paper, we lowered our television camera from *Günyel*'s stern. Only one of the targets proved to be a possible wreck, a scatter of Byzantine pottery not worth excavating. I was more than discouraged. As the weeks passed, most of my companions had to return to their jobs.

Then our two-person, double-lock recompression chamber arrived from America, a gift of Cleveland businessman Alex Nason. With three Turkish and two American divers, I moved from *Günyel* to the larger 20-m (66-ft) trawler *Kardeşler*, onto whose deck we strapped the chamber and its supporting compressor and air bank. Now we could dive.

We followed the proven method of finding wrecks by interviewing local sponge divers. By talking to the divers of just 20 sponge boats, we calculated that we were learning about any antiquities they had seen during 10,000 hours on the seabed that year.

Retired sponge-diver Mehmet Aşkın soon led us to the wrecks at Bozburun and Serçe Limanı whose excavations are described in this book. Others followed. But Cumhur Ilik, a young Turkish diver on my team, had no background in archaeology. He had been a cabin boy on my first underwater excavation, at Cape Gelidonya in 1960, had turned to sponge diving for a few years, and in 1973 was a charter boat captain. His idea of shipwrecks, when he joined us, was of modern vessels, whose

Below **Interviewing sponge divers proved more efficient than using sonar: retired diver Mehmet Aşkın (center) directed the author and Yüksel Eğdemir (right), from the Turkish Ministry of Culture, to the nearby Bozburun wreck and two wrecks at Serçe Limanı.**

Diver Joe Alexander examines a 7th-century cargo of Byzantine roof tiles in Turkey's Gökova Bay during our initial 1973 survey.

bronze or brass fittings and propellers could be salvaged and sold for scrap. But after diving with us on a cargo of ancient tiles, he voiced surprise, and said he knew of other places like that. Pressed for more information, he recalled two large jars he had seen only once, seven years before, about 30 m (99 ft) deep, at a place called Şeytan Deresi, in English "Devil Creek." By the end of the survey, in November, we had found a dozen wrecks, at least a third of them worthy of archaeological excavation.

The year on Cyprus passed quickly. Dick Steffy sold his business completely to join the fledgling institute for a pauper's salary. Fred van Doorninck joined us for part of the year to continue research on the Byzantine shipwreck.

In the summer of 1974, we planned to complete the excavation of the 4th-century Yassıada wreck, and we had a good contingent of paying field-school students, including David Switzer, a professor of history at Plymouth State College, and Faith Hentschel, a Yale University doctoral candidate. The excavation was only days old when the outbreak of war on Cyprus ended it – and our idyllic situation on that lovely island.

The Katzevs moved to Greece, Dick Steffy moved back to his hometown of Denver, Pennsylvania, and I simply followed him with my family, all of us war refugees. Some people urged me to give up and simply return to teaching, but instead I convinced our Board of Directors to hire Robin Piercy, Michael Katzev's right-hand man on Cyprus, and Donald Frey, my right-hand man in Turkey.

AINA Director Elizabeth Whitehead proposed that we find a university home, where AINA would be affiliated but would retain its own corporate structure, like the Whitehead Medical Institute her husband had just founded at the Massachusetts Institute of Technology. But how does one shop for a university home? I had no idea, but the word got out, and soon we were approached by a number of universities.

Nautical Archaeology as an Academic Discipline

Texas A&M University made by far the most generous offer, proposing to establish a separate graduate program in nautical archaeology, with Dick Steffy, Fred van Doorninck, and me joining the faculty, each of us teaching either in the spring or fall, but free to pursue AINA research during the other term, paid by AINA; we would also offer summer field courses.

In our case, the cloud of war had more than one silver lining:

First, we learned not to put all of our eggs in one geographical basket, and soon were accepting invitations to work in North America and in Africa. I asked David Switzer to direct the first excavation of a Revolutionary War vessel in the United States, in Penobscot Bay, Maine; Dave describes his excavation in this book. Then I asked Don Frey and Robin Piercy to examine a Portuguese shipwreck at Mombasa, Kenya, where AINA had been invited by the director of the Fort Jesus Museum; Robin, too, describes his subsequent excavation in this book.

Second, the Turkish military initially allowed AINA to continue its work at Şeytan Deresi, but only if we used Turkish students as our volunteer staff. Don Frey chose ten students, and then brought multi-talented Donald Keith to Turkey to teach them to dive. Not long thereafter, Tufan Turanlı and Cemal Pulak joined AINA. Tufan later found the wreck described by Deborah Carlson in these pages, and Cemal Pulak writes about his excavation for the Institute of the Bronze Age shipwreck at Uluburun; some years later another of the students, Ayhan Sicimolğu, who had gone

Japan, Malaysia, Mexico, the Netherlands, New Zealand, Peru, Portugal, South Africa, Switzerland, Turkey, and the United Kingdom.

Not long after affiliating with Texas A&M University, the Institute shortened its name simply to the Institute of Nautical Archaeology (INA) to reflect more accurately the international nature of its staff, sponsors, and projects. INA has since conducted projects in Albania, the Bahamas, Bahrain, Bulgaria, the Caymans, Cyprus, the Dominican Republic, Egypt, Eritrea, Georgia, Israel, Italy, Jamaica, Kenya, Lebanon, Malta, Mexico, Morocco, the Netherlands, Panama, Portugal, Turkey, the Turks and Caicos Islands, and from the Great Lakes to the Gulf of Mexico in the United States; additionally, it has conducted joint projects with national agencies in Greece and Mexico.

The INA Center in Bodrum

In Bodrum, Turkey, Don Frey, while serving as INA's second president, raised the funds to acquire a beautiful piece of land and start a building project, which I continued while serving again briefly as president. Today INA has a five-building campus with offices, dormitory, four-story library building, conservation laboratory, and computer center. Cemal Pulak, Fred van Doorninck, Tufan Turanlı and I bought adjacent plots of land on a small lane adjoining the INA campus, where we have built our own homes.

We also added a small fleet in Turkey. We bought *Virazon* outright, and acquired a new two-person submersible, *Carolyn*, whose occupants sit in a clear acrylic sphere able to look in all directions except directly behind. To carry and launch *Carolyn*, we built a 15-m (50-ft) steel catamaran, named *Millawanda* after the Bronze Age name for Miletus on the Turkish coast. In just one month in 2001, surveying from *Carolyn*, we located 14 ancient wrecks and 10 possible wrecks, while re-examining a dozen wrecks we already knew.

INA also established a modern conservation center in Alexandria, Egypt, now operated by the Egyptian government.

In just a month INA's two-person submersible *Carolyn*, during a 2001 survey off the Turkish coast, helped to locate 14 ancient wrecks and 10 possible wrecks, while revisiting a dozen known wrecks. Here the sub approaches a medieval cargo of at least 32 immense millstones.

into business, joined the Institute's Board of Directors.

Third, affiliating with Texas A&M University relieved to some extent the institute's financial burden because of some shared costs, although in the years since the affiliation, the Institute's income has risen from $50,000 a year (for *everything*, including salaries) to $1–2 million a year.

Fourth, during negotiations with Texas A&M University, we mutually decided to add a New World archaeologist to our team. Our choice was Dr Donny Hamilton, then at the University of Texas at Austin in charge of conserving artifacts from the Spanish fleet that sank off Padre Island in 1554. This led Texas A&M and the Institute not only to become world leaders in archaeological conservation, with both teaching and innovative research laboratories, but to conduct a ten-year excavation of Port Royal, Jamaica, which Donny describes here. As I write these words, Donny is president of INA.

Fifth, Michael, Fred, and I had done most of our work while we were still graduate students, and now, with a virtual department devoted to our field, we had a self-replacing stable of nautical archaeology thoroughbreds able to direct their own projects. Among the former students who have contributed to this book are Robert Neyland, underwater archaeologist for the US Navy, who went on to direct the recovery and conservation of the Civil War submarine *Hunley*; Fred Hocker, now at the *Vasa* Museum in Stockholm, Sweden; Bill Charlton, a retired Marine Corps Officer and INA Divemaster; Elizabeth Greene, teaching at Wellesley College; Jerome Hall, on the faculty of the University of San Diego; Margaret Leshikar-Denton, an archaeologist at the Cayman Islands National Museum; Cheryl Ward, on the faculty at Florida State University; Brett Phaneuf, now a graduate student in oceanography; and, finally, Deborah Carlson, Filipe Castro, Kevin Crisman, and Cemal Pulak, all members of the Texas A&M nautical archaeology faculty – Dick Steffy, Fred van Doorninck, and I having graciously made room for them by retiring!

Other graduate students in the Texas A&M Nautical Archaeology Program have come from Albania, Belgium, Bulgaria, Canada, China, Denmark, Greece, Jamaica,

Graduates of the graduate program in Nautical Archaeology at Texas A&M University, with field experience gained on INA projects, have gone on to successful careers. Dr Robert Neyland, assisted by other former Texas A&M students, directed the raising and conservation of the Confederate submarine *H.L. Hunley*, the first submarine ever to sink an enemy vessel. Shortly after sinking the USS *Housatonic* in 1864, during the American Civil War, the *Hunley* disappeared for over a century in Charleston Harbor, South Carolina.

Spreading the Discipline

Other archaeologists who gained their first field experience with us, studied with us, or pursued postgraduate studies at Texas A&M University, have gone on to direct their own major projects. They include some of the authors of this book.

John Broadwater, sonar operator on INA's first field project, a 1973 survey of the Turkish coast, and later a member of an INA excavation team working in the York River, Virginia, is now Manager of the *Monitor* National Marine Sanctuary for the National Oceanic and Atmospheric Administration, and was recently in charge of raising the turret of that famed Civil War ironclad. In these pages he describes his excavation of the British ship *Betsy*, scuttled in the York River in the closing days of the American Revolution.

Jeremy Green, whose introduction to underwater archaeology was with me at Yassıada in 1969, soon afterward became head of the Department of Marine Archaeology at the Western Australian Maritime Museum in Fremantle. In addition to his own excavation of the Dutch East Indiaman *Batavia*, now beautifully conserved and restored in his museum, and the Far Eastern research he describes here, he has played important roles, as an INA Research Associate, in INA excavations at Mombasa, Kenya, and at both Tektaş Burnu and Pabuç Burnu in Turkey.

Nergis Günsenin, who while still a high-school student assisted INA's excavation at Serçe Limanı, Turkey, went on to earn a doctorate at the Sorbonne and, later, a professorship at Istanbul University; as an INA Adjunct Professor, she provides field experience for Texas A&M graduate students on her excavations, and INA accepts her students for training in Bodrum, Turkey.

Ralph Pedersen, while still a graduate student at Texas A&M not only worked at Uluburun, Turkey, but directed an INA survey in Bahrain and excavated a Byzantine wreck off

Below **The crew of the Civil War ironclad USS *Monitor* relax on deck after her 1862 battle with the Confederate ironclad CSS *Virginia* (ex-USS *Merrimack*).**

Bottom **The *Monitor*'s turret, when recovered in 2002, still contained its two 11-inch Dahlgren guns, gun carriages, and more than 100 artifacts, in addition to the remains of two of the crew.**

Eritrea. Since obtaining his doctorate, he has studied the thousand-year-old hull of a sailing barge at Kadakkarapally, near Chertala in Kerala, India.

Robert S. Neyland, although mentioned earlier for his work as Head of the Underwater Branch of the Department of the Navy on the Civil War submarine *Hunley* in Charleston, South Carolina (illustrated and described on page 23) had already, while still a student at Texas A&M University, conducted the excavation of a 17th-century wreck in the Netherlands that he describes here.

Paul Johnston worked as a graduate student volunteer on INA projects at Serçe Limanı, Turkey, and in Penobscot Bay, Maine, and the York River, Virginia, before earning a doctorate at the University of Pennsylvania and becoming Curator of Maritime History at the Smithsonian Institution's National Museum of American History, for which he excavated the remains of the royal yacht off Hawaii.

After receiving an M.A. from Texas A&M University, Kenneth Cassavoy returned to his native Canada where he studied the remarkably preserved War of 1812 *Hamilton* and *Scourge* in Lake Ontario, and, as this is written, is excavating at Southampton on Lake Huron the earliest warship yet found in the Upper Lakes, probably the British Navy brig *General Hunter* built in 1806.

Zhang Wei, who studied with us at Texas A&M University in 1989, now heads underwater archaeology in China for the National Museum of Chinese History in Beijing, for which he has directed excavations of 14th- and 13th-century ships laden with large cargoes of beautifully preserved porcelain.

Donald H. Keith, after his start as a diving instructor at Şeytan Deresi, went on to excavate what was the oldest known shipwreck in the Western hemisphere, at Molasses Reef in the Turks and Caicos Islands, where he established on Grand Turk

Below left **Archaeologists George Bass, Zhang Wei, and Ao Jie examine some of the ceramics excavated in the Yellow Sea and the South China Sea by Zhang Wei's team, now displayed in a museum in the Ocean Visitor Hotel in Yangjiang, a tourist center on the South China Sea.**

Above **Former INA Executive Director Kenneth Cassavoy stands on the stern of the excavated hull of a War of 1812 ship, believed to be the British brig *General Hunter*.**

Below **Divers under the direction of INA's Donald Keith raise a cannon from the early 16th-century Molasses Reef Wreck in the Turks and Caicos Islands, at the time the oldest known shipwreck in the New World.**

Island a permanent display of that wreck in the Turks and Caicos National Museum. After earning a doctorate at Texas A&M University, he formed his own group, Ships of Discovery, based at the Corpus Christi Museum in Texas.

Jeffrey Royal, with experience on the Bozburun excavation, described in this book, and with a doctorate from Texas A&M University, took a position as Archaeological Director of the RPM Foundation, established by George Robb, a member of the INA Board of Directors. The Foundation has archaeological research vessels in both the Caribbean and Mediterranean, and its close collaboration with INA should lead to astonishing discoveries on both sides of the Atlantic.

Oğuz Alpözen, who as an Istanbul University undergraduate student joined us at Yassıada in 1962 to learn to dive, and worked with us for years thereafter, has been director of the Bodrum Museum of Underwater Archaeology for more than 20 years. The museum, with separate galleries devoted to all of the shipwrecks excavated by INA off the Turkish coast, has become under his leadership the most visited archaeological museum in Turkey.

The Future

The dream of an institute of nautical archaeology has become a reality far beyond my wildest expectations. Now I dream of INA research vessels in both the New and Old Worlds, the first American research vessels designed specifically for the humanities, vessels large enough to carry and launch submersibles like our current *Carolyn*, vessels that will lead to unimaginable discoveries. I dream of an endowment to guarantee their continued operation.

We will never run out of worthy sites. If only one vessel sank in every year of every decade of every century of every millennium since the first seafarers sailed out from their cave dwellings in Greece 11,000 years ago, we would have 11,000 wrecks in the Aegean alone. But hundreds of ships have sunk in Aegean storms in a single day. We cannot calculate the number of wrecks in that one sea. The number of wrecks beneath the Seven Seas is truly unimaginable.

Archaeologists, however, face the constant threat of the looting of historic wrecks by treasure hunters for personal gain rather than for the benefit of humankind. Every known wreck from the period of discovery of the New World, for example, has been destroyed or badly damaged by those seeking non-existent gold in them. With false promises of paying off the debts of nations by the treasures they will find and share, they often profit most from the finances they have received from their investors. No country has ever benefited as much from treasure hunting as from true archaeology, which results in museums that attract thousands, even millions, of visitors, each one of whom boosts the local economy by paying for hotels, taxis, restaurants, and souvenirs, in addition to their museum tickets.

One day, INA will have excavated a wreck of every century of the past, and then can turn its attention to tracing the evolution of specific types of ships, from warships to ferries to fishing boats. This will contribute to an increasing number of informative museum displays around the world. But the ultimate product, shelves filled with large volumes written on these vessels and their contents, will provide for the world not only the ultimate histories of watercraft, but the ultimate histories of virtually everything ever made by humans.

Excavations of the three Bronze Age shipwrecks described here have resulted in a puzzle, a ridiculed hypothesis, and a royal cargo beyond imagination. Archaeologists divide the Bronze Age into three periods, Early (around 3000 to 2000 BC), Middle (around 2000 to 1600 BC), and Late (around 1600 to 1000 BC). The Bronze Age people who inhabited the island of Crete are called Minoan (after the legendary King Minos of Crete), and those on the Greek mainland, southern Italy, and the western coast of Asia Minor (modern Turkey) are called Helladic. The Late Helladics are also known today as Mycenaeans, after King Agamemnon's great citadel at Mycenae.

The Bronze Age civilizations of the eastern Mediterranean were clearly dependent on watercraft. Only by water could islanders go anywhere, and since the invention of the sail, around 3500 BC, it has been far easier and cheaper to move people and cargoes over water than over land.

Greek archaeologists have excavated an Early Helladic cargo of pottery off the island of Dokos; have discovered a Minoan cargo; and have excavated a cargo of Minoan, Mycenaean, and Cypriot pottery from around 1200 BC off Point Iria in the Peloponnesus.

Three Bronze Age wrecks studied by the Institute of Nautical Archaeology off the southwest Turkish coast, described in the following pages, include a site whose date and very nature remain puzzles. No wooden hull remains lay beneath the scatter of large jars on the seabed at Şeytan Deresi, suggesting that the pottery spilled from a capsized vessel – in which case the site should not really be called a shipwreck – or that the hull was made of such fragile material, such as sewn animal hides, that none of it survived. Only two of the jars closely resemble any known jars, suggesting that the pottery was made by a local culture that has not yet been discovered and identified on land. The two jars are near duplicates of a jar found on Crete, but it was called Neolithic (pre-Bronze Age) by its excavator. Other Şeytan Deresi pots resemble ceramics from around 1600 BC on Crete, in the interior of Asia Minor, and at Troy. Yet a thermoluminescence dating of fragments of the pots places them in the Late Roman or Byzantine period! Are two spills of pottery involved? Puzzling, indeed.

The other two wrecks investigated by the Institute of Nautical Archaeology have made substantial contributions to our knowledge of the Bronze Age. These are the wrecks at Cape Gelidonya and at Uluburun.

The Cape Gelidonya wreck has a solid place in the history of nautical archaeology, being the first ancient Mediterranean shipwreck excavated in its entirety on the seabed, and being the first excavated by a diving archaeologist. It, like the Dokos and

Archaeologists excavating at Uluburun. In the foreground, a diver measures some of the many copper ingots that were found. The diver in the background hovers near one of the ship's heavy stone anchors, while fanning sand away from a second. Airlifts rise up behind him.

Point Iria wrecks mentioned above, was discovered by Peter Throckmorton, whose vision led to the original excavation of the site by the University of Pennsylvania Museum. When I excavated the site with Peter, I was still a graduate student at that university, but after founding the Institute of Nautical Archaeology (INA) I returned to the site several times with INA colleagues, making additional discoveries and interpretations, which allows inclusion of the site in this book. The Cape Gelidonya excavation, which led me to recognize a significant but at that time unsuspected Semitic presence in the Bronze Age Aegean, was proof that underwater archaeology could rewrite history, although my initial publication of this presence was criticized and even ridiculed. I did not think I would live to see my once controversial ideas validated, as they were by the Uluburun wreck.

The wreck at Uluburun was voted one of the ten greatest archaeological discoveries of the 20th century – along with King Tut's tomb and Machu Picchu – in a poll of archaeologists taken by *Discovering Archaeology* magazine. It, perhaps more than any other underwater site, has shown how shipwrecks can provide unique information about the past, contributing to such diverse fields as Egyptology, Homeric studies, and biblical studies, and to the histories of metallurgy, metrology, glass, ceramics, foodstuffs, weapons, tools, musical instruments, trade, international relations, technology, and much more.

The Cape Gelidonya and Uluburun wrecks revealed how ships were built at the time of the Trojan War, although not being Mycenaean they may not have been of the types of which Helen's face launched a thousand.

Above **A beautifully preserved sword is raised from the depths of the Mediterranean by archaeologist Faith Hentschel during excavation of the Uluburun wreck.**

Right **Places mentioned in this section, with the featured wrecks in bold.**

Şeytan Deresi

Date c 1600 BC?
Depth 27–33 m (89–109 ft)
Found by Cumhur Ilik, 1965
Excavation 1975
Cargo storage jars, krater, pitchers
Hull unknown

An Enigma at Devil Creek: Şeytan Deresi, Turkey

GEORGE F. BASS

If it hadn't been so cold, we never would have seen them. The two jars sparked little interest. But on a cold November evening in 1973, bundled in jackets on the deck of the Turkish trawler *Kardeşler*, we looked for any excuse to stop for the evening and perhaps warm ourselves over glasses of *rakı*.

We'd been living on fishing boats for three months, eating on deck from communal pots and sleeping in fish holds. We were on our way to examine a reported Roman wreck in Turkey's Gökova Bay when we realized we were passing Şeytan Deresi. The Roman wreck was still two hours away.

"Maybe Cumhur's jars are worth a photograph," suggested Yüksel Eğdemir, the diving commissioner assigned to us by the Turkish Ministry of Culture. "This is where he says he saw them."

I doubted that Cumhur Ilik could spot again jars he had seen only once, seven years earlier, when he was diving for sponges at a depth of 33 m (109 ft). But it was getting colder. I asked Captain Mehmet Turguttekin to stop for the night.

Next morning, with *Kardeşler* anchored nearby, Cumhur uncannily led Yüksel and me, with no guideposts, directly to the jars. One was a *krater*, a large bowl for mixing wine and water. I reached for its rim, but Yüksel pulled me away, pointing to the large moray eel living inside and looking more than annoyed by uninvited visitors.

After placing lead markers in the depressions they left in the seabed, we raised the *krater*, along with a large, intact storage jar, and part of what proved to be a smaller, two-handled jar. I was not sure of their dates, but the faint black spiral painted on a single sherd made me think of the Late Bronze Age (1600 to 1000 BC). At the same time, we picked up broken bits of Roman amphoras, the kind of rubbish found everywhere on the sea floor. Colleagues in Turkey and Cyprus all told me that the *krater* could not possibly be earlier than the 8th century BC, so when I first mentioned the site in print, I said it was from the Iron Age.

Above **During the survey that led to the discoveries at Şeytan Deresi, the 10-m (33-ft) fishing boat *Günyel*, anchored in the cove, was used for sonar work, while the larger *Kardeşler*, heading out to sea, was equipped for diving, with compressors and recompression chamber on its deck.** *Right* **The survey team dined on *Kardeşler*'s deck and slept in the trawler's fish hold. Enjoying a meal of beans are, clockwise from left, Cumhur Ilik, George Bass, John Gifford, and Yüksel Eğdemir.**

Return to Devil Creek

Turkish place names like Karatoprak and Kızılağaç sound so exotic, not like Big Lake, Coldspring, Grapevine, Longview, and Sweetwater in Texas. But translated into English, they are just as prosaic: Black Earth and Red Tree. *Şeytan* (pronounced Sheytan) is the same as our Satan, and *dere* means stream, so I call Şeytan Deresi simply "Devil Creek." I'm not sure of the name's origin, but we usually encountered winds when we arrived there, and Captain Mehmet recalled seeing a waterspout there when he was a boy.

I returned to Devil Creek in 1975, for INA's first full-scale excavation. With me were several veterans, and ten Turkish students chosen by Don Frey, who had been teaching physics at Robert College in Istanbul.

We built a camp of woven mats and tents in a nearby pine forest, heavily screened against constant swarms of yellow jackets that stung everyone at least once. Although the Turkish students had to learn to dive, I was struck by their multi-talented ability to do anything asked of them, from wiring the camp to repairing the generator to running the photographic darkroom. All were excellent cooks.

To support the compressors and recompression chamber, we moored over the site the old 15-m (50-ft) wooden barge we had used in the 1960s when we excavated at Yassıada for the University of Pennsylvania Museum. Then we put our underwater telephone booth and airlifts in place, laid down a metal grid to break the site into coherent squares for systematic excavation, and began to dig.

A Puzzling Site

We found nothing – absolutely nothing – other than more pottery, mostly jars and mostly close together. Some, however, were scattered. One of six large jars lay about 30 m (99 ft) from the other five, only 27 m (89 ft) deep, as if it had floated there separately. Inside was a fragment of pottery that joined a broken pot in the main concentration; we suppose it had been carried to the isolated jar by an octopus that once made its home there. In addition, there were smaller two-handled jars and a couple of pitchers.

Above **A 15-m (50-ft) wooden barge served as a dive platform, holding on its deck the white air-bank for a recompression chamber, high- and low-pressure compressors, and storage spaces for diving equipment. The barge was used for excavations off the Turkish coast for nearly two decades.**

Right **One of six large storage jars lay in isolation about 30 m (99 ft) from the major concentration of pottery. An octopus has pulled rocks and broken pottery into its mouth to protect its home inside.**

Top **At the Bodrum Museum, excavation director George Bass repairs one of the large jars, and Ann Bass mends a pitcher, before they color the white plaster used to fill gaps. The smaller jar with two horizontal handles,** *above,* **closely resembles a jar found on Crete.**

The sand was deep enough to have covered and protected remains of a wooden hull, which suggests that a small, local craft capsized, spilled out its cargo, and floated away. I do not think of the site as a shipwreck.

After looking for published parallels for our pottery during a term at the University of Cambridge, I decided that my first assessment of the site was correct, that it dated to the Bronze Age. Comparing similar pieces found at Troy and Beycesultan in Turkey, as well as at sites in northern Greece and on Crete, I concluded that the pottery dated to around 1600 BC.

Some colleagues, however, continued to doubt this early date. So in 1996 I had the Research Laboratory for Archaeology and the History of Art in Oxford date two sherds by means of thermoluminescence. One sherd dated to between AD 110 and 640 and the other to between AD 510 and 770, giving a possible date of around AD 600 for the site, putting it well into the Byzantine period – 2,200 years later than I had thought possible!

I invited Roxani Margariti, a brilliant Greek student, to write her Texas A&M University M.A. thesis on the site. She, like me, concluded that the pottery was made in the first half of the 16th century BC, at the beginning of the Late Bronze Age. In the course of her research, she found the report of an excavation on Crete, published in a Greek archaeological journal, with the picture of a two-handled jar exactly like our smaller jars – the most perfect parallel for any of our pottery – but the caption below the picture says that the jar is Neolithic, before 3000 BC, or more than 1,000 years earlier! Alas, the jar is not mentioned in the text of the report.

We plan to have more samples dated by thermoluminescence, while trying to contact the excavator of the "Neolithic" jar to learn the exact context in which it was found.

Archaeological detective work can be long and tedious. One day, however, I am sure we will understand this still puzzling site.

Discovering a Royal Ship from the Age of King Tut: Uluburun, Turkey

CEMAL PULAK

"I think we have another Bronze Age wreck," I said to George Bass, without complete conviction. It was 1982. We were on the island of Yassıada, excavating an Ottoman shipwreck.

Word had reached me that a Bodrum sponge diver, Mehmet Çakır, had discovered "metal biscuits with ears" 45 m (148 ft) deep off Uluburun ("Grand Promontory") near the Turkish town of Kaş. Mehmet could not have realized that he had stumbled onto the remains of the world's oldest seagoing ship, the excavation of which would take INA 11 years and nearly 22,500 dives to complete. His captain, however, immediately recognized the metal slabs Mehmet described as being four-handled copper ingots of the kind INA archaeologists had been sketching for him and asking him about for years. Such ingots are typical of the Late Bronze Age, especially between 1450 and 1200 BC.

Unaware of what to expect, we included Uluburun for inspection in INA's 1983 survey of the Turkish coast. As I kicked downward, the water became colder and darker. In the monochromatic blue light of the depths, I could not make out anything remotely resembling a shipwreck among the seaweed-cloaked rocks. Was this just one more false report, the single ingot raised from the site shortly after its discovery an isolated find? Suddenly, one of the rocky outcrops metamorphosed into rows of

Left **Excavation director Cemal Pulak (left) examines a Canaanite flask with George Bass, who initiated the eleven-year excavation in 1984. The ship carried items from Syria-Palestine, Greece, Cyprus, Egypt, Mesopotamia, and other lands from tropical Africa to northern Europe.**

Above **Hanging precariously to the cliff against which the Uluburun ship crashed 33 centuries earlier, a camp provided ample and comfortable living and working spaces for an average of 25 people only meters away from the ancient wreck.**

Opposite **Nearly 150 two-handled Canaanite jars in the cargo were transporting terebinth resin, a substance burned as incense in antiquity, and vegetable oil, but one jar was filled with glass beads and several others with olives. Terebinth resin comes from a tree related to the better known pistachio.**

Uluburun

Date late 14th century BC
Depth 41–61 m (135–200 ft)
Found by Mehmet Çakır
Excavation 1984–1994
Number of dives 22,500
Number of hours on wreck 6,613
Conservation 1984–present
Hull c 15 m (49 ft) long

copper ingots stacked as originally stowed in the hull of a ship. I focused my gaze and saw more ingots jutting out from seemingly sterile sandy patches. Everywhere I looked there were ingots; we counted 84 during our week-long survey of the site, but never guessed that beneath the sand and marine encrustation were a staggering 354 four-handled ingots, several times more than all the ingots of their type found until then in the entire Mediterranean region!

I saw two-handled pottery jars with the pointed bases typical of Canaanite containers. Higher and lower on the steeply sloping seabed lay huge storage jars, several at around 50–55 m (165–182 ft) deep. Hand-fanning sand from a rectangular stone slab, I uncovered a rectangular hole that revealed it to be a stone anchor weighing about 200 kg (440 lb). Overwhelmed with the excitement of discovery, I found it difficult to leave these new treasures when the time came to surface; my 20-minute dive seemed like seconds. But I was to return to excavate the wreck from 1984 to 1994, living for months at a time in a small "village" we built on the steep cliff above. George directed the first campaign, and then turned the project over to me.

Two large stone anchors at the site's deeper end suggested the ship's bow, with its stern at the highest extremity. Based on the cargo, it appeared that the ship was sailing

- Copper oxhide ingots
- Copper bun ingots
- Tin ingots
- Stone anchors
- Ceramics
- Ebony logs

Painstaking recording of the positions of thousands of artifacts over many years resulted in this plan of the wreck site.

from the coast of Syria-Palestine or Cyprus and was headed in a northwesterly direction when it failed to clear craggy Uluburun. Perhaps the ship was dashed against the rocky promontory by a fierce south wind that unexpectedly rose in summer, when the prevailing wind blows from the northwest.

Early finds on the wreck suggested that the Uluburun ship plied the Mediterranean towards the end of the 14th century BC, one of the most active and colorful periods of the ancient world. During this century Late Bronze Age Greeks were constructing the great palace at Mycenae from which they received their name: Mycenaeans. They established trading outposts and colonized the islands and shores of the Aegean and Ionian Seas from Asia Minor to southern Italy. To the east lived the seafaring Canaanites, a term used to denote generally the Semitic peoples along the Syro-Palestinian coast during the second millennium BC. They traded extensively with Egypt, Cyprus, Crete, and lands beyond, and their ports served as hubs for overland trade routes connecting Egypt, Mesopotamia, and the Hittite Empire. In this century Egypt was ruled by the heretic pharaoh Akhenaten, whose queen was the beautiful Nefertiti. During Akhenaten's reign Egypt's foreign influence waned, but it was in his city on the Nile, known today as el-Amarna, that 382 clay tablets inscribed in cuneiform were found. Some 350 of them, known as the Amarna letters, offer a vivid portrait of Egypt's diplomatic relations with Cypriot, Hittite, Kassite, Assyrian, and other rulers, as well as with vassals in Syria and Palestine. While the exact nature of international trade during this period is not fully understood, and the presence of private enterprise is suggested by textual evidence, the Amarna tablets show that much of the trade at palace level was conducted as exchanges of "royal gifts."

"…this ship [is] the king's"

> *The minister of Alashiya (Cyprus) to the minister of Egypt, from a clay tablet found at el-Amarna, Egypt*

The Uluburun ship's cargo seems to represent a royal dispatch of enormously valuable raw materials and manufactured goods, matching many of the royal gifts listed in the Amarna letters.

"I will bring to thee as a present two hundred talents of copper"

> *The king of Alashiya (Cyprus) to an Egyptian pharaoh, from a clay tablet found at el- Amarna, one of several mentioning shipments of copper ingots*

The Uluburun ship's cargo consisted mostly of raw materials – trade items that before the excavation were known primarily, and in some places solely, from ancient texts or Egyptian tomb paintings. The major cargo was 10 tons of Cypriot copper in the form of flat, four-handled ingots and similar, but previously unknown, two-handled ingots, weighing on average about 25 kg (55 lb), approximately an ancient talent. In addition there were more than 120 smaller plano-convex discoid, or "bun," ingots of copper.

"…tribute to [Tutankhamun] offered by Syria"

> *Inscription beneath a painting in the tomb of Huy, Egyptian viceroy to Nubia, showing a Syrian bearing a four-handled copper ingot*

Syrian merchants and tribute-bearers carrying four-handled ingots are depicted in Egyptian tomb paintings. Similar ingots are found throughout the eastern and

central Mediterranean, from southern Germany and France to Mesopotamia, and from Egypt to the Black Sea. Those of the 15th century BC, with less prominent handles, are from unknown sources, but all of those from the 14th and 13th centuries BC are apparently from Cyprus, as shown by lead-isotope analyses by Noël Gale and Sophie Stos at Oxford University's Isotrace Laboratory.

Originally stowed in four transverse rows across the Uluburun ship's hold, the ingots in each row overlapped one another like roof shingles, the direction of overlap alternating from layer to layer to prevent slippage during transit.

In addition to the copper, the ship yielded the earliest well-dated tin ingots. Most occur in the four-handled form, often cut into quarters, each quarter retaining one handle. Others are rectangular slabs, or sections cut from ingots of indiscernible shape. One, however, is shaped like a stone anchor with a large hole at one end, reminding us of bearers in Egyptian tomb paintings carrying similar metal ingots previously identified as silver or lead. Because in some cases the tin has assumed the consistency of toothpaste, which we carefully scooped from the seabed with teaspoons, it is not possible to know the exact amount of tin carried on the ship, but we recovered a ton. When alloyed with the copper, this would have made 11 tons of bronze in the standard 10 to 1 ratio of copper to tin.

Remarkable finds were made on the seabed. The ceramic flask is Near Eastern in origin and the two-handled cup is Mycenaean Greek, but the origin of the bi-conical gold chalice remains undetermined.

The source of our tin has not yet been determined. Preliminary results of Noël Gale's lead-isotope analyses indicate that it was not derived from known sources in eastern Europe, Spain or Cornwall – but ancient texts from western Asia hint at tin sources somewhere to the east, perhaps in Iran, or even Afghanistan or central Asia, from which it was transported overland to the Mediterranean by donkey caravans. This lends weight to the supposition that the ingots' shape was designed for ease of handling and for transportation by pack animals.

The Uluburun ship also carried about 150 Canaanite jars, vessels widely distributed over Syria-Palestine, Egypt, Cyprus, and Greece, which served as containers for shipping all sorts of liquids and solid commodities. The shipwrecked jars fall into three general sizes, with three quarters of them representing the smallest size, having an average capacity of 6.7 liters, the medium size about twice that volume, and the largest about four times the smallest value.

One jar was filled with glass beads, and several with olives, but about half of them contained a yellowish material chemically identified as terebinth resin from the *Pistacia* tree group, which grows around much of the Mediterranean. This resin cargo, which originally weighed about half a ton, revealed for the first time another raw material that was part of the complex eastern Mediterranean trade of the Late Bronze Age.

We carefully decanted each jar we raised of its sand and silt, which we searched for tiny finds before passing it through a series of fine-mesh sieves to recover every seed, some smaller than a pin's head such as figs and black cumin, and other minuscule bits missed during the visual sorting. During these processes, I spotted small land snails in the resin. Francisco Welter-Schultes, a malacologist at the Zoologisches Institut in

Berlin, identified one as a species with an extremely limited geographical distribution, which has changed little during the last 10,000 years. These snails, entrapped in the resin as it oozed out of the cuts made in trees, suggest that our resin was gathered from regions to the west-northwest of the Dead Sea in Israel, a suggestion strengthened by analysis of the plant pollen extracted from the resin.

Jars labeled *sntr* in Egyptian hieroglyphs are depicted in an Egyptian tomb painting of royal storerooms displaying Canaanite tributes. Decades ago a French Egyptologist translated *sntr* as terebinth resin, which he said was recorded as brought to Egypt from the Near East, primarily for use as incense. Over a five-year period in the annals of pharaoh Thutmose III, the volume of *sntr* received averaged 9,250 liters per year, approximately twenty times the amount carried aboard the Uluburun ship.

"Payment to the palace, 1,320 liters of ki-ta-no; *still owed, 240 + liters"*

> *Record of payment to royal stores, written in Mycenaean Greek on a clay tablet found in the palace at Knossos, Crete*

Terebinth resin may also correspond to Mycenaean *ki-ta-no*, which had been interpreted as meaning nuts related to the modern pistachio. Palace inventories on Crete record enormous quantities of it, more than 10,000 liters in one case. No large quantities of *Pistacia* nuts have been found at Bronze Age sites, however, and since the word *ki-ta-no* was written with a symbol suggesting that it was an aromatic or a condiment, it may be that resin, rather than nuts, was inventoried. Was terebinth resin used as incense in the Aegean as in Egypt? Or was it used in the manufacture of scented oils, as today in parts of the Near East?

"The king, my lord, has written to me about the mekku-*stone that is in my possession, but I have already given one weighing one hundred [units] to the king, my lord"*

> *Prince Abi-milki of Tyre to Egyptian pharaoh Akhenaten, from a clay tablet found at el-Amarna*

Some 170 cup-cake shaped glass ingots approximately 15 cm (6 in) in diameter and 6.5 cm (2.5 in) thick were found on the wreck. They are among the earliest intact glass ingots known. Cobalt blue, turquoise, lavender, and amber, they are quite likely the *mekku* and *ehlipakku* mentioned in Amarna letters sent from Tyre, Akko, and Ashkelon, among others, to Egypt, and listed in other Near Eastern tablets as exports from the region. Their colors must have been favored for their likeness to the highly sought semi-precious stones and material of their day: lapis lazuli, turquoise, amethyst, and amber. When cakes of lapis lazuli and turquoise are shown as tribute in Egyptian art, they are sometimes called "genuine" in Egyptian hieroglyphs; our discovery has led Egyptologists to believe that glass imitations of those precious stones are depicted if the word "genuine" does not appear. Robert Brill of the Corning Museum of Glass reports that our ingots of cobalt blue are chemically identical to contemporary blue Egyptian vessels and blue Mycenaean relief beads, suggesting a common source – perhaps Near Eastern glassmakers who kept secret the formulas for the "simulated" stones they exported.

A computer-generated version of the ship, by Shih-Han Samuel Lin, allows archaeologists to move cargo, some of which had slid down the steep slope of the seabed, into positions that would have provided the best ballast.

A well-preserved cobalt-blue glass ingot, cast to imitate rare lapis lazuli mined in Afghanistan. Such ingots would have been melted down and formed into a variety of objects or vessels.

"One hundred pieces of ebony I have dispatched"

Amenhotep III to King Tarkhundaradu of Arzawa, from a tablet found at el-Amarna

Small dark logs of what the Egyptians called ebony, known today as African blackwood (*Dalbergia melanoxylon*), were another unique find. Egyptian tomb paintings show such logs being brought as tribute to the pharaoh from Nubia, south of Egypt, and furniture in King Tutankhamun's famous tomb is made of ebony. The skilled craftsmen needed to shape this hard material would only have been in the employ of palaces. Ebony was exclusively for elite consumption, then, and along with ivory comprised some of the prestige goods carried aboard the Uluburun ship.

"Now, as a present for thee…one elephant's tusk…I have sent"

The minister of Alashiya (Cyprus) to the minister of Egypt, from a tablet found at el-Amarna

Other raw materials include a 20-cm (8-in) length of neatly sawn elephant tusk. More than a dozen hippopotamus teeth, both canines and incisors, were also recovered.

Below left **Faith Hentschel holds one of the logs of African blackwood, which the ancient Egyptians called "ebony," but which differs from the wood called ebony today.**

Below right **INA archaeologist Sheila Matthews measures a section of elephant tusk as Faith Hentschel looks on. Raw ivory on board also included hippopotamus teeth.**

The large number of hippopotamus teeth surprised us, for archaeologists had assumed that most Late Bronze Age ivory came from African and Asian elephants. After we published our findings, several contemporaneous ivory collections in museums were restudied with the unexpected discovery that hippopotamus ivory had been used more frequently than elephant ivory, especially for smaller pieces, in one collection accounting for 75 percent.

Other raw materials of animal origin included thousands of tiny opercula, the button-like plates attached to the feet of marine mollusks that serve as protective doors when the animals retract into their shells. They seldom survive in the archaeological record. Ours were from murex snails, but they were found in clusters without the corresponding numbers of dead murex shells nearby, some in recognizable patterns suggesting that they had been stored in bags that had long since disintegrated. We later learned that opercula were another ingredient of incense. Ours were almost certainly by-products of the Canaanite industry that extracted the legendary purple dye from murex glands.

We also found fragments of seven tortoise carapaces that had been modified into sounding-boxes for stringed musical instruments, probably lutes, and three ostrich eggshells that were probably modified into ornate vases by the addition of glass or metal bases and necks, now lost.

There were also manufactured goods on board. At least three of nine large storage jars contained Cypriot export pottery. Four faience drinking cups were crafted as the heads of rams and, in one case, the head of a woman. Copper and/or bronze vessels of several types, although poorly preserved, also appear to have been in the cargo, some found nestled one inside another.

The best preserved of four faience drinking cups shaped like ram's heads. Such vessels were used for ceremonial purposes.

The Uluburun wreck yielded the largest collection of Canaanite jewelry of any excavated site. The larger pendant depicts a fertility goddess with gazelles in her hands, and the smaller carries a typical Canaanite star-and-ray design of the type depicted at the necks of Canaanites in Egyptian tomb paintings.

"...fourteen seals of beautiful hulalu [stone], overlaid with gold"

Gifts listed on a tablet from King Tushratta of Mitanni to Pharaoh Akhenaten, found at el-Amarna

An astonishingly rich collection of both usable and scrap gold Canaanite jewelry (a few of Egyptian origin) surfaced during the excavation: pectorals, medallions, pendants, beads, a small ring ingot, and an assortment of cut and deformed fragments. One pendant bears the repoussé figure of a nude female holding a gazelle in each hand, almost certainly a Canaanite fertility goddess. Among four gold medallions is the largest known Canaanite gold medallion. A gold pectoral, in the shape of a falcon with a hooded cobra clutched in each claw, is worked in repoussé and granulation. A goblet, the single largest gold object from the ship, is of uncertain origin.

Nine cylinder seals – of hematite, quartz, stone, and faience – probably belonged to those on the ship. Their geographically widespread places of manufacture need not indicate a crew of diverse origins, however, for such items could have been obtained from different regions while others were passed down from one generation to another. For example, the oldest seal, of hematite (a black iron ore), is of Babylonian origin. Dominique Collon of the British Museum noted that it was made in the 18th century BC, originally depicting a king facing a goddess with the

Above **This 17-cm (6.7-in) tall bronze statuette of a goddess, partly clad in gold foil, may have been the ship's protective deity. The position of her hands indicates a gesture of blessing.**

small figure of a priest between them; she further noted that probably in the 14th century, in Assyria, a new scene incorporating a winged griffin-demon and a warrior with a sickle sword was engraved over a cuneiform inscription alongside the old, by now worn, scene. Two cylinder seals of quartz show the Kassites, foreign invaders who ruled Babylonia around the time the Uluburun ship sank.

"The Beautiful one has come"
Literal translation of the name Nefertiti

Egyptian objects of gold, electrum, silver, and steatite were also found. The most significant is a unique gold scarab inscribed with the name of Nefertiti, wife of the pharaoh Akhenaten. It is considered to be one of the most important Egyptian discoveries ever made in the eastern Mediterranean outside Egypt. Other scarabs, mostly older than the wreck, refer to Thutmose I or have either unreadable combinations of signs or good-luck and prophylactic signs.

Additional finds include two duck-shaped ivory cosmetic boxes, the ivory figurine of a female acrobat with her feet on her head, and more tin vessels than had previously been found throughout the entire Bronze Age Near East and Aegean. Beads of glass, agate, carnelian, quartz, gold, bone, Baltic amber, seashell, ostrich eggshell, and faience were raised by the thousands. A bronze female figurine, with hands extended forward, and with the head, neck, hands, and feet covered with gold foil also appeared. Probably representing a deity, she may have served to protect the ship from peril.

Left **One of two duck-shaped ivory containers that were found on the Uluburun wreck. Each has pivoting wings that served as a lid for its body cavity, which contained cosmetics.**

Weapons on board included arrows, spears, maces, daggers, an axe, a single armor scale of Near Eastern type, and swords. The bronze swords are of interest as they represent three unrelated types. Two are typical 14th-century Aegean products. The best preserved is a heavy Canaanite weapon with ivory and ebony inlay in its hilt; three daggers similar to it resemble a dagger from a 14th-century tomb in Israel. The last and most poorly preserved sword is similar to swords found in southern Italy and Sicily.

A large number of tools, which included sickles, awls, drill bits, a saw, a pair of tongs, chisels, axes, double axes, a plowshare, whetstones, and adzes, came mostly from the aft section of the ship. Virtually all are either of Near Eastern types or are shapes ubiquitous in the Eastern Mediterranean, but a few point to an Aegean connection.

Most of the Uluburun ship's cargo could have been taken on at a port in Syria-Palestine or Cyprus, but the origin of the cargo does not necessarily reveal the homeport of the ship that carried it. The latter is best revealed by the 24 stone anchors carried on the ship, which are of a type virtually unknown in the Aegean, but are often found in the sea or built into temples on land in Syria-Palestine and on Cyprus. Moreover, the ship itself was built of Lebanese cedar, a tree indigenous to the mountains of Lebanon, southern Turkey, and central Cyprus. Cultic and ritualistic objects aboard the ship, such as the probable bronze female deity, an ivory trumpet carved from a hippopotamus tooth in the likeness of a ram's horn, and a pair of bronze finger cymbals are probably also of Canaanite origin. Canaanite, too, are the oil lamps

Above **The thick-bladed bronze sword with flanged hilt inlaid with ivory and Egyptian ebony (right), is Canaanite, as is the dagger with hilt plates of an unidentified wood; the dagger's missing pommel was discovered later and attached to it. The lighter sword on the left, with fine midrib and grooves, is Mycenaean.**

Right **An archaeologist excavates delicate finds trapped between copper ingots (in the foreground) and two stone anchors in the general area of the ship's mast.**

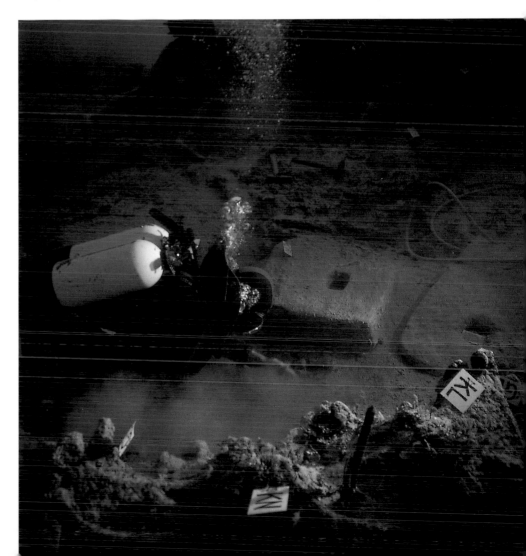

used on board, revealing the crew's preference for this lamp type over the more abundant Cypriot variety carried in pristine condition as cargo inside one of the large storage jars that was used, like a modern china barrel, to transport new Cypriot pottery.

Approximately 150 weights from Uluburun comprise the most complete groups of contemporaneous Late Bronze Age weights from a single site. As such, all standards and sets necessary for a merchant venture should be present. Most of the weights are of hematite or stone carved into known geometric shapes of the period, but the assemblage includes the largest set of Bronze Age zoomorphic weights, cast in bronze and sometimes filled with lead; these include a sphinx, bulls, cows, a calf, ducks, frogs, lions, a fly, and even the figure of a cow herder kneeling before three of his calves. While the bronze weights have suffered damage from corrosion, the other weights are generally well preserved and mostly correspond to a weight system based on a unit mass of 9.3 g, the standard commonly used along the Syro-Palestinian coast, on Cyprus and in Egypt. The numbers of sets suggest that there were at least three or possibly four merchants on the ship. Three sets of copper or bronze pans for balances, one pair nested and encased in its wooden sleeve, strengthen this view. The weights may be taken as nearly conclusive evidence of Canaanite or Near Eastern merchants on the ship. With one exception, no weights conform to the Aegean mass standard.

Foodstuffs, whether as cargo or for shipboard use, include almonds, pine nuts, figs, olives, grapes (or raisins or wine), black cumin, sumac, coriander, and whole pomegranates, along with a few grains of wheat and barley. Lead net sinkers, netting needles, fishhooks, a barbed spear and a trident of bronze indicate that the crew fished.

Estimated to have been about 15 m (49 ft) long and built of cedar, the Uluburun ship was constructed in the "shell-first" method with pegged mortise-and-tenon joints holding its planks together and to the keel. Used in Greco-Roman ships, this edge-joined planking technique contrasts with the more familiar "skeleton-first" construction method, whereby the planking is formed around and fastened to a pre-erected frame. In spite of our detailed examination of the hull remains, no evidence for any framing has emerged. Perhaps the preserved hull section is not large enough to include frames (ribs) or bulkheads, or evidence for securing such elements to the planking. The keel of the ship, which is wider than it is high, originally protruded into the hull rather that outward, as in later construction. This timber would have served as the ship's spine, as well as protecting the planks and supporting the ship when beached or hauled ashore. Unlike keels of later sailing ships, however, it would have done little to help the ship hold course or point nearer the wind under sail – in other words, it appears rudimentary in design rather than a keel in the traditional sense.

"Then he fenced in the whole from stem to stern with willow withies to be a defense against the waves, and strewed much brush thereon"
Odyssey, Book 5.256–7

Remains of a wicker fence call to mind the weather fencing on Syrian ships depicted in nearly contemporary Egyptian tomb paintings, and of the wicker fence

Above **The ship's cedar planks were held together by oak tenons inserted into mortises and then locked in place with oak pegs.**

Right **"Then he fenced in the whole from stem to stern with willow withies," Odyssey, Book 5.256–7. The Uluburun ship's wicker fence was still preserved on the seabed.**

Below **A diver illuminates some of the ship's mortise-and-tenon joined hull planks as they were found on the seabed. The keel protruded farther inboard than outboard. No evidence for framing was found.**

constructed by Odysseus to keep the waves out of his vessel. Like the brush mentioned by Homer, a layer of thorny burnet was found under the rows of copper ingots, and under it we found many sticks of branches, sometimes with bark, twigs and even leaves preserved, laid perpendicular to the ship's planking. The brushwood and sticks served as dunnage to protect the ship's planks from the heavy metal ingots and other cargo in the ship's hold.

Based on ceramic evidence, it appears that the Uluburun ship sank toward the end of the Amarna period or shortly thereafter. The unique gold scarab of Nefertiti indicates that it could not have sunk before her time. The earliest date for the scarab could be 1376–1358 BC, or 1339–1327 BC, depending on the chronology used. The scarab was found near a jeweler's hoard of scrap gold, silver, and electrum. If it was part of this hoard, the Uluburun ship probably sank after Nefertiti's reign, at a time when her scarab would have been worthless except for its gold value. It is hoped that ongoing precision carbon dating of short-lived items such as olive pits, resin, and brushwood, coupled with tree-ring sequencing, will provide an accurate date for the ship's sinking. For now, we may say that the ship sank at the end of the 14th century BC, around 1300 BC.

The Uluburun ship, therefore, sailed during a well-documented segment of history, and inferences from the Amarna letters as well as evidence from Egyptian tomb paintings can aid us in better understanding the nature of its voyage. The only clear depiction of a Mediterranean merchant venture is the mid-14th century BC scene in the tomb of Kenamun, the "Mayor of Thebes" in Egypt and "Superintendent of the Granaries" under Amenhotep III, which illustrates the arrival of a Syrian merchant fleet in Egypt. Porters unload cargo including Canaanite amphoras and a "pilgrim flask" that are similar to those found on the Uluburun wreck. Medallions on the necks of some of the crew resemble pendants we recovered during the excavation, and the large Uluburun storage jars found with their contents of intact Cypriot pottery allow us to speculate about the large jars depicted on the Syrian ships' decks. Perhaps coincidentally, the ships are shown with four merchants, identified by their long cloak-like garments and looped belts, the number suggested for the Uluburun ship by the balance weights. One man, probably the chief merchant, is

Above **A remarkable find was this unique gold scarab inscribed with the name of Nefertiti, chief wife of the Egyptian heretic pharaoh Akhenaten. It proves that the ship could not have sunk before Akhenaten's reign, but an even later date is likely since the scarab was found near a jeweler's hoard of scrap gold, electrum, and silver.**

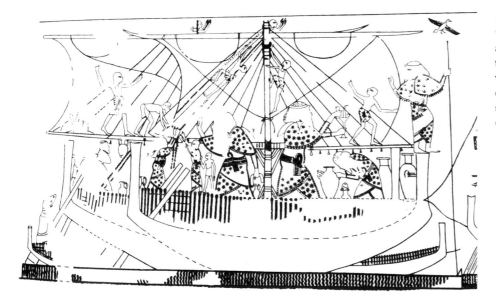

Left **A scene in the tomb of Kenamun, the "Mayor of Thebes," depicts Syrian ships arriving in Egypt. The excavation at Uluburun found wicker fencing for deflecting spray like that shown on the Kenamun ships (and described by Homer), and also gold medallions similar to those shown at the necks of the crew.**

engaged in an on-board ceremony, presumably in thanks for the successful conclusion of the journey.

Other Egyptian tomb paintings depict Syrian tribute bearers carrying elephant tusks, ebony logs, two-handled Canaanite jars, and other vessels of the types found on the wreck.

"…he sent him to Lycia and gave him baneful signs in a folding wooden tablet"
Iliad, Book 6.169

A boxwood diptych, consisting of two boards joined by a three-piece ivory hinge, unfortunately with its interior beeswax writing surfaces missing, was found in a large jar that had contained whole pomegranates. Although of the type mentioned by Homer in his only reference to writing, it, and part of another diptych, are most

Above **A boxwood diptych with ivory hinge. The recessed inner faces were scored to hold in place beeswax writing surfaces on which a scribe wrote with a stylus. Such diptychs continued in use until medieval times, but the earliest known wooden example before the Uluburun excavation was found in a well at Nimrud, Iraq, dating to around 700 BC.**

likely Near Eastern in origin. On the other hand, pairs of personal and utilitarian items of Mycenaean origin point to the presence of two Mycenaeans aboard the ship, perhaps as envoys. That they were not merchants engaged in trade is shown by the absence of their personal weight sets based on the Aegean standard. An Aegean connection for the Uluburun ship that extends all the way into the northern Balkans and the western Black Sea region is suggested by the recovery from the wreck of spears of a type found in northern Greece, and a ceremonial scepter-mace of a type known from Romania and Bulgaria, and believed to bestow social prestige on its bearer.

In sum, the Uluburun shipwreck demonstrates how essential and strategic raw materials, as well as other raw materials and manufactured goods, were dispersed from the Near East via maritime routes to the Aegean and beyond during the Late Bronze Age. In navigating this route, ships mostly hugged the southern coast of Turkey (sailing past Cape Gelidonya, as shown by the wreck of around 1200 BC, described on pages 48–55), and then rounded Uluburun before passing the southwestern corner of Turkey. The ships then continued west to Greece or sailed north into the Aegean Sea. Almost all the items on board our ship, cargo or otherwise, could have been taken on at a single Canaanite or Cypriot port, with some of the goods probably in transshipment. It is possible that ports in both areas were visited before the ship sailed toward a region west of Cyprus, but its ultimate destination can be only surmised. Perhaps it was Rhodes, an important redistribution center for the Aegean; or Crete, where Cypriot pottery like that on board has been found and which

Below **A gold pendant with granulated decoration in the form of a falcon clutching a pair of hooded cobras. The same motif, but with the cobras more clearly defined, appears on Canaanite jewelry excavated on land.**

is known from texts to have been visited by ships from the major Syrian port at Ugarit (near Latakia); or, more likely, it was a major Mycenaean port on the Greek mainland that could receive a cargo of such magnitude.

The objects found on the ship – from northern Europe to tropical Africa, and from as far west as Sicily and at least as far east as Mesopotamia – include products of nine or ten ancient cultures. This extraordinary cargo was probably placed in care of an official who represented a king's interests – and who probably engaged in some private trade of his own on the side. It is likely that the Mycenaeans on board were emissaries or messengers sent by a Mycenaean palace with the explicit purpose of securing and escorting, presumably to a Mycenaean port, the goods on the Uluburun ship.

Cargo from the Age of Bronze: Cape Gelidonya, Turkey

GEORGE F. BASS

Cape Gelidonya

Date late 13th century BC
Depth 26–28 m (86–92 ft)
Found by Kemal Aras
Excavation 1960
Cost $18,000
Cargo copper, tin, scrap bronze
Hull size unknown

The place of the Cape Gelidonya shipwreck in the history of underwater archaeology, as the first ancient wreck excavated in its entirety on the seabed, is less important to me than how its excavation rewrote a significant part of the history of the Bronze Age.

In the introduction to this book, I describe how the excavation came about: how Peter Throckmorton reported a wreck of the Late Bronze Age (1600 to 1000 BC) to the University of Pennsylvania Museum, how I was asked to learn to dive and become archaeologist in charge of its excavation, and how I took the first six lessons of a ten-lesson YMCA diving course before heading for Turkey with Peter in the spring of 1960. I did not describe the physical and intellectual adventures that followed.

In mid-June I sailed on a sponge-diving boat from Bodrum, then the sponging center of Turkey, accompanied by a vessel that normally dragged for sponges with a net attached to a metal axle on wheels. Neither boat was more than 10 m (33 ft) long. I had no inkling that my life was changing forever.

The wreck lay 26–28 m (86–92 ft) deep between two of five small, barren islands that run out from the cape, today known as Taşlıkburun, but we needed a source of fresh water for drinking, bathing, and cooking, and for leeching corrosive salts out of the artifacts we hoped to find. About an hour's sail from the wreck I spotted two damp patches in the sand on a narrow beach surrounded by high cliffs. We dug into the sand until we had two streams of fresh, cold water, which we dammed to form two basins. Between them we pitched our camp.

The Beach

I was still only a student. I'd never even dived in open water before I arrived in Turkey. No one had ever done on the seabed what we hoped to do. It had been difficult to attract funding. So our camp for eight people was mostly what Peter and I scrounged from a US Air Force base near Istanbul: part of a canvas mess tent, some discarded cot mattresses, torn parachutes we strung up for shade, and an electric generator that powered the darkroom we installed in a shallow cave at the base of the cliff. The wooden crates in which our diving equipment arrived from America served as furniture.

Without refrigeration, in a natural oven that reached 110°F (43°C) most mornings, we lived on little more than beans, rice, tomatoes, olives, and watermelon for three months, sending one of our two boats weekly to a distant village for supplies. We were a multi-national team, from the United States, Britain, France, and Turkey, joined later by Waldemar Illing, a powerful German diver who, when he had time, supplemented our diet by spearing fish.

Below **The expedition's home for three months was a narrow strip of beach about an hour's sail from the wreck site. Seen here on a calm day, it was abandoned when the first south wind of autumn sent waves crashing over it.**

Below right **Excavation director George Bass (left) and Peter Throckmorton puzzle over bits of wood and corroded bronze implements in the camp's simple "conservation laboratory."**

I had married Ann Singletary shortly before sailing to Turkey. She joined me after completing her master's degree in music, carrying two suitcases, one of clothes and one of music – expecting to find a piano?

French diver Claude Duthuit had the only pup tent.

"Take it, George," he gallantly offered. "It's your honeymoon."

Claude remains my closest friend!

The Excavation

Daily we sailed to the site, where we had permanently moored metal oil drums to which we tied our boats. We dived 40 minutes in the morning and 28 minutes in the afternoon, working hard on the seabed, with only a few minutes of decompression after each dive. Without a physician, or recompression chamber, or even medicinal oxygen, we must have had a guardian angel, for we suffered no cases of the bends.

When our little high-pressure compressor broke down and had to be sent to the nearest machine shop, an overnight sail away, we could no longer fill scuba tanks. Peter and I attached a hose to the sponge-boat's originally hand-cranked compressor, having made gaskets from old leather shoes, and continued to dive, although we were in what our pilot book said was the strongest current in the Mediterranean. We held on for dear life descending and ascending a rope running to the bottom, our bodies flapping like laundry on a windy day, and took turns bracing ourselves between rocks to hold our partner's hose so that he or she could let go and work with freed hands.

Chief diver Frédéric Dumas, on loan from Jacques-Yves Cousteau, was regarded as the world's greatest diver. He told Peter and me we were crazy, and refused to dive with our jury-rigged gear. Normally, however, we dived with scuba.

Laboriously we mapped the site by measuring with meter tapes from spikes we drove into the rock around the mostly metal cargo. This cargo was embedded in rock-hard seabed concretion that had built up in thickness over the years. Dumas suggested that we bring the cargo to the surface still encased in this concretion, so that we could extract it more carefully back at camp. From that time we hammered and chiseled to free massive lumps of concretion that we raised with air-filled lifting balloons, and then fitted back together on the beach.

The depth of sand was not sufficient to have covered and protected from shipworms and other marine borers the ship's wooden hull, although we found a few scraps of wood and, under some of the metal cargo, layers of twigs with the bark still preserved. This explained the brushwood Odysseus spread out in a ship he built, which had puzzled classicists. The twigs formed dunnage, a cushion for the cargo.

We removed sand with airlifts, nearly vertical metal pipes to whose lower ends we pumped air from the surface through hoses; as the air entered the pipes, it formed bubbles which rushed upward, creating a suction that pulled in both water and whatever sand we swept into the pipes' lower ends.

We had all but completed the excavation before the first south wind of autumn sent waves crashing completely across our narrow beach in mid-September, driving us from the Cape.

Above **With an ordinary pencil Claude Duthuit draws on a sheet of frosted plastic the positions of artifacts lying in a rocky gully.**

Below **The cargo was brought to the surface still embedded in large chunks of concretion that were put back together at the camp like pieces of a giant jigsaw puzzle. Ann Bass removes concretion, revealing copper ingots.**

Fatal Final Voyage

We had excavated a ton of metal. Thirty-four flat, four-handled ingots of almost pure Cypriot copper, weighing on average 25 kg (55 lb), were still stacked as they had been in the ship 3,200 years before. A material like white toothpaste was later shown, by chemical analysis, to be the remains of tin, probably tin ingots. Mixed with the ingots

Below **A bronze swage, 10 cm (3.9 in) long, was used like a small anvil for shaping metal. Sockets for tools were hammered out at one end.** *Above center* **Stone hammers 6 and 8 cm (2.4 and 3.1 in) in diameter, displayed with modern wooden hafts, resemble more recent hammers used for working metals.** *Below center* **Pan-balance weights of stone were based on Near Eastern weight standards.** *Above right* **The remarkably preserved bottom of a woven basket that held scrap bronze in the cargo.** *Center right* **Scarabs were Syro-Palestinian imitations of Egyptian scarabs.** *Below right* **A stone seal about the diameter of a pencil is like those once worn at the wrists of Near Eastern merchants. It is shown with modern string and modern clay onto which it has been rolled.**

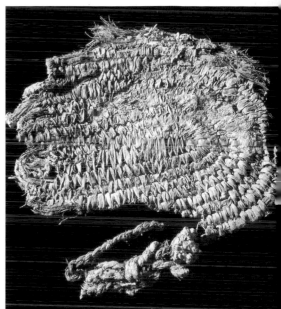

were broken bronze tools made on the island of Cyprus and carried in baskets, one of which we found remarkably preserved. The copper and tin, ingredients for making new bronze, and the scrap bronze, were all intended to be melted down and cast in molds to form new bronze objects.

The discovery of a grooved and pierced bronze swage (a kind of small anvil), two stone hammerheads of types sometimes used in metalworking, a whetstone, numerous stone polishers, and a large, close-grained stone with flat top that could have served as an anvil suggested that a traveling smith, or tinker, may have been on the ship's last voyage.

At one end of the site, which we believe to have been the living quarters of the ship, probably at the stern, we found the personal possessions of those on board – along with olive pits that had been spat into the bilge. About 60 small stone objects, some shaped like domed marshmallows and others like pointed American footballs flattened on one side so they would not roll, were merchants' weights for pan balances. The ship's saucer-like lamp, its rim pinched to form a spout to hold in place a wick that once floated on oil inside, was intact, but most of the pottery was broken. Each of two stone mortars was carved with a spout and three stubby legs.

From here, too, came unbroken metal objects such as a bronze razor and a small chisel once used for cutting mortises, four scarabs and a scarab-shaped plaque, and a cylindrical stone seal of the kind rolled out on clay documents as a kind of signature by Near Eastern merchants. An astragalus, or knucklebone, of a sheep or goat, reminded us of the game of knucklebones still played, like dice, in Europe. In antiquity, knucklebones were also used in divination, to receive a sign from the gods, and I wonder if it was by tossing a knucklebone that "fair-haired Menelaus" received such a sign when he debated which route to sail in the *Odyssey* (Book 3.173).

Anyone reading this can date a photograph to the early 20th century or to the late 20th century from the style of clothes, hairdos, or automobiles in it. Archaeologists similarly date artifacts, for styles have always changed. Thus, we knew early on that the ship sank around 1200 BC, probably just before, a date later verified by the radiocarbon dating of some of the twigs.

Rewriting History

At the time of the excavation, virtually all Classical archaeologists and ancient historians held that Late Bronze Age Greeks, today called Mycenaeans after Agamemnon's great citadel at Mycenae, monopolized maritime commerce in the eastern Mediterranean in the 14th and 13th centuries BC. They further believed that Semitic traders and seafarers, best represented by Phoenicians, did not begin their famed seafaring activities until the Iron Age, after 1000 BC, and more especially after 800 BC. Indeed, the main reason most scholars have dated Homer's composition or compilation of the *Odyssey* to the Iron Age, long after the Bronze Age events described in his epic poems, is his frequent mention of Phoenician seafarers, merchants, and metal smiths.

Small wonder that throughout the excavation, my colleagues and I assumed we were excavating a Mycenaean ship.

It was not until I began to study the stone weights that I had my first stirrings of doubt. Before hand-held calculators, I sometimes sat up through the night doing long division, trying to learn the standards of the weights. Just as today, where some nations use pounds and others use kilograms, there were various weight standards in antiquity. When I realized that the Cape Gelidonya weights were often multiples of 9.32 g, an Egyptian *qedet* used throughout the Near East and Cyprus, or 10.3 g, a Syrian *nesef*, I wondered why a Mycenaean merchant carried Near Eastern weights; anthropological studies show that merchants traditionally carry their own, familiar weights, even when they travel abroad.

From library research I learned that our terracotta lamp was probably Canaanite, and that the stone mortars had been manufactured on the Syro-Palestinian coast where the Canaanites lived. An Egyptologist determined that our scarabs were not Egyptian, but were Syro-Palestinian imitations of Egyptian scarabs, the hieroglyphs on them only meaningless decorations. Lastly, two scholars recognized the cylinder seal as having been carved in north Syria, although it seemed to be centuries older than the wreck, probably an heirloom passed from father to son. The bronze razor was another personal possession of Near Eastern origin.

With surprise I concluded, from these personal possessions, that our ship was Canaanite or proto-Phoenician or Syrian – in other words, of Near Eastern origin. A single ship, of course, is not a fleet, nor can it rewrite history. Our shipwreck was only the catalyst that led me to question prevailing views of scholars around the world.

Above **Like tribute bearers in ancient Egyptian tomb paintings, Turkish sponge-divers carry copper ingots from the wreck to the waiting hands of Captain Kemal Aras, discoverer of the site, for transport to storage and eventual display in Bodrum.**

Below **The ship's sole source of light after dark was a terracotta Canaanite bowl with pinched rim to hold a wick floating on olive oil inside.**

I re-examined virtually all published Egyptian tomb paintings and found that in the 14th and 13th centuries BC, four-handled copper ingots brought as tribute to the pharaoh are identified as Syrian, in one case even shown being borne from a Syrian ship. Another painting depicts a Syrian merchant fleet newly arrived in Egypt. Nowhere do we see Greeks. I turned to hundreds of 14th-century BC cuneiform documents excavated at el-Amarna in Egypt. They describe gift cargoes from various Near Eastern lands, without mention of Greece. I later learned that in Bronze Age Greek, written in what scholars call Linear B script, there is not even a word for merchant.

What had been the evidence before 1960 for the presumed Mycenaean monopoly on maritime commerce? The frequent finds of Mycenaean pottery throughout the Near East, including Egypt and Cyprus. Because there were not similar finds of Near Eastern goods in Greece, it was assumed that Mycenaean ships carried all this pottery.

To me there was a flaw in this reasoning. That Mycenaean pottery reached the Near East was unquestioned, but nothing proved it was carried there in Mycenaean ships. Further, I doubted that Mycenaean sailors were sailing around the eastern Mediterranean giving out free samples of their pottery. Something of equal value had to be coming back to Greece in return. Yet that something had to be invisible to the archaeologist. My published doctoral dissertation suggested that the invisible cargoes must have been raw materials – copper, tin, ivory, gold, cloth, and spices – things that left no trace in the archaeological record because soon after reaching port they were quickly consumed or manufactured into objects of the land or culture that imported them.

My publication received universally unfavorable reviews by Classical archaeologists. Luckily, I lived long enough to begin the excavation of another Late Bronze Age ship, one that sank about a century earlier, off the very next cape to the west, at Uluburun. Cemal Pulak, who directed most of its excavation and is responsible for its interpretation and publication, describes it elsewhere in this book. Its 20 tons of raw materials – copper, tin, ivory, ebony, glass, resins, shell, and spices and other foodstuffs – carried on a ship of almost undoubted Near Eastern origin,

On a return visit to the wreck nearly three decades after its excavation, the Institute of Nautical Archaeology's research vessel *Virazon* is anchored directly over the site, which lies between two of five small islands that extend out from the cape, seen in the distance.

convinced most scholars of an appreciable Semitic presence in the Bronze Age Aegean. Because of underwater archaeology, Homer's Phoenicians are no longer anachronistic.

Return to the Cape

By the 1980s, the Institute of Nautical Archaeology (INA) had its own research vessel, *Virazon*, fully outfitted with diving and underwater excavation equipment, including a double-lock recompression chamber. In 1987, while we were excavating the Uluburun site, Claude Duthuit, by now an INA director, suggested:

"Why don't we run over to Gelidonya with *Virazon*, just for nostalgia."

Cemal Pulak, to whom I had by now entrusted the excavation at Uluburun, came with us – and immediately found a sword, the first weapon from the site, which we had

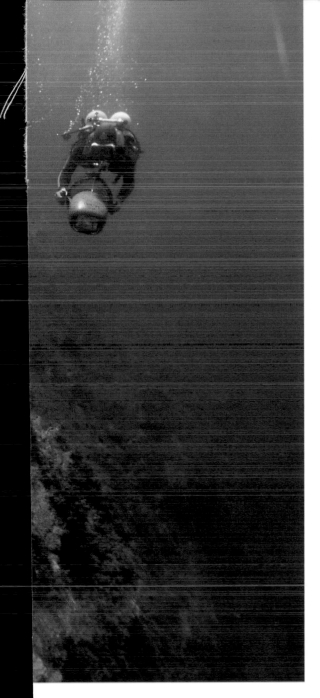

somehow overlooked nearly two decades earlier. With a better metal detector than we had in 1960, INA's Tufan Turanlı found additional metal finds, some trailing toward a pinnacle of rock that reached nearly to the surface and almost certainly tore open the bottom of the Bronze Age ship. Motorized underwater scooters now allowed INA divers to search far from the original cargo during almost annual visits to the Cape.

Discoveries were also being made in College Station. In 1990, Peter Throckmorton died quietly in his sleep, leaving his library, notes, and photographs to INA. Cemal Pulak soon recognized in photographs of scanty wood remains evidence that the Cape Gelidonya hull was constructed like his earlier Uluburun hull, in the same technique as that used to build the much later Kyrenia ship, also described in this book.

In 1994, Don Frey and Murat Tilev, using scooters, located the Cape Gelidonya ship's large stone anchor. It is of a type found throughout the Near East and Cyprus, both under water and on land, but in the Aegean only at a Bronze Age site on Crete that seems to have served as a harbor for Near Eastern traders. If we had found the anchor in 1960, perhaps my assigning a Near Eastern origin to the Cape Gelidonya wreck would not have been so controversial.

Above **On visits to Cape Gelidonya in the 1980s and 1990s, divers with motorized underwater scooters were able to explore far beyond the original excavation site, allowing them to discover the ship's stone anchor.**

Right **Although the cargo found at Cape Gelidonya weighed only a tenth of that at Uluburun, the Cape Gelidonya ship's anchor, being weighed on *Virazon* by Cemal Pulak, was heavier than any found on the earlier wreck.**

Ancient Greece depended on the ships that brought essential grain to her ports from the Black Sea, transported and supplied her colonists throughout much of the Mediterranean, and defeated her enemies in naval engagements. Without ships, Athens could not have become the definitive icon of Greek splendor. The Institute of Nautical Archaeology remains at the forefront of writing a detailed history of ancient Greek ships.

Excavations of 6th-century BC vessels found in Italian and French waters revealed construction methods unlike those associated with Classical shipbuilding of the 5th century BC and later. Their planks, instead of being fastened together by mortise-and-tenon joints, were laced together through pre-cut holes along the edges of the planks. Some scholars hypothesized that this was a peculiar Western Mediterranean tradition, perhaps representing and/or reflecting an Etruscan tradition, and that mortise-and-tenon joints continued in the Eastern Mediterranean from the Bronze Age (as we have seen in the Uluburun and Cape Gelidonya hulls) through the 4th century BC (as we shall see in the Kyrenia hull).

As described here by Elizabeth Greene, INA excavated for the first time in the Aegean a 6th-century BC shipwreck, at Pabuç Burnu on the Turkish coast. Almost certainly Greek, the hull was laced. We can now say with some confidence, therefore, that Greek ships of the Archaic Period (7th and 6th centuries BC) that preceded the glorious Classical Period (5th and 4th centuries BC) were all or mostly laced. And we may now assume that the 6th-century ships excavated in the Western Mediterranean were also Greek.

While Texas A&M University graduate student Sam Mark was working in the field with INA, he published two controversial articles proposing that the ships described by Homer were laced. Is it possible, then, that laced Greek hulls were the norm in the Bronze Age, the time of the Trojan War, and that Greeks borrowed mortise-and-tenon construction from Near Eastern Phoenicians in later Classical times? We need to find a Mycenaean hull, but when we do, I suspect that it will be laced, from a time when Near Eastern ships were already mortise-and-tenon joined.

INA has conducted the first complete seabed excavation of a Greek wreck from the 5th century BC, the century of the Parthenon, of philosopher Socrates, of political leader Pericles, and of dramatists Sophocles and Euripides. Deborah Carlson describes the Tektaş Burnu wreck and its excavation here.

The Kyrenia ship, built in the 4th century BC, has become the hallmark of nautical archaeology in the Mediterranean. It not only was the first shipwreck of its period fully excavated, but it was the first ancient hull ever raised from the Mediterranean

Archaeology student Deniz Soyarslan raises a large shallow bowl from the Pabuç Burnu shipwreck site. Items such as this, intended for shipboard use, are frequently found in the galley area of a wreck, usually located toward the stern of the vessel.

Above **Three rows of millstones from Nisyros lie centered over the Kyrenia ship's keel, serving for trade and ballast. Rhodian amphoras are stacked above them.**

Below **Places mentioned in this section, with the featured wrecks in bold.**

and reassembled on land. Further, two full-scale replicas have been built to show the public, from Greece and Cyprus to the United States and Japan, the exact appearance of the ships on which the ancient Greeks were so dependent. Even more, one of these replicas sailed from Greece to Cyprus and back, demonstrating its seaworthiness when going through a gale. Susan Womer Katzev, a driving force in the ship's excavation and conservation along with her late husband Michael, has taken time from completing the definitive scholarly publication of the site to share some of the highlights of the project here.

Although it sank about a quarter century later, it seems that the Kyrenia ship was built before the death of Alexander the Great in 323 BC. Thus we consider it a Classical Greek ship. After Alexander's death, three of his generals divided his empire among themselves, starting the two-century age known today as the Hellenistic Period.

INA has partly excavated two Hellenistic wrecks, one in Italy, at La Secca di Capistello, described here by Donald Frey, and the other at Serçe Limanı, Turkey, described by Cemal Pulak. Because of extreme conditions – the depth of the former and the fact that the latter was found to be partly covered by a rockslide of huge boulders – neither of these excavations has yet been completed.

As these lines are being written, INA archaeologists off the coast of Turkey are examining other 6th- and 5th-century BC wrecks to see if any are worthy of full-scale excavation. Annual surveys have revealed the locations of over 150 ancient wrecks on just a small part of that coast, but we believe that a wreck should not be touched unless it offers much new information about the past.

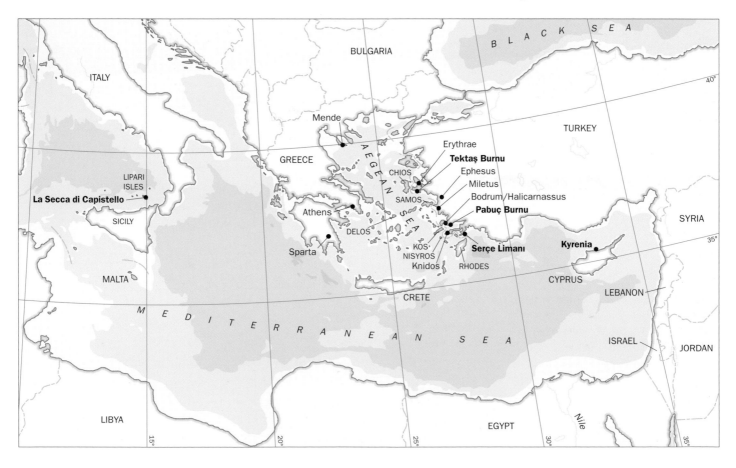

An Archaic Ship Finally Reaches Port: Pabuç Burnu, Turkey

ELIZABETH GREENE

From INA's submersible *Carolyn*, Feyyaz Subay and George Bass (right) watch Mutlu Gunay uncovering an amphora from the Pabuç Burnu site during the 2001 survey.

"Is it really a shipwreck?" photographer Don Frey wondered aloud. Don had just surfaced from an exploratory dive to investigate a scatter of ceramics reported by Turkish diver Selim Dincer. Intact and broken amphoras, or two-handled storage jars, dotted the sloping surface of the seabed 40 m (132 ft) underwater off the coast of Pabuç Burnu. "Shoe Point," shaped like a curved sandal, lies about 35 km (21 miles) from Bodrum, the site of ancient Halicarnassus, where the tomb built by King Mausolus became one of the seven wonders of the ancient world.

George Bass, director of the 2001 survey, felt sure it was a wreck when, from the submersible *Carolyn*, he watched Mutlu Gunay lift an amphora from the sand, revealing a nearly intact wine pitcher beneath. These must mark more than the cargo jettisoned from a ship in distress. The team's spirits rose higher after Mark Lawall, an amphora expert at the University of Manitoba, dated an emailed photograph of one of the jars to the mid-6th century BC. No shipwreck from the Archaic Period, which laid the foundation for the glory of Classical Greece, had ever been excavated in the Eastern Mediterranean!

As George and I wrote proposals for the project, we wondered, "What picture can we draw of Archaic trade?" From land excavations and literature, scholars construct images of the Greek tyrants who acquired exotic items through gift-exchange, much like the aristocrats of Homer's *Iliad* and *Odyssey*. We imagined the treasures we might find: the richly painted wine cups of lyric poets who composed songs for drinking parties, or the bronzes dedicated in great sanctuaries like Hera's temple on the island of Samos. But the fact that we conducted two seasons of excavation without discovering any commodity that could be labeled as luxurious forced us to consider what other goods moved throughout the Mediterranean.

The Cargo

Instead of painted pottery or the precious metals valued by an elite aristocracy, the majority of artifacts found on the Pabuç Burnu shipwreck are intact and broken amphoras, crafted perhaps at the nearby sites of Knidos, Ephesus, or Miletus. Ancient documents give a sense of the goods transported by the traders of the Greek East: Miletus was famed for its wool, Chios for its wine, Rhodes for sponges, Knidos for herbs, and Kos for raisins. Indeed, the sieved contents of our amphoras yielded grape seeds and olive pits – hints to stores of wine and oil, capped by tree bark stoppers. On the seabed, loose seeds suggest another cargo of foodstuffs, loaded on the ship in sacks along with other now-lost organic goods.

Day after day of excavation yielded thousands of amphora sherds, their scattered

Left **While waiting at the decompression stop, archaeologists take the opportunity to examine their finds, including this fragment of a fineware drinking cup decorated with black glaze.**

distribution perhaps caused by the trawling nets of modern fishermen. In a discrete area of the site, lying on the upper slope of the seabed, a number of rough pitchers, cooking bowls, and cups mark the ship's galley, or kitchen area, in the stern of the vessel. These locally produced wares were likely used by members of the ship's crew for cooking, dining, and shipboard sacrifice, rather than destined for trade. A lone stone anchor stock, located in the center of the site, suggests a moderate-sized vessel, slightly smaller than the 22 m (73 ft) spread of ceramic remains. All of these remains were placed on a three-dimensional site plan made from digital photography and computer modeling.

Above **These large shallow bowls or *mortaria*, discovered in what was probably the ship's galley area, may have been used on board by the ship's crew for preparing food.**

Left **Over 200 intact and broken transport amphoras once carried the ship's primary cargo of wine or olive oil. From their size, shape, and diagnostic features, amphora specialist Mark Lawall suggests an origin in nearby Knidos, Ephesus, Miletus, or even Halicarnassus.**

Right **Discovered in the center of the wreck site, this large stone anchor stock weighs about 115 kg (250 lb). It would have helped the anchor's wooden flukes, now consumed by marine organisms, grab the sea floor.**

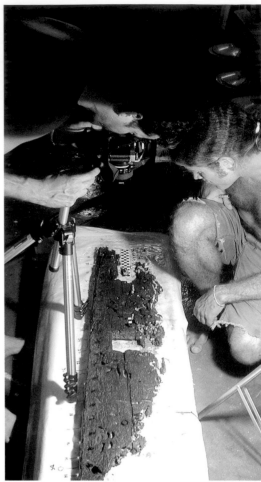

Above **INA Conservator Asaf Oron aids Assistant Excavation Director Mark Polzer (right) in his recording of the hull remains. On the edge of the plank, the lacing holes indicative of the ship's construction are clearly visible.**

Left **Archaeologist Robin Piercy excavates one of six fragmentary planks from the ship's hull. This one measures over 2 m (6.6 ft) in length and preserves evidence of the lacing techniques used to hold the vessel together.**

Construction

Don's initial doubts about the site were fully resolved by the middle of the first excavation campaign, when he sent up a note from the decompression stop. "Today *is* the day! I've found the hull." With excitement, Robin Piercy and I began work in the area on our next dive. As we moved sand with airlifts, Robin bubbled at me enthusiastically through his regulator, then made sewing motions with his free hand. Through our masks, we saw triangular holes on the edges of the plank that marked its construction; the ship's pine planks had been laced together like a sneaker, an appropriate find off the coast of Shoe Point.

Echoes of Homeric poetry ran through my mind as I looked at the plank. Before his departure from the island of Calypso, the hero Odysseus builds a boat for his journey:

He felled twenty trees in all, and shaped them with his bronze axe,
and smoothed them expertly, and trued them straight to a chalkline.
Meanwhile Calypso, the shining goddess, brought him an auger
and he bored through them all and fitted them to each other
with dowels, and then with cords he lashed his boat together
(*Odyssey*, Book 5.244–48)

As Assistant Excavation Director Mark Polzer has determined through careful research on the hull remains, construction features of the Pabuç Burnu wreck call such details to mind: widely spaced dowels join the planks in preparation for the laces that held them together. It may be cords and rotting hull planks like these that King Agamemnon laments in the second book of the *Iliad* (2.135), as he describes the damage wrought to the ships by nine long years of disuse at Troy. Before the East Greek tyrants such as Polycrates of Samos adopted sturdier "modern" building techniques (or mortise-and-tenon joints, as on the Kyrenia ship) in the late 6th century BC for their multi-level triremes, they appear to have laced their vessels together.

What boats did the Greeks imagine the heroes of Homeric poetry sailed? What vessels carried wandering sages like Thales and Pythagoras? And what cargoes did ships bear other than wisdom or the spoils of war? Ventures must have included the occasional jaunts of local farmers, like those to whom the Archaic poet Hesiod offers advice. Recommending journeys in late summer, after the harvest and before the autumn rains, Hesiod cautions (*Works and Days* 689–91), "Do not put all your goods in hollow ships; leave the greater part behind and put the smaller part on board; for it is a bad business to face disaster among the sea's waves." With its cargo of wine, olive oil, grapes, and organics stored in locally crafted amphoras, the wreck at Pabuç Burnu may represent just such a voyage: of a moderate-sized merchant vessel, carrying goods from a collective of farmers, that met ruin on the wine-dark seas.

Below **Mark Polzer's study of the hull remains suggests this reconstruction. Dowels and tenons formed the preliminary method of joinery before the hull planks were laced together. Lashed frames were then inserted to reinforce the vessel.**

Left **On this 6th-century BC Attic black figure cup in the British Museum, a pirate galley powered by sail and oars chases down a tubby merchant vessel that may resemble the Pabuç Burnu ship.**

A Wreck from the Golden Age of Greece: Tektaş Burnu, Turkey

DEBORAH CARLSON

Tektaş Burnu

Date 440–425 BC
Depth 38–45 m (125–149 ft)
Found by INA survey, 1996
Excavation 1999–2001
Number of dives 5,046
Amphoras 213

I will never forget the first time I saw the cliffs at Tektaş Burnu. It was June of 1999 and three of us – Murat Tilev, William Murray, and myself – had been sent ahead as a scouting party to assess the site's livability. What greeted us was a towering wall of razor-sharp, jagged spires of rock separated by deep, dark crevices. Weeks earlier, Murat, with several workmen, had driven pieces of angle iron into the rock and welded them together as a steel framework that, he hoped, would serve as the foundation for a dive platform. Within weeks, however, waves had utterly destroyed this experimental platform, pitching the arc welder into the sea, and leaving behind

Below **The *Artemis*, a wooden-hulled US Navy minesweeper-turned-passenger ship that housed the 1999 team, anchored in the lee of Tektaş Burnu, the "Cape of the Lone Rock." In the distance is the lone island that gives the cape its name.**

Above **The so-called Siren Vase of *c* 480 BC shows Odysseus tied to the mast of his ship while the singing Sirens attempt to divert him and his shipmates. The bow is outfitted with eyes similar to those found at Tektaş Burnu.**

Below right **Once on the sea bed, divers often removed their fins in order to negotiate the amphora mound without damaging artifacts or compromising visibility.**

only gnarled bits of steel that looked to me like tiny, twisted pipe cleaners.

What had brought us to Tektaş Burnu – Turkish for "Cape of the Lone Rock" – were the remains of a Greek shipwreck from the 5th century BC, what archaeologists call the Classical Period. This was the century in which the Greeks decisively defeated the invading Persian army, and Athens built a vast maritime empire funded in large part by tribute exacted from all Greek cities allied against the Persians. But the Athenians' domineering tactics earned them the resentment of the Spartans, and by the last quarter of the 5th century the two Greek superpowers had dissolved into civil war – the Peloponnesian War.

Shipping of both commercial and strategic goods played a vital role in the history of Classical Greece, yet no 5th-century shipwreck had been excavated in its entirety in the Aegean Sea.

The Tektaş Burnu wreck had been found in 1996, during one of INA's annual surveys of the Turkish coast, this one directed by Tufan Turanlı. As with most ancient shipwrecks, all that was visible of the ship was a portion of its cargo – a small mound of about 60 amphoras heaped on a sloping ledge between 38 and 45 m (125 and 149 ft) deep. The amphora mound was so small that on my first dive to the wreck in 1999 I swam right past it! Divers on the 1996 survey raised two amphoras from the site:

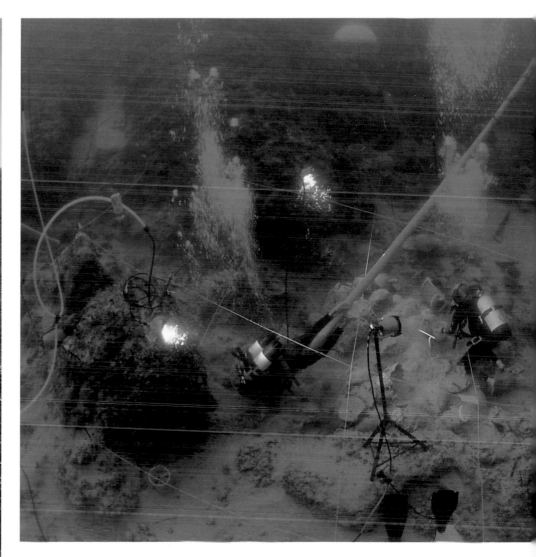

A Wreck from the Golden Age of Greece: Tektaş Burnu, Turkey **65**

one could not be identified with certainty, but the other had been produced in the northern Greek city of Mende some time between 450 and 425 BC. The team was surprised to find that the Mendean amphora was filled with dark, gooey pine tar, still viscous and odorous after nearly 2,500 years on the seabed!

As the field director, it was my job to report our impressions of that unforgettable visit in 1999 to the overall director of the project, George Bass. It was clear to all who had visited the site that the construction of any facilities on the rocks above the wreck would require a substantial investment of time and labor. George decided that we could simultaneously initiate both excavation of the wreck and construction of a camp if we could find a ship large enough to house our team of more than 30 students, professionals and INA staff. The challenge was to find such a vessel.

Preparations

After weeks of searching, we found the *Artemis*, a decrepit, 45 m (150 ft) long, wooden-hulled former US Navy minesweeper, which had been converted into a passenger ship that could accommodate upwards of 50 people in 28 berths.

Unfortunately, the challenge of finding the *Artemis* proved to be nothing compared with the daily stress of living aboard. Electrical failures were routine, and the pumps never worked properly, so that fresh water seldom reached the galley or bathrooms, and bilge water had to be pumped out manually, leaving the cabins on the lower deck in a chronic state of unbearable sogginess. Project historian William Murray, inspecting the *Artemis* during the ship's first days at Tektaş Burnu, observed: "There is a shark's bite out of the ship's stern, and the patch looks like someone nailed

Above **The 2000 camp at Tektaş Burnu became a permanent summer home for almost 30 people. The structures nearest the sea are the artifact conservation facility and dive platform, while the higher buildings include dormitories and a galley for meals and meetings.**

half of a ping-pong table to the transom and then stuffed Styrofoam around the edges on the starboard quarter." In addition to a smattering of other, smaller holes in the hull, the bowlines were badly frayed, and the rusty anchor chain terminated in an anchor of unknown size and dubious quality. The anchor was put to the test, however, during an extremely windy morning in August, when I emerged from my cabin and saw that the camp was unusually far away. A quick check revealed that both bowlines had parted and the ship was drifting frighteningly close to the rocky coast. It seems the *Artemis* might well have become the second ship wrecked at Tektaş Burnu, if the rusty anchor chain had not held long enough for us to secure new lines to shore.

The unpredictable and increasingly unpleasant living conditions aboard the *Artemis* hastened camp construction on the rocks, guided by the creative genius of INA's Robin Piercy. Unfortunately, the pace of progress on the seabed was conspicuously slower, due to a delay that year in the issuance of our excavation permit. As if sensing our frustration, however, the Turkish Ministry of Culture granted us permission to prepare the site for excavation, which meant that our team was able to dive on the wreck to set up safety equipment and install datum stakes and towers in preparation for mapping the site.

When our excavation permit arrived toward the middle of August, the majority of the team was set to return to their respective universities, leaving a small group to carry out the excavation. We moved ashore and watched *Artemis* steam away – forever, as it turned out, since she later ran aground, a total loss.

Initial Excavation

Though few in number, initial finds provided an unexpectedly accurate snapshot of the ship's cargo: large transport amphoras, smaller flat-bottomed jugs called table amphoras, oil lamps, shallow one-handled bowls, and black glazed drinking cups. Each amphora, once raised, was carefully emptied and its contents sieved in search of botanical remains such as grape seeds and pollen grains. In the case of one

Above **Archaeologist Elizabeth Greene produces one of more than a dozen table amphoras excavated from the wreck. Most were lined with pitch, suggesting that they were intended for transporting and serving wine.**

Left **Travis Mason and Mutlu Gunay examine the contents of an amphora after sieving for macrobotanical remains. On occasion archaeologists recovered small nails, tacks, and pottery fragments that had been pulled inside amphoras by resident octopuses – one amphora even produced an intact oil lamp.**

Right **Among the ceramic table wares in the cargo were a dozen unused lamps with nozzles for wicks and open bowls for oil. These may be products of the nearby island of Chios.**

Mendean amphora, sieving proved impossible because the jar was chock-full of butchered cattle bones, mostly ribs and tail bones – presumably the remains of salted beef, an uncommon commodity in the ancient world, and a powerful reminder that transport amphoras were used to ship far more than just wine and olive oil (and pine tar!).

A fascinating artifact appeared during the 1999 excavation campaign in the loose sand at the shallow end of the wreck: a white marble disk about the size of a saucer, incised with concentric lines and pierced through the middle by a large lead spike. Many of us were initially quite puzzled by the find, and various interpretations were advanced: was it an axle, part of a child's toy, or an obscure calendrical device? Perhaps it was the lid of an elaborate box or part of an ancient sculpture? Team members Troy Nowak and Jeremy Green simultaneously but independently identified the mysterious object as one of the ship's two eyes, or *ophthalmoi*, which would have adorned the bow of the vessel on either side of the stem. This contradicted the view that eyes in antiquity were simply painted on ships, as they are in the Mediterranean today. The second *ophthalmos* was discovered the following year, just meters away from where the first had surfaced.

Trials of Camp Life

Life on the rocks at Tektaş Burnu had its own set of challenges, which included biting flies, grasshoppers the size of a human fist, seasonal moth swarms, and the occasional rat, snake and scorpion. The winds that had snapped the bowlines of the *Artemis* were the *meltem*, which typically arrived after lunch and could agitate the sea sufficiently to make afternoon diving a harrowing experience. The "Cape of the Lone Rock" lay virtually totally exposed to the northwest – the source of the *meltem*, which could reach gale force overnight and was consequently responsible for many sleepless nights in camp. But these occasional hardships were offset by evenings of staggering sunsets and nights under a breathtaking canopy of stars.

Despite our initial success in taming the raw wilderness of Tektaş Burnu – which George deemed the most inhospitable place he has ever worked – we did receive an occasional reminder that Poseidon was ultimately the one in charge. As the 1999 season drew to a close, we opted to leave most of the camp structures standing, knowing that we would return to Tektaş Burnu the following summer. In an effort to protect the two enormous one-ton generators that had been hoisted onto shore in order to power the camp, we hauled them up and far away from the water, covering them with plastic sheets and huge metal cases. Still, to our dismay, rough seas brought by winter storms plucked one of these two massive machines from the rocks and hurled it into the sea more than 40 m (132 ft) down.

Productive Dives

We salvaged the lost generator, along with the welder that had earlier suffered the same fate, and returned to Tektaş Burnu in June of 2000 for what was to be our most productive summer. In just 12 weeks, our team of more than two dozen archaeologists excavated the bulk of the amphora mound and much of the surrounding area, systematically uncovering, mapping and raising an impressive array of artifacts that included cooking pots, drinking cups, and a large decorated

Above **Archaeologist Ken Trethewey uncovers the second of the ship's two marble eyes, or** *ophthalmoi.* **Ancient Greek mariners gave eyes to a ship to help it see its way through treacherous seas, a phenomenon that is still common in parts of the Mediterranean.**

Right In camp, team members spent hours mapping and digitally modeling artifacts to produce an accurate final site plan of the wreck, shown overleaf.

Above **This Greek *alabastron*, an alabaster container for perfumed oil, came from the ship's stern area.**

Below **Each of the Tektaş Burnu anchors was manufactured by pouring molten lead into a wooden stock. Earlier anchor stocks, like those from Pabuç Burnu, were of stone, while later anchors often had stocks made entirely of lead. Four lead cores are all that remain of the anchors after more than two millennia on the seabed (*below right*). Each of the two cores to the right has a cylindrical casting bolt protruding from its center, which indicates that the original wooden stock was about 4 cm (1.5 in) thick.**

decanter called an *askos*. Other objects seemed to be of a more personal nature: a lone alabaster bottle for holding perfumed oil, small square tiles of animal bone (perhaps gaming pieces), and an unusual ceramic lamp, different from the others, with a thick, heavy base and deep oil well that made it ideal for use on board a ship at sea. Scattered about the wreck in sets of two or four we located 14 notched lead bars, the remnants of five wooden anchor stocks, which had been hollowed out and filled with molten lead to give the anchor weight.

Working dives at Tektaş Burnu typically lasted 20 minutes, and on an average day about 15 divers would visit the wreck in both the morning and afternoon, meaning that we spent a combined daily total of at least ten hours under water. But one team member, who made her debut at Tektaş Burnu in 2000, was unlike any of us inasmuch as she could stay on the bottom for hours on end. She was *Carolyn*, a two-person

submersible that joined the INA fleet primarily as a survey tool, but which proved to be a useful addition to the excavation at Tektaş Burnu. The *Carolyn* made it possible for George or myself to study the progress of the excavation over a period of hours, instead of mere minutes, and make suggestions or alterations in order to improve our level of efficiency.

Working under water is really all about striking a balance between precision and speed, organizing your dive, your equipment, and your thoughts so as not to waste a second of time on the seabed. At Tektaş Burnu, one aspect of the excavation that was made markedly more efficient was the mapping of the site, which relied on a system of photogrammetry designed by Tufan Turanlı and fine-tuned by Jeremy Green and Sheila Matthews. In essence, Tufan or Jeremy recorded the provenience of each object using calibrated digital cameras, and then processed the digital images to create a three-dimensional map of coordinates. In a separate process, Sheila digitally modeled each artifact individually, and then inserted the image onto the pre-existing coordinates, creating a very realistic computer-generated site plan with centimeter accuracy.

We returned to Tektaş Burnu with a small team to complete the excavation in 2001. By this third season, our camp had become a kind of palatial summer retreat complete with a dishwasher and flushing toilets. Only the dive platform, which was nearest sea level, had to be rebuilt at the beginning of every summer. The 2001 season, however, brought with it some particularly inclement weather, and just days after the completion of our new dive platform, the enormous swells of a fast-approaching storm dismantled the platform in less than an hour. On the wreck, it seemed even the local marine life was ready for us to depart Tektaş Burnu. When on one dive I descended to excavate a small cluster of three amphoras, I arrived to find a 3-m (10-ft) long moray eel coiled like a cobra ready to strike. I might have found the courage to stand tall, had not Robin Piercy earlier been bitten on the foot by another moray!

EPY

George is fond of saying that the most exciting archaeological discoveries are made in the library, sometimes long after the excavation is finished. To be honest, this rubric had always struck me as something one says to conciliate those who have not experienced the thrill (and exhaustion) of three months in the field. But I will admit now that, for me, the most meaningful moment of the Tektaş Burnu shipwreck excavation occurred neither at Tektaş Burnu nor during the excavation, but in the Bodrum Museum of Underwater Archaeology, one year after the excavation was over.

It was the first study season, and three of us – Kristine Trego, Catharine Corder, and myself – were busy taking artifact photographs and gathering volumetric data on more than 100 intact transport amphoras. While measuring the capacity of one jar, Kristine noticed that it had been stamped on the neck with an unusual mark: a circle framing the Greek letters EPY – Epsilon, Rho, Upsilon. We immediately recognized this as the abbreviation of Erythrae, an ancient Greek city on the western coast of Turkey not far from Tektaş Burnu.

In antiquity, Erythrae and 11 neighboring cities and islands along the western coast of Turkey were part of a region called Ionia. It was the Ionian Greeks who, by revolting from the Persian Empire in 499 BC, precipitated the Persian invasion of

Above **A digital site plan – another INA first – shows how the vessel came to rest between two large rock outcrops in an area roughly 12 m (36 ft) long and 4 m (12 ft) wide. The rocks kept the hull exposed to marine organisms which devoured the wood.**

Above right **An artist's rendering of the ship sinking at Tektaş Burnu. The absence of any plainly personal items on the wreck suggests that the crew had sufficient time to escape with their possessions.**

Left **The only lettered amphora stamp from Tektaş Burnu carries the Greek letters Epsilon, Rho, Upsilon and represents Erythrae, one of the 12 cities of Ionia. Other amphora stamps from the wreck include simple circles and a leaf motif.**

mainland Greece and, ultimately, the Athenian defeat of the Persians 20 years later.

Erythrae's closest neighbor to the west was the island of Chios, visible from Tektaş Burnu on all but the haziest summer days. During the course of the excavation, trips to the Chios Archaeological Museum revealed that several pottery types from Tektaş Burnu had strong Chian parallels, while the presence of a lone Chian amphora enabled us to refine the date of the wreck to between 440 and 425 BC.

The discovery of the EPY amphora stamp not only permitted the identification of a previously unattributed amphora type, but also offered proof of what many of us had long suspected: that the Tektaş Burnu ship was a modest, local merchantman carrying a cargo of wine, pine tar, and East Greek pottery and following a coastal course, probably southward, when it was wrecked off the unforgiving rocky coast of Ionia.

During the second Tektaş Burnu study season, in 2003, Kristine and I were walking along a quay of the Bodrum harbor one evening when we spied a small boat, not more than 10 m (33 ft) long, dwarfed by the *gulets* and their colorful banners advertising exotic daily charters. On the stern of this modest vessel sat an old sailor on a makeshift stool, heating his dinner in a pot by the dim light of a small lamp. Kristine and I stopped, transfixed by the sight of what seemed to us to be a perfect modern rendering of the small-scale merchant venture that ended nearly 2,500 years ago at Tektaş Burnu.

Resurrecting an Ancient Greek Ship: Kyrenia, Cyprus

SUSAN WOMER KATZEV

"The bow plank that was a glowing golden color just last week…it's turning brown. Oxygen must be getting to the wood. We don't dare leave that hull on the bottom over another winter. But how are we going to raise her?" Laina Wylde Swiny, architect in charge of mapping the ancient ship, up from her morning dive, voiced our worst fears. Were we about to lose the precious treasure lying 27 m (90 ft) below…the most perfectly preserved ancient Greek ship ever found?

It all began in the autumn of 1965. Town councilman Andreas Cariolou, diving for sponges, chanced upon a mound of 80 graceful amphoras emerging from a carpet of eel grass on the flat seabed less than a mile from Kyrenia, his home on the north coast of Cyprus. For two years he kept his secret until meeting my husband Michael Katzev and me and guiding us over the wreck. In the most dramatic dive of our lives we were alone with the ancient jars, now homes for darting squirrelfish, untouched by man for 2,300 years.

Two summers of excavation peeled away layers of cargo, dining wares, tools, ship's rigging, and even four bone eyelets from a sailor's sandals. Cradling them like open hands was the still curving ship that had borne them from foreign ports and at last took them to the sea floor. Sixty percent of the ship and more than 75 percent of her representative timbers lay exposed. How could we raise the softened wood before the coming autumn storms?

The ship had sunk on an even keel, her cargo intact, striking the soft bottom and then rolling onto her port side. While currents slowly buried and preserved that side, the bow and stern broke away under the weight of an anchor, amphoras, millstones, and iron ingots. Then the exposed starboard side, easy prey to teredo worms, fell

Kyrenia

Built c 325–315 BC
Sunk c 295–285 BC
Depth 27–30 m (89–99 ft)
Found by Andreas Cariolou
Excavation 1968–1969
Conservation 1969–1974
Team 54 (international)
Total cost $300,000
Hull 14 m (47 ft) long, 4.2 m (14.5 ft) wide

Right **With plastic grid frames and one last amphora still in place, the preserved hull is ready for lifting. This bow view shows how the ship broke apart. To the right on the better preserved port side jagged lead sheathing projects beyond the ribs. A few years before sinking this last repair was meant to keep her watertight.**

Opposite above **The author's first dive over the mound of amphoras from Rhodes that was the tombstone for the Kyrenia Ship.**

outward, breaking off from the keel and leaving most of the cargo compressed in the better-preserved port side. Could we raise each side intact? We learned through the American Embassy that no helicopter in the Mediterranean was capable of hoisting 5 tons of our ship off the bottom. We would have to take the delicate hull apart piece by piece.

With rolls of Dymo tape, Laina labeled every scrap of wood. Using three different methods of mapping for insurance, our 54-member team recorded the hull with stereo photos, manual triangulation, and a new invention of movable vertical rods called "the cheesecutter".

As the first autumn storm strained the moorings of our diving barge, the last lifting trays of wood broke surface and reached the safety of a fresh-water holding pool inside a vaulted gallery of the massive Crusader castle that dominates Kyrenia harbor. Like first parents we scrubbed, bathed, and photographed each timber, then catalogued and made full-scale tracings of each side until thousands of pieces of the old ship were safely recorded. It took seven people five years. Our goal was to preserve and reassemble the original ship inside this gallery.

"We cannot settle for less than 100 percent saturation," said conservator Frances Talbot Vassiliades, fresh from studies at London University. "Look how this test piece twisted and shrank at lower concentrations...we cannot risk doing that just to save time. So let's start figuring on years, not months of treatment." The saturation would be with a water-soluble wax called polyethylene glycol, PEG for short. Visits to European labs had shown that PEG was our only hope. But no one had yet reached 100 percent saturation. So riddled was our ship's Aleppo pine with ancient teredo worms that the timbers easily soaked up the preservative in heated tanks. Almonds treated in seven months, but hull members demanded over a year for each tank load.

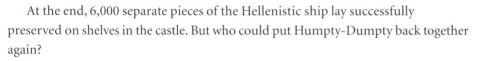

At the end, 6,000 separate pieces of the Hellenistic ship lay successfully preserved on shelves in the castle. But who could put Humpty-Dumpty back together again?

Just as Michael Katzev's first lecture in Cyprus had brought the tip leading to Andreas and this spectacular wreck, Michael's lecture in Lancaster, Pennsylvania, attracted the attention of electrical contractor J. Richard Steffy. Dick Steffy's basement models were already testing construction theories for the Yassıada Byzantine ship, but the chance to work on an actual hull sparked him to leave his comfortable business, move with his wife and two sons to Cyprus, and immerse himself in unraveling the secrets contained in the ship's timbers.

The Ship Speaks

Over four years, aided by Michael and apprentices Robin Piercy and Chip Vincent, Dick pieced the Kyrenia ship back together, pinning the brittle wax-treated timbers to each other using stainless steel rods. "The men who built the Kyrenia ship were real craftsmen," he says. "In fact they were sculptors. Today we are in a hurry and we penny-pinch to use the least materials. So we start a ship by building a skeleton of ribs, or "frames," bolted to the keel, and then we wrap sawn boards around the outside to plank the ship. Kyrenia's builders adzed those outer planks first. They carved away over 70 percent of the original wood to sculpt the entire outer shell, without an interior framework."

Like weaving a basket upwards, the shipwrights joined the first carved plank to the keel using mortise cuttings linked with oak tenons spaced every 12 cm (4.7 in). Pegs locked them together. It took nearly 4,000 mortise-and-tenon joints to attach all the

Far left **Unloading tanks of now waxy wood, team members Laina Wylde Swiny (left), David Steffy, author Susan Katzev and Netia Piercy sponge off excess wax, then bag the timbers to cool slowly.** Left **Pieces of the ship's flooring lie atop full-scale tracings on archival mylar. Found fragmented from the weight under water of the millstones and amphoras, these planks bear 22 carved Greek letters, their meaning a mystery.** Right **Masking tape alignments guide Dick Steffy as he drills a long stainless steel rod to join the wax-filled original timbers.** Far right **The late excavation director Michael Katzev (left) discusses the ship's original lines with Dick Steffy. Katzev's 30 years of research on the ship will be published in INA's Nautical Archaeology Series by a team of specialists.**

Above **The hull fully reconstructed, representing over four years' work by Dick Steffy and his apprentices.**

pre-carved planks edge to edge over the whole 14 m (47 ft) length of the ship, fitting them so tightly that no caulking was needed. Only after eight or nine of the 13 planking rows were securely linked did the Greeks shape the first ribs to fit inside the shell. Driving pure copper spikes from outside through the ribs and clenching them down like staples, the builders locked the ribs in place to stiffen the ship. But the shell of planks was the ship's true strength.

Life on Board

Launched close to the year Alexander died, 323 BC, our merchantman must have moved tons of cargo through the eastern Mediterranean in the turbulent years when Alexander's surviving generals were carving his empire into kingdoms of their own.

Rhodes, the most prosperous island in the region, whose merchants the orator Lycurgus said, "sail the entire civilized world for trade," used her navy and diplomacy to remain independent of the generals. I believe our merchant captain could have homeported in one of her thriving harbors and that his name began with the letters EUP, which he scratched into the base of a plate designed for dipping tidbits of fish into a spicy sauce. He needed to be literate to keep his books and deal with harbor documents. We found his inkwell and perhaps a personalized wine amphora marked EU. Much of the ship's black glazed pottery lay in two distinct areas – the far bow and stern. A short deck in the bow carried a wooden anchor, its stock filled with poured lead as on the Tektaş Burnu ship (see page 69). Clusters of small folded lead weights tell us that one of two fishing nets was on this deck. In foul weather, the crew slept in the open space below, among seven amphoras from Samos filled with over 10,000 almonds.

How many men lived aboard this trader, 14 m (47 ft) long by 4.2 m (14.5 ft) wide? Four oil jugs, four identical drinking cups, four salt dishes, four wine pitchers and four wooden spoons tell the story of a captain and three sailors.

Aft of the foredeck rose the single mast carrying a broad square sail, which reefed upwards through lead brail rings like a Venetian blind. Beside the mast lay logs useful for making on board repairs and iron tools to shape them. Dick thinks a ton or two of cargo is missing from the bow, probably perishables such as food stuffs or cloth.

Loading Up

I picture our captain and crew at Rhodes loading for their last voyage. They already had the almond-filled Samian jars stowed bow and stern, along with the perishables mentioned above, and a leftover shipment of 29 heavy millstones fashioned on the nearby volcanic island of Nisyros. The odd number, and a lack of matching pairs, suggests that they were sold singly to replace bakers' broken stones, meanwhile serving as ballast in three rows centered over the keel.

Now they filled the open hold with Rhodian amphoras, their conical shape handy for wedging in across the wide-bellied ship. Some jars were stamped on their handles with names of potters, magistrates, or traders, and all had been swirled inside with hot, black pine pitch to make them watertight. The wine they carried – most likely the popular table wine Rhodes exported north to the Black Sea and south to Egypt – took on the resin flavor that survives as "retsina" in modern Greece.

Each full amphora weighs 41 kg (90 lb). We think a circular bronze strap and ring were the end of a hoist our crew used to lift each jar off the dock, swing it inside, and lower it into the neat stacking pattern we found. On Cyprus we made replica amphoras and practiced loading them with all 17 tons of cargo found on the original ship into a sailing replica named *Kyrenia Liberty*. *Liberty* is equipped with her own hoist, called a "mast derrick." Using pulleys and a hook just like one found in excavation, a crew of four could load a grain mill or offload a full amphora in just 20 seconds. At this rate the entire cargo could easily be loaded in a morning. All together over 380 amphoras in ten different shapes were aboard when the ship left harbor heading east to Cyprus. Just-harvested millet, grape seeds and almonds tell us the season was September or October, and coins and amphoras indicate the year was about 295 to 285 BC.

The helmsman on the aft deck steered with two oars called "quarter rudders." We found the blade of the starboard rudder lying outside the collapsed stern. Through the hatch near his feet, the captain could drop down into the only closed cabin. Here was a cargo of nearly pure iron ingots; a spare sail, its many lead rings sewn in rows; spare rope and tackle; and a bow drill and other ship's tools. All were preserved inside a large concretion that formed around the iron ingots. A tiny votive lamp, the captain's inkwell, an elegant bronze ladle ending in a duck's head, a fish hook, and many studded nails, possibly decorating a wooden box, were cemented in the mass. The captain's drinking cup and inscribed plate lay nearby.

Here, too, was a marble ceremonial basin resembling a modern birdbath. Such basins are found in sanctuaries and shipwrecks, reminding us of references to ceremonies asking and thanking Poseidon for safe passage. Perhaps our captain was prepared to give thanks for safe arrival in Kyrenia. Whether he ever entered the harbor we will never know.

Above **Jill Scott Black holds the smallest of the ten types of amphoras. The different shapes identified the city or island producing them and can even reveal the approximate date.**

Below **The ship's pottery served a crew of four. Behind the ladle is a specialty plate designed for dipping tidbits of fish into sauce in the center depression, its base inscribed EUP. Above it, the captain's inkwell.**

Why Did She Sink?

"All those years of voyaging had taken their toll," Dick learned. "The Kyrenia ship was tired and weak." After many repairs, with a patched bow and years of teredo worm damage, she had been sheathed in lead as a last effort to keep her watertight. The golden plank Laina had seen was a recent repair. But under the millstones, years of bilge water had softened the old ship's backbone, and the lack of attachment between ribs and keel proved the ship's "Achilles heel."

Did the captain, knowing of the accumulated ravages from decades at sea, decide to give it all up and scuttle his ship to cover up some shady deal?

The riddle of her sinking, within sight of Kyrenia, remains unsolved. Violent storms drive down from the Taurus mountains of southern Turkey without warning, and Kyrenia's ancient harbor may have been dangerously exposed. Before the modern breakwater was built the locals always put to sea in the face of incoming storms. Perhaps our merchantman was attempting this maneuver when her old hull finally failed. With no natural hazards to wreck her, this seemed the best explanation until, years into studying the artifacts, we came upon unexpected finds.

"Spears! These are spearheads or maybe javelin tips, and there are eight of them. Look, four have lead sheathing, even scraps of wood attached, and one tip is bent. What were spears doing underneath the hull?" Michael had just sawn apart small lumps of iron concretion that had lain on our storeroom shelves since being found some years after the ship was raised. Then he cleaned iron dust from inside the molds and made rubber casts of the rusty

Above **Found beneath the hull, eight iron spearhead or javelin tips survived to be cast in those rubber replicas. Their presence hints at piracy to explain the ship's sinking.**

Below **A reconstruction of the ship as she may have looked, with cutaway areas to show the cargo and construction techniques used. Lead sheathing ensured that the hull remained watertight.**

RICHARD SCHLECHT

Left **Fitting outer planks together over close-spaced tenons, shipyard owner Manolis Psaros (below) and master shipwright Michaelis Oikonomou of Perama, Greece, recreate ancient shell-first construction.**

originals – light javelin heads. Had the ship sunk on the site of a previous naval battle? Unlikely. But what if these javelins had been imbedded in our hull during a pirate attack? In a Greek vase painting a pirate ship appears ready to ram a merchantman in her starboard bow. In this area of our ship no wood survived, but our worm-riddled bow would have offered little resistance. Possibly attackers drove javelins into the hull to pull their craft alongside for boarding. With the bow slowly taking water, there would have been time for pirates to snatch up valuables and take captive the four mariners, leaving the ship to sink. Slave markets prospered in Delos, Crete, Syria and the nearby south Turkish coast. But in a kinder scenario, captives could also be ransomed back to their families.

In Alexander's wake, his Macedonian general Antigonus, with his son Demetrius, were now at war with the Egyptian general Ptolemy I. Caught between were the islands of Cyprus and Rhodes. In 306 BC Demetrius captured Cyprus from Ptolemy, then turned his attention to independent Rhodes, sending ships to seize any merchants sailing to Egypt from Rhodes. When the Rhodians refused to yield, Demetrius besieged their island for a year, spreading the noose of his navy and pirates to intercept Rhodian shipping. With Ptolemy's aid the Rhodians broke the siege, preserving their sovereignty. But the seas of the eastern Mediterranean teemed with pirates for years to come.

Piracy would explain why certain things one might expect to find are missing from the wreck. Only seven bronze coins minted 306 to 294 BC were found. These were small change, not the high values needed for business. And how could a ship trade without several sizes of bronze balance scales and sets of weights? This most basic equipment found on other wrecks is absent in ours. What happened to the personal possessions of our crew? Four sandal eyelets and two bronze beads were hardly the belongings of four men.

Another sinister surprise waited on the storeroom shelves. A folded lead sheet known as a "curse tablet" had been slipped inside a lead envelope and pierced with a copper spike. Its find spot suggests the spike was driven into the ship's main crossbeam, then clenched downward to hold the curse in place.

Similar tablets found throughout the Greek and Roman world were inscribed with morbid spells naming the curser's enemies and begging gods of the underworld to wreak miseries upon them and their families, dragging their tortured souls down into hell. Tablets found uninscribed, like ours, are thought to be the work of illiterates. Inside our tablet were two pieces of white string, perhaps to bind the accursed down. All materials for the tablet were on board…fish net string, lead sheathing, and the copper spike. Was a seaman disgruntled with the captain? Or had illiterate pirates incanted a spell to bind the sinking ship into the sea? If so, they succeeded…but only for 2,300 years. The old ship has risen to display again the masterful craftsmanship of her builders, and to honor the men who shared her life.

Saturation Diving for Archaeology:
La Secca di Capistello, Italy

DONALD A. FREY

La Secca di Capistello

Date 3rd century BC
Depth 59–80 m (195–264 ft)
Excavation 1976–1977
Mixed gas dives 5.5 hours on site
Saturation dives 3 teams,
157 hours on site

I had second thoughts as I stood in my vertical steel coffin and heard the hatch bolted shut. The re-breathing mask strapped over my face only added to my claustrophobia in the cramped Robertina diving bell. Two days earlier I had helped lower the bell to 250 m (825 ft) and seen it come up dry inside. This time I would descend only 65 m (215 ft), where stresses would be considerably reduced. But what would happen if a porthole struck a rock on the slopes below?

As the bell descended I thought about my meetings with Giunio Santi, Director of Subsea Oil Services (SSOS) of Milan. He believed that the deep divers SSOS continually trained would be better motivated if they had something more interesting to occupy them than artificial tasks on the seabed. At the same time, these trainees could excavate deeper than INA divers. We decided to join forces.

Now, on a hot August day in 1976, I was descending into the cool, blue sea to monitor SSOS divers excavating a 3rd-century BC Hellenistic ship that had wrecked at La Secca di Capistello, a reef off Lipari in the Aeolian Sea north of Sicily. Through the bell's ports, I watched and photographed teams of SSOS trainees as they airlifted the sediment covering an intact layer of amphoras. I had chosen the wreck for excavation because it seemed less pillaged than other wrecks I had seen, with George Bass and Robin Piercy, on an INA/SSOS survey several months earlier.

The trainees were learning mixed-gas diving. When breathing compressed air SSOS divers do not work deeper than 50 m (165 ft). But with a nitrogen-free mixture of helium and oxygen, divers can descend hundreds of meters. The expense of mixed-gas diving, and the requisite technical support, had until now precluded archaeologists from excavating shipwrecks deeper than 50 m (165 ft); indeed, an attempt to excavate this wreck on air had ended with the deaths of two German archaeologists in a 1969 diving accident.

In 1977, I returned to La Secca di Capistello with a team being trained for saturation diving. During the previous year, trainees' bottom time was limited to 20 minutes by the need to decompress at the end of each dive, in order to release gradually the nitrogen in their blood that could otherwise form fatal bubbles. Saturation diving overcomes this. At every depth there is a limited amount of dissolved gas the blood will hold – a saturation point. Divers can take advantage of this by diving and living at the same pressure not for minutes, but for *weeks*, before resurfacing through a single, lengthy decompression. On the SSOS training ship *Corsair*, divers lived in a chamber filled with a mixture of helium and oxygen maintained at a pressure equal to that of 60 m (198 ft) of water. Daily they entered a personnel transfer capsule (PTC) locked onto the chamber with the same pressure

Above Teams of four Italian divers lived for a week at a time inside a pressurized chamber on the training ship *Corsair*, and were lowered in this pressurized PTC (personnel transfer capsule) to the wreck, where they could work outside for hours without daily decompression.

Left Don Frey enters the Robertina diving bell to be lowered to the site for observation of work in progress.

Below Saturation diving allowed careful excavation of cargo and hull at greater depths than scuba divers can work.

of gas inside. Sealed in the PTC and lowered to the seabed, divers then took turns working outside while breathing the gas mixture through umbilical hoses.

During 21 days, three different groups of four divers lived in the chamber. Each morning and afternoon a two-man team descended to the site to work for about four hours. Sometimes one of the INA archaeologists – Faith Hentschel, Donald Keith, and Michael Katzev – observed the work from the PTC, or from a maneuverable two-person submersible. At other times, we followed progress by closed-circuit television, giving instructions over the divers' umbilicals.

Using closed-circuit television we also obtained exceptionally clear videotapes. These, along with sharp, time-exposure photographs taken by the divers from portable photo towers, allowed us, on *Corsair*, to draw a site plan. As expected, the hull was built in the shell-first manner common to Greco-Roman vessels, its planks held together by mortise-and-tenon joints.

Many of the Greco-Italic amphoras, whose contents included olives, grapes, and pistachio nuts, still had cork stoppers. We could date the cargo to the first quarter of the 3rd century BC by the shapes and decorations of ceramic drinking cups, fish plates, lamps, and black-glazed Campanian wares.

Our La Secca di Capistello excavation was at its time the deepest ever conducted under archaeological controls, and the first use of saturation diving for archaeology. INA had opened a new door to underwater excavations.

Digging into an Avalanche: The Hellenistic Wreck at Serçe Limanı, Turkey

CEMAL PULAK

Serçe Limanı Hellenistic Wreck

Sunk	280–275 BC
Depth	35–37 m (115–121 ft)
Found by	Mehmet Aşkın
Survey	1973, 1977
Excavation	1979–1980
Amphoras onboard ship	c 1,000
Number of dives	c 1,800
Hull	c 18 m (60 ft) long

We were 36 m (118 ft) deep, on a nearly barren seabed. Large boulders lay landward of us. George Bass signaled that we were on the Hellenistic wreck. I strained to see what he had seen, but could make out only occasional amphora fragments, the bits of pottery found nearly everywhere along this coast. Seeing my puzzlement, George chose a spot and began to fan furiously by hand, lifting billowing plumes of milky silt, which quickly engulfed him. As the silt cloud moved slowly away, I could make out features through the haze. I caught George's eyes beaming through his mask. He pointed at the gaping hole he had dug in seconds. In it were the intact amphoras, one on top of the other, of a wreck.

A rocky promontory flattened by sledge hammers served as a dive platform with double-lock recompression chamber and air banks (right), and bins for diving equipment. The two hoses leading into the sea provided surface-delivered air to archaeologists working on the wreck.

We were in Serçe Limanı ("Sparrow Harbor"), a natural harbor on the southwestern coast of Turkey, to excavate the 11th-century medieval shipwreck described in this book. I had asked George to show me the Hellenistic wreck, about 150 m (500 ft) away. Sponge-diver Mehmet Aşkın had described it to him four years earlier, in 1973, when Mehmet also guided George to the medieval wreck. A single visible amphora then dated this site to 280–275 BC, but Mehmet said at least 200 other amphoras had been removed by looters.

We briefly explored the Hellenistic site in 1978, but full-scale excavation began in 1979, as an adjunct to work on the 11th-century wreck. That year our diving barge, a veteran of projects since 1961, had to be scrapped, so we dived from land. Precipitous cliffs with razor-sharp edges, however, discouraged us from building a dive platform close to the wreck, so with sledge hammers we leveled a nearby area of rocky promontory to hold our air compressors and double-lock recompression chamber. Even divers using hookah (surface-delivered air) swam the 150 m (500 ft) to and from the wreck with scuba, leaving the long hookah hoses permanently in place on the site.

In the final season of excavation in 1980, conducted from INA's *Virazon* rather than from shore, we learned that the wreck runs under a rockslide of multi-ton boulders. Fearing that the removal of additional boulders might start a new slide, we discontinued the excavation.

Excavators struggle to remove a huge boulder from the site with lifting bags and air-filled 55-gallon steel drums. The excavation was discontinued from fear that removing boulders might start a new rock slide, endangering the wreck and the divers.

Cemal Pulak exposes one of 27 bulbous jars dispersed among the ship's ballast stones and wine jars from Knidos. The striated rectangular rock is the lower block of a two-part mill whose upper hopper block is obscured by the diver. Such finds suggest that this area corresponded to the ship's galley.

We had learned that the Hellenistic ship was a mid-sized merchantman carrying wine in amphoras made at Knidos on Turkey's southwestern coast; about half of the pitch-lined amphoras still preserved grape seeds.

As the site was not fully excavated, we can only approximate the ship's size and capacity by the amphoras. We recovered approximately 400 of them, in two sizes, of which roughly 120 large and 24 small amphoras were intact. Each large amphora held about 37 liters of wine and each empty amphora weighed about 14 kg (31 lb), totaling 51 kg (112 lb); each small amphora carried 10 liters and weighed about 5.4 kg (12 lb), totaling 15.4 kg (34 lb). Another 400 amphoras probably remain on the seabed, which, along with the 200 or so reputedly looted from the site, bring the total to some 1,000 amphoras. If we assume that the ratio of large to small amphoras is the same for the entire site, then the total cargo of full amphoras weighed about 44 tons.

Several large sections of crumpled lead sheets, only 1 to 1.5 mm thick, indicated that the wooden hull was sheathed in lead for water tightness and protection from marine borers. The lead was placed over an inner lining of pitch-impregnated fabric of wool or hemp, and secured with small copper tacks. Lead sheathing was used from the end of the 4th century BC until about the 2nd century AD, our wreck providing one of its earliest examples.

At one extremity of the site, we encountered hull wood 1.5 m (5 ft) below the surface. With it was a section of lead pipe 6 to 8 cm (2.4 to 3.1 in) in diameter, most probably for discharging bilge water raised to deck level by the ship's pump. If so, this is the earliest evidence for the use of a bilge pump. Neighboring finds included a marble trip-ring for freeing anchor cables and fishnets, the upper and lower blocks of a hopper-rubber mill, and a flat quern. Glazed and plain ceramic pitchers, bowls, jugs, and dishes also appeared. All these finds were probably in the ship's galley. Twenty-seven small globular jars also found here, however, are too numerous to have belonged to the crew, and may represent a secondary cargo of unguents on the ship.

We hope one day to overcome the logistical difficulties of the site so that work can be resumed on this unique and important shipwreck.

Above **A large marble trip-ring probably facilitated the freeing of snagged fishnets or the ship's anchor cable if it became fouled.**

Right **Ann Bass assembles Knidian wine amphoras from hundreds of sherds. The ship carried an estimated 1,000 amphoras of two sizes, the larger containing about 37 liters of wine, and the smaller about 10 liters.**

Below **Twenty-seven bulbous jars, without handles, may represent a secondary cargo of unguents.**

I once found wooden hulls somewhat boring, and left the interpretation of often small and unattractive bits of wood to my expert colleagues Fred van Doorninck, J. Richard (Dick) Steffy, and Cemal Pulak, while I studied and published the "more glamorous" cargoes and personal possessions found inside the hulls. Slowly I came to accept that the ship itself – the Greek *naus* – is often the most important and exciting artifact on any shipwreck site. In the following pages, you will see how INA archaeologists have for the first time traced the evolution from ancient to modern ships – although I hope you will also be dazzled by the "more glamorous" artifacts from shipwrecks such as the 11th-century Serçe Limanı "Glass Wreck."

Because of excellent excavations and publications by French, Italian, and Spanish archaeologists of Roman shipwrecks off their own coasts, the Institute of Nautical Archaeology has not undertaken the excavation of a Roman wreck. INA's only involvement with the Roman-period fishing boat excavated by Shelley Wachsmann, when he was still Underwater Inspector for the Israel Antiquities Authority, was the model of the boat he had built by INA's Bill Charlton, a veteran of the Uluburun, Bozburun, and Tektaş Burnu excavations. Because of biblical associations, the Sea of Galilee Boat is one of the best-known ancient craft discovered anywhere.

The hulls of most ancient shipwrecks are only partially preserved. Marine borers devoured all their exposed wood long ago. That is why I find so exciting the incredibly preserved Early Byzantine ships found by Robert Ballard in the anaerobic depths of the Black Sea, where such borers do not live. When these ships can be fully uncovered, they will provide unprecedented knowledge of Byzantine ships to specialists like his colleague Cheryl Ward.

Between the 4th century AD, when Constantine moved his capital from Rome to Byzantium (later named Constantinople and now Istanbul), and the fall of that city to the Turks in 1453, the Byzantine period is sometimes seen as a transitional period between the ancient and modern eras. It was, indeed, a transitional period for ship construction, for it saw hull design evolve slowly from ancient shell-first construction to modern frame-first construction.

A late 4th- or early 5th-century wreck at Yassıada, Turkey, excavated first by the University of Pennsylvania Museum and then INA, showed the beginnings of the evolution toward modern hull construction. The mortise-and-tenon joints that held its planks together were smaller and farther apart than in the hulls of ships from at least the Late Bronze Age through Classical Greek and Roman times. In other words, the strength of the Yassıada hull was more dependent on its internal framework, or skeleton, than before. This trend continued with a 7th-century wreck also excavated

Over 30 m (99 ft) below the surface of the Aegean Sea, excavation director Fred Hocker puzzles over a group of pitchers found in the stern of the Bozburun wreck, perhaps the remains of the captain's last meal before he abandoned his ship.

at Yassıada by the University of Pennsylvania Museum and INA. The hull of this wreck, described by Fred van Doorninck, was truly transitional, built in the ancient manner below the waterline and in the modern manner above.

Exactly when the full transition from ancient to modern design was complete remains unknown. The 11th-century ship that sank in Serçe Limanı, Turkey, is the first fully excavated "modern ship," built in the same manner as the ships that took Columbus across the Atlantic and Magellan around the world. Shelley Wachsmann, however, has found a partial 5th- or 6th-century hull in Tantura Lagoon, Israel, that shows no evidence of mortise-and-tenon joinery.

The 9th-century shipwreck excavated by INA President Fred Hocker at Bozburun, Turkey, was thought to be an even earlier example of a modern ship than the 11th-century Serçe Limanı ship, until Fred van Doorninck, who studied and published the latter hull, as well as the two Yassıada hulls, intently examined the Bozburun planks while they were still soaking in fresh water, and discovered that they had been held edge to edge by wooden pegs similar to the tenons of earlier hulls.

Now Nergis Günsenin, with modest support from INA, is excavating a 13th-century Late Byzantine shipwreck at Çamaltı Burnu in Turkey's Sea of Marmara. Her hull specialist is Jay Rosloff, who studied nautical archaeology with us at Texas A&M University and later excavated the hull of a ship of around 400 BC in Israel.

By now the reader must wonder what these Turkish words *burnu* and *burun* mean (as in Taşlıkburun, Uluburun, Pabuç Burnu, Tektaş Burnu, Bozburun, Çamaltı Burnu). It's the same word, meaning "cape" or "promontory," which simply takes a different form if preceded by an adjective.

Above **Cemal Pulak holds a demijohn from the Serçe Limanı Glass Wreck. Perhaps the largest glass vessel surviving from antiquity, it was mended from pieces identified among perhaps a million glass shards.**

Right **Places mentioned in this section, with the featured wrecks in bold.**

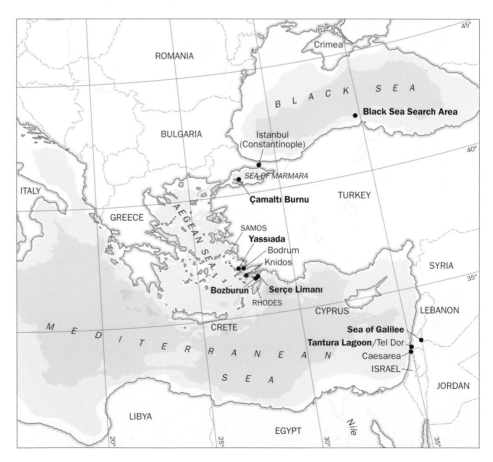

Sea of Galilee Boat

Date 1st century BC–1st century AD
Excavation 1986
Excavated by Israel Antiquities Authority
Length c 8 m (26.5 ft)
Model built 1991–1992
Material European pear wood
Displayed Yigal Allon Museum
Scale 1:10

Modeling the Fishing Boat from the Sea of Galilee, Israel

WILLIAM H. CHARLTON JR

Probably no ancient vessel has attracted more world-wide interest than the 2,000-year-old fishing boat that Shelley Wachsmann excavated from the shore of the Sea of Galilee – Israel's Lake Kinneret – in 1986. This modest vessel, only about 8 m (26.5 ft) long, provided for the first time direct evidence for the kind of boat Jesus and his disciples used on this very sea.

It had been an old boat, partly dismantled in a boatyard before being abandoned. Spotted by the brothers Moshe and Yuval Lufan in the lake's muddy shore in 1986, when the water was unusually low, the hull was partly excavated in place and then coated with polyurethane foam and floated 485 m (1,600 ft) from its find spot to the nearby Yigal Allon Museum, where it was conserved with polyethylene glycol.

In 1990, when Dr Wachsmann left his position as Underwater Inspector for the Israel Antiquities Authority to join INA and the faculty of the Nautical Archaeology Program at Texas A&M University, he brought with him the dream of having a scale

Below **The hull remains of the ancient Galilee boat on display in Israel's Yigal Allon Museum. The hull is cradled in its own purpose-built stainless-steel support structure.**

model of the Galilee Boat to display alongside the original. Shortly after our first meeting he asked me to build such a model.

The Model

Now, I hadn't done any modeling in wood since making model airplanes out of balsa wood in my youth (and almost cutting a finger off doing it). This certainly looked like a long, detailed, and much more difficult project. Did I still have the patience, especially since I was working on a graduate degree in nautical archaeology? The knowledge and experience I would gain in the techniques of the ancient shipwright far outweighed any apprehensions I might have had. So I consented.

I began the project in the Ship Reconstruction Laboratory of the Nautical Archaeology Program in mid-January of 1991. The model was to be in 1:10 scale, its design based on a set of preliminary lines drawings made by INA's Dick Steffy during the boat's excavation. The high, incurving sternpost and cutwater prow, as well as the single mast and large rectangular sail, were based on a contemporary mosaic found at the nearby town of Migdal.

My next consideration was the type of wood to use. The original planks were of cedar and the ribs were of oak. Always a concern in model building, however, is the *scale effect*; wide-grained woods just don't look right in a model of reduced scale, and detract from the model's appearance. I would need a close-grained wood. And not knowing the climatic conditions under which the model would be displayed in the museum, I needed a dimensionally stable wood – one that would not shrink or swell, to any great degree, with changes in relative humidity. European pear wood (*Pyrus communis*) fitted both of my requirements.

As I got down to cutting and shaping wood, I discovered how easy it is to break pieces at this small scale. The original hull had been formed in the shell-first fashion typical of its period, with its sides built up one plank at a time with mortise-and-tenon joints – the joints that told Shelley Wachsmann he was looking at an ancient boat when he first saw it. Now I faced the problem of how to simulate the edge-joinery on the original. This was solved by the use of small, three-way edge clamps.

Hand-carved frame members (ribs) are modeled on those from the ancient boat. Small three-way edge clamps can be seen holding a hull plank in place.

Right The contemporary Migdal Mosaic gave hints for many features on the model, including the single mast and rectangular sail, the incurving sternpost and cutwater prow, and the two oars and one steering oar on each side.

As the planking worked its way up the sides, I learned how frustrating it was to have a plank snap in my fingers as it was almost bent to shape. This began happening routinely because the bends required to fit the planks into the sternpost were so radical. I quickly learned that I could soak a roughly-shaped plank in water for 24 hours and then gently massage in the required curves and bends with my hands, clamp the piece into place on the model, and allow it to dry overnight and take the desired shape. It then remained only to trim the piece to its final shape and glue it in place.

The project took almost a year and a half, during which time a small group of local supporters developed a keen interest in the model. This resulted in the sail being hand-woven out of linen by a local weaver, and the ropes being hand-laid from fibers of the Torrey Yucca plant (*Yucca Torreyi*) by an INA secretary.

The model is now on permanent display with the boat itself in the Yigal Allon Museum, Kibbutz Ginosar, Israel.

Far left The author nears completion of the model, installing the starboard-side steering oar.

Left The model with the wind in its sail, as the ancient boat may have looked while sailing on the Sea of Galilee.

Modeling the Fishing Boat from the Sea of Galilee, Israel **91**

The Ship of Georgios, Priest and Sea Captain: Yassıada, Turkey

FREDERICK VAN DOORNINCK

I was a first-year doctoral student in Classical archaeology at the University of Pennsylvania in 1961 when fellow graduate student George Bass invited me to join him in the excavation of a 7th-century Byzantine shipwreck in Turkey.

The wreck, he said, lay on a slope 32–39 m (106–129 ft) deep off Yassıada, a small coastal island in the southeastern Aegean. It, like perhaps a dozen other ships of antiquity, was the victim of a treacherous reef that nears the surface about 125 m (400 ft) away from the island. Kemal Aras, a sponge diver from nearby Bodrum, then the sponging center of Turkey, had shown the wreck to Peter Throckmorton in 1958.

Although my previous diving experience was limited to a little snorkeling at Eniwetok in the Pacific, where I had been assigned in the US Army, I eagerly accepted George's invitation.

Soon we were pounding daily through white-capped waves, sometimes against gale-force winds, on the two-hour trip from Bodrum to the wreck site. Our team lived in a rented house in Bodrum, then a town of 5,000 people, but today a bustling tourist center whose summer population reaches 200,000. We took turns, however, in pairs, sleeping as guards on the splintered deck of an old 15-m (50-ft) wooden barge we had anchored directly over the wreck – luckily in the lee of the island.

George's experiences at Cape Gelidonya the previous summer had made him realize that shipwreck excavation had little future as a discipline without better methods of mapping wreck sites. The Byzantine wreck presented a well-preserved amphora mound ideal for developing new techniques.

Excavating and Mapping the Wreck

In 1961, we experimented with various mapping devices, including square metal frames divided into grids by wires stretched across them. We placed these over artifacts on the seabed and then, hovering over each grid square, in turn, we made accurate drawings with pencils on frosted plastic paper. Grid photographs added details. We plotted the three-dimensional locations of grid corners with crude, iron-pipe alidades, like those used by surveyors on land, and measured the distances of artifacts beneath the grids with meter sticks. Before summer's end, we were mapping exposed parts of the ship's fragmented hull.

The daily four-hour commute took so much time that we seldom had a full night's sleep; Ann Bass was up each morning at half past four to buy fresh bread at a nearby bakery for breakfast. Fatigue may have contributed to diving-instructor Larry Joline's serious case of the bends.

In 1962, therefore, we built a camp on Yassıada (literally "Flat Island"), setting a

Yassıada
7th-Century Wreck

Date AD 625/626 or slightly later
Excavation 1961–1964
Found by Kemal Aras
Depth 32–39 m (106–129 ft)
Hull c 21 m (69 ft) long
Amphoras onboard ship c 900
Number of dives 3,533
Cost $95,000

Left **Diving off the wooden barge in 1961. One diver carries a bouquet of plastic tags with wire stems used to identify artifacts in grid photographs.**

Below left **The two-person submersible, *Asherah*, stereo-mapping the Byzantine wreck. Mounted toward either end of a long bracket are a camera and stroboscopic light; in the middle, a television camera monitors the photography.**

Below right **Fred van Doorninck, his fins removed to minimize wreck damage, measures the vertical distance of tagged artifacts beneath a 3-m (10-ft) square grid.**

policy, which we have followed for four decades, of living as close to our diving sites as possible.

That year we also used an improved mapping system. We erected and leveled on pipe legs nine angle-iron frames, each measuring 6 m (20 ft) by 2 m (6.6 ft), like giant steps running up the 1:4 slope on which the wreck lay. We slid 4-m (13-ft) high photo towers over these steps, taking pictures down through the towers' square, wire grid bases. Although still time-consuming, this system yielded a highly accurate three-dimensional wreck plan.

It was in that year that I volunteered to attempt a reconstruction of the quite fragmentary hull for my PhD dissertation. I was put in charge of all wreck plans as Assistant Excavation Director.

To reduce mapping time further, we developed a system of stereophotogrammetry during the last two summers of excavation. We floated a horizontal bar at a precise height over the wreck and suspended a camera from it on a gimbal. We then took vertical photographs at calibrated intervals along the bar, each two pictures forming a stereo pair. It was the first use of stereo-photography for three-dimensional mapping under water, leading to a US Navy grant that allowed us to refine the technique in order to map a neighboring 4th-century Byzantine wreck at Yassıada with a pair of cameras mounted on the two-person submersible, *Asherah*.

A Fast and Well Appointed Ship

When the 7th-century ship sank, it landed on a steep slope. Listing to port, with her bow pointing upslope, she slid down until her stern bottom dug into sand. The forward half of the hull remained on bedrock and did not survive, but much of the stern half did survive, some up to deck level, protected from marine borers by the sand.

Using the seabed evidence, along with detailed drawings made on land of all the significant hull remains, I reconstructed the hull's general shape aft of midships. My restoration of the missing bow, however, produced something less than seaworthy. This was remedied by a series of scale models built by volunteer consultant Dick Steffy; these confirmed most of my reconstruction and successfully projected the hull lines into the bow.

Although the ship, at just under 21 m (69 ft) long, could carry some 60 tons, her hull, with a slim 4:1 length-to-width ratio and a maximum breadth well aft of midships, was primarily designed for speed.

Economy took precedence over appearance in building the hull. Four pairs of heavier planks called wales and most timbers lining the ship's interior were little more than half logs. Construction methods were much more economical than in earlier Greco-Roman hull construction, where the outer shell of planking was built first by edge-joining the planks together with large mortise-and-tenon joints fixed in place by pegs. In this hull, the joints were much smaller, more widely spaced, unpegged, and used only up to the waterline, above which the planking was simply nailed to already erected frames (or ribs). The skeleton of keel and frames rather than the shell was now the principal source of hull strength, representing a transitional stage in the evolution from ancient to modern hull construction.

The ship had been well equipped. Despite her small size, she carried 11 iron anchors. Four bower anchors were ready for use, two on either bulwark just forward of midships. Stacked on deck between them was a set of spares and, at the bottom, three sheet anchors for use as a last resort in storms.

The distribution patterns of tiles, metal and ceramic vessels, and other items found at the stern revealed the dimensions and layout of an elaborate galley set low within the hull. A large tile firebox with adjustable iron grill occupied the port half of the galley floor. A superstructure rising above deck level to give access and interior light to the galley was roofed with tiles. Galley wares included at least 16 pantry jars and the ship's water jar, a mortar and pestle, 21 cooking pots, two cauldrons, a bake pan of copper, several copper or bronze pitchers, 18 ceramic pitchers and jugs, a half-dozen spouted jars, and four or five settings of fine tableware.

A storage locker in the galley's forward wall contained the ship's valuables: 16 gold and 50 copper coins, three steelyards and a set of balance-pan weights, a carpenter's chest containing all the tools needed for ship repairs, 16 unused lamps perhaps to be used as dedications in churches and shrines en route, and a bronze censer surmounted by a cross. The latest copper coin had been minted in the year 625/626. An inscription on the largest steelyard gives the name and title of its owner: Georgios, priest sea captain. A boatswain's locker, just aft of the galley, contained a grapnel for the ship's boat, tools for use in foraging for water and firewood on land, needles and lead weights for repairing fish nets, and lead weights and lures for deepwater line fishing.

The Last Voyage: A New Interpretation

The ship was carrying approximately 900 amphoras. Some 700 were globular jars stacked three deep in the hold; the rest were cylindrical jars placed horizontally between the necks of the top layer. We raised only 110 amphoras during the excavation. Their pitch-coated interiors suggested they had contained wine, and in

Top **The counterweight of the ship's largest steelyard, a bust of Athena wearing her helmet and Medusa's head, is here shown with some gold coins from the wreck.**

Above **The inscription on the bar of the largest steelyard reveals that the ship's captain, Georgios, was also a priest.**

Opposite **A basket of amphoras from the 4th-century Byzantine wreck is made ready for lifting by balloon. In the foreground are globular amphoras from the 7th-century wreck.**

Below **One of the tiles from the roof of the ship's galley, here being mended by Ann Bass, had a round, collared hole through which smoke from the galley firebox escaped.**

the excavation report, *Yassi Ada: A Seventh-Century Byzantine Shipwreck* (1982), we state that the ship probably had been a coastal trader involved in wine commerce.

A chance discovery in 1980 of graffiti on many of the raised amphoras, which had been mostly hidden by concretion, was to lead to a very different conclusion. The newly established presence of a permanent INA staff in Bodrum soon made possible the recovery of 570 of the amphoras still on the site and a new amphora study under my direction that entailed a thorough cleaning and cataloguing, including drawings of all distinct types and sizes, capacity measurements and the collecting of the organic contents of intact amphoras. Recording of graffiti was mostly done by my wife, Betty Jean. Peter van Alfen published a study of the cylindrical amphoras in 1996; he and I continue the study of the globular amphoras.

What we learned about the amphoras and their contents was unexpected and not easily explained. The recovery on average of just under a dozen grape seeds from the intact amphoras indicates that most, if not all, amphoras in the cargo were carrying low-grade wine. Differences in decoration, typology and fabric revealed 11 distinct types of cylindrical and some 40 distinct types of globular amphoras. Approximately 80 percent of the globular amphoras had been made shortly before the ship's sinking, but other globular types had been made at least several decades earlier. Graffiti indicate that many of the recently made amphoras had earlier carried olives, possibly preserved in sweet wine, and some of these jars contained, along with grape seeds, degraded bits of olive pits. Some older jars had once held lentils. Several dozen different marks of ownership occur on the globular amphoras, some jars having had more than one owner.

As we learned more about the unusual nature of the ship's cargo, we began to comprehend the unusual nature of the ship itself. In the early 1990s, at the urging of the Bodrum Museum Director, Oğuz Alpözen, INA, under the direction of Fred Hocker and Taras Pevny, constructed a full-scale replica of the ship's stern. Building the replica led to a better appreciation of the hull's highly streamlined design.

I now believe that the ship, with her priest-captain, belonged to the church and

Above **George Bass inspects globular amphoras from the 7th-century Byzantine wreck as they are lifted onto the deck of INA's research vessel, *Virazon*.**

Loft Texas A&M faculty and students, the Bodrum Museum staff, and Turkish archaeology students all had a hand in building a full-scale replica of the ship's stern.

Right The replica of the galley complex with its tile roof, tile firebox and storage facilities and the after part of the hold with its cargo of amphoras gives visitors to the museum a vivid impression of what shipboard life was like.

had been designed for speed and the feeding of passengers so that it might transport churchmen as well as cargo; the tile galley roof added a touch of suitable elegance. The ship sank near the end of a long war with Persia, a war so costly that the church had to lend major assistance in provisioning the army, partly through levies of produce from church-owned lands. Particularly in view of rather frequent allusions to the Christian faith among the amphora graffiti, it appears likely that the ship's cargo of low-grade wine in recycled amphoras had been a part of this effort.

Below A 1:10 scale replica of the ship showing the internal hull construction on the port side, the general structure of the stern galley complex (left), and the location of the bower anchors and pile of anchor spares on the deck just forward of midships.

The Graveyard of Ships: Tantura Lagoon, Israel

SHELLEY WACHSMANN

The flash came from above as I examined the planking of a newly discovered hull. My first thought was, who in the world is using our flash unit to take underwater photographs? Then I remembered that I had taken the unit to Tel Aviv for repair. By the time I saw the second flash, I was looking straight up and realized that I was witnessing lightning strikes as viewed from underwater. Moments later I was rushing the team out of the lagoon….

Tantura Lagoon is one of the few natural harbors along Israel's remarkably straight and shallow Mediterranean coastline. Its protected waters have served as an anchorage for Tel Dor, one of the largest ancient mounds in Israel, as well as for Dor's immediate environs. This region has been almost continuously inhabited for 4,000 years, and few other Mediterranean ports have the potential for hiding remains from such a breadth of history. Now, with a team of faculty, staff, and students – from INA, Texas A&M University, and Haifa University's Recanati Center for Maritime Studies (now, The Leon Recanati Institute for Maritime Studies) – I was coaxing some of that history from beneath the cove's shifting sands.

Remarkably, in an area only about the size of a basketball court, we uncovered remains of seven different hulls! To find them, we used a hydraulic probe, consisting of a pipe connected by a hose to a pump. This simple tool proved more effective than any electronic method available in locating waterlogged timbers under as much as 2 m (6.6 ft) of sand. Trenches sunk over the timbers revealed buried hulls. In two cases we located lead-filled wooden anchor stocks, in this area the archaeological equivalent of finding "needles in a haystack."

With but one exception, the wrecks date from the 4th to the 10th centuries AD. We studied two hulls in particular detail. The Tantura A wreck consists of about a quarter of the bottom of a small coaster, apparently of local origin, dating from the mid-5th to the mid-6th century AD. Originally, it was probably about 12 m (36 ft) long.

Right **Tantura Lagoon has so filled up with sand over the centuries that at times the excavators had to dig holes in which to dive. This aerial photo shows the excavation of the Tantura B shipwreck in extremely shallow water. Among the finds was this intact jar** (*left*)**, found lying next to the keelson.** *Below* **Team member Andrew Lacovera examines the wreck. The hull's narrow lines strongly suggest that it was a galley.**

Opposite below **The hull of the Tantura A shipwreck had come to rest on the 52-kg (115-lb) stone stock of a wooden anchor, which predates the vessel by about a millennium.**

We were surprised to find that the hull planking and keel contained no evidence of mortise-and-tenon joinery, which at the time of its discovery was considered a hallmark of contemporaneous ship construction. This led to some concern that the ship might be of later date than originally determined, but the subsequent discovery of Byzantine-period pottery stuck to the hull with resin, together with a series of radiocarbon dates, clearly confirmed the early date range. This makes the Tantura A wreck one of the oldest recorded hulls discovered in Mediterranean waters that had been built in the innovative methods that were to evolve more fully and eventually become the standard in the medieval period.

The Tantura B hull lies about 10 m (33 ft) west of Tantura A. It appears to be part of a large vessel dating to the first half of the 9th century AD. Its unusual combination of angles, breadths, and what appears to be a lack of longitudinal stiffening make it unlike any other known Mediterranean hull. This led noted hull reconstructor Dick Steffy to propose that we may have part of an oared galley, a particular rarity in the archaeological record. We speculate that Tantura B may have been one of the Andalusian Arab vessels used to raid Crete during the early 9th century, leading to the island's Arab conquest around AD 824.

As on land, we repeatedly found stratified artifacts in the lagoon. Indeed, in 1996, we learned that the Tantura B hull rested on an earlier vessel – known as Tantura C – which dates to the early 4th century AD.

The ships that we examined in Tantura Lagoon from 1994 to 1996 show evidence of traumatic ends. All appear to have sunk when forced against a lee shore during storms.

Perhaps each vessel had tried to make a desperate run for safety between the lagoon's islands and had been smashed on the rocks before being battered into the lagoon by the pounding waves. Once flushed into the lagoon, large sections of hull were quickly buried in the shifting sands, preserving them and their contents, through the centuries, in an anaerobic embrace.

Sampling a Byzantine Vintage: Bozburun, Turkey

FRED HOCKER

Bozburun

Built   AD **874**
Sunk   c AD **880**
Depth   **30–35 m (99–115 ft)**
Found by   Mehmet Aşkın
Excavation   **1995–1998**
Number of dives   **8,500**
Cost (fieldwork)   **$400,000**
Cargo   c **1200–1500 amphoras**
Hull   c **15 m (49 ft) long,**
c **5 m (16 ft) wide**

The early summer wind had blown steadily out of the northwest, as it often did in the Aegean, but now, just as they were approaching the entrance to the harbor, the wind veered abruptly to the northeast. They would not make the harbor. The captain turned west to run before the squall for the shelter of Crescent Island, but he did not count on the sudden shift in wind jibing the sail and cracking the yard. Unable to sail and being blown onto a rocky lee shore, he had no option but to anchor and wait out the wind or make repairs. First one anchor was dropped, and then another, but the channel was deep with a sloping bottom, and the anchors would not bite. The ship's head did turn into the wind, but the stern now came closer to the limestone cliffs with each wave, until it was driven onto the rocks. Water began to flood through sprung seams. With the stern pounding on the shore, the crew tried to save the ship by lightening it, throwing cargo overboard, but the damage was too great. There was only enough time to gather up their valuables and scramble ashore. They huddled on a small spur bulging from the cliff face and waited for a local boat to rescue them, while they watched their broken ship disappear.

How can we know the details of a wreck that happened more than 1,000 years ago? The sailors are long gone, only the bottom of the ship survives, and the cargo, amphoras that once contained wine, seems uniform and unremarkable. Partly it is from our own experience of four summers on the same rocky spur, excavating the shipwreck. We are sailors too, and felt the prevailing northwesterly wind. But when it veers around toward the northeast, the cliffs on either side of narrow Hisarönü Bay divert it and keep it flowing into the bay from the west until it veers far enough to come through the passes to the northeast. Then it shifts suddenly and with little warning. This happens most often in late spring and early summer, before the wind settles into its stable summer pattern. It is still not inherently dangerous, as it is possible to run back down the channel and get into the safety of the lee of one of the islands. Something else had to have happened to the ship.

The wreck, itself, offers clues, although it is not *what* was on the bottom of the Aegean that is so enlightening, but *where* it was, and even more so, what was *not* there. Most of the amphoras were in a compact mound, the classic Mediterranean wreck, but many were spread out, some around the corner of the rocky spur, and a few even under the hull. The last had been thrown overboard and sank before the ship came down on top of them. The ship itself lay at the bottom of the cliff, with its stern pointed at the rocks. What was missing is the final key. There was only one anchor still on the ship, at the bow. Most medieval ships found in the Mediterranean have a large stack of spare anchors on deck, but this ship had already cast all but one, a clear sign of desperation. There were no coins, no objects of value, and almost no personal possessions, although such things are common on other wrecks – the crew had escaped, and had had time to collect the things important to them.

What the Finds Can Tell Us

But why excavate such a dull site? No gold, no jewelry, no exotic goods or artwork, just day after day of amphoras and amphora sherds. Some 960 amphoras and over 2 tons of sherds, to be exact. However, what *is* there on the bottom tells another story, about what happened before the ship ran into trouble. That story is part of one of the

Left **Sue Schulze attaches identification tags to the handles of amphoras, still stacked in the bottom of the ship's hold where 9th-century stevedores left them.**

Right **One of three tiny glass goblets found in the stern, too fine for regular shipboard use but perfect for entertaining important guests or prospective buyers in port.**

Below **A selection of earthenware jugs from the galley, most for serving wine, but one (front row, left) was full of whole grapes, still plump and juicy after over 1,100 years.**

great political and economic conflicts of the Middle Ages, the life-or-death struggle between the Byzantine Empire and the Muslim Caliphates for dominance in the eastern Mediterranean. This little ship and its cargo of wine came along at one of the turning points in that struggle, when an exhausted Empire came back from the dead, re-established its long-distance economy, and began to re-conquer its lost territory. The Bozburun ship is one of the few pieces of evidence that might tell us how that happened.

George Bass was the first archaeologist to see the wreck, when Mehmet Aşkın, a local sponge diver, took him to it on INA's first shipwreck survey in 1973. It was the "next" wreck on INA's long-term plan for many years, but George and Don Frey kept finding ever more spectacular sites. By the time Cemal Pulak finished the excavation of the Bronze Age wreck at Uluburun in 1994, I was ready to look at this medieval wreck. In a way, it was a return to INA's roots, excavating a site very similar to the Byzantine wreck at Yassıada, but building on the knowledge that George, Fred van Doorninck and Dick Steffy had squeezed out of that site and others and then taught me when I was a student at Texas A&M University.

When we arrived in May of 1995, the area had only just become accessible by road. Local villagers still harvested wheat by hand from terraced fields, and tourist traffic was light. We established camp on one edge of the village of Selimiye and Robin Piercy built a three-story dive platform on the same rocky spur where those sailors had once huddled. We could dive from shore, only a short boat ride from camp, which greatly simplified logistics. We also had space for a large field conservation lab, where finds could be registered and initial cleaning could take place, reducing pressure on our Bodrum conservation lab in the winter.

The site itself was relatively simple to excavate. It was "only" 30–35 m (99–115 ft) deep, shallow for an INA project in Turkey, and the wreck lay on a clean, sandy slope. We dived for 30 to 40 minutes at a time, twice a day, sometimes breathing a special mixture of air called nitrox, with an unusually high ratio of oxygen, enabling us to dive longer without increasing our chances of suffering the bends. As we airlifted away the sand and exposed the cargo, we learned that the upper layers had been battered by fishing-boat anchors over the years, but the material below was in good condition. By the second season, we had cleared enough of the broken material to see that the amphoras had been at least two layers deep, that there was a galley in the stern, and that well-preserved hull remains lay underneath. By the third season, it was clear that the lower layer of cargo was still in its original position. I was busy that year excavating the stern, where part of the hull was appearing, but our divemaster, Bill Charlton, told me one day I should take a look at the middle of the site where he was working.

The next day, I went on the first dive, before the water became murky from airlifting, and did an overall site inspection before going to my little patch of wood. The overall shape of the wreck was clear when I was still 20 m (66 ft) above it. As I got closer, I could see the bottom layer of amphoras marching solemnly down the slope in orderly files, their handles aligned like soldiers on parade, just as the stevedores had stacked them 1,100 years ago. It was easy to imagine ropes running through the handles to keep them in place.

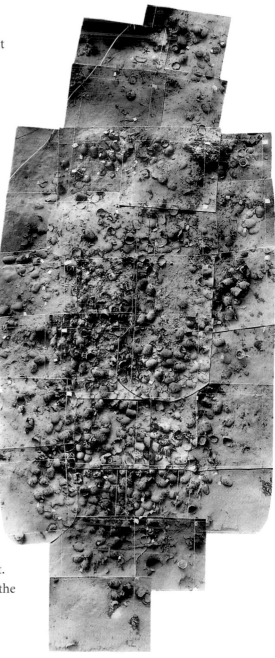

Opposite **Our three-story, split-level dive platform clinging to the same rocky spur that claimed the Bozburun ship. Robin Piercy, a Turkish stonemason, and a team of archaeology students used five weeks and over 8 tons of hand-mixed concrete to construct it.**

Below **A photomosaic of the Bozburun shipwreck as it looked soon after George Bass first surveyed it, a weed-covered mound of amphoras. The wreck slopes from the stern (top of picture), at 30 m (99 ft) depth, to the bow, at 35 m (115 ft).**

Above **The Bozburun project was a popular attraction for the media – hosting five TV crews, from the US, Turkey and Japan. Here excavation director Fred Hocker prepares to take a Turkish journalist on a guest dive.**

Below **While most of the amphoras were full of red wine, one, found in the galley, contained olives. These were probably provisions for the crew rather than cargo, but carried in the same kind of Crimean amphora.**

Below right **Pine bark was used both for amphora stoppers, which were sealed in place with pitch, and for fishing net floats (top).**

Bad Amphoras, Worse Wine

Over the years, we had become familiar with the uniformly bad quality of these jars. They were small, egg-shaped, made from poor clay, and unevenly fired. They tended to break if not kept wet and handled very carefully. What was remarkable was where they came from, what was inside them, and what was written on them.

The jars and the wine in them were not from any of the traditional Aegean vineyards, from Rhodes or Samos or Knidos. They had been made in kilns in the Crimea, at the northern end of the Black Sea, thousands of kilometers away. That area was a distant outpost of the Greek world, but clearly still connected to the main Aegean heart of the Empire. Long-distance trade had to have recovered significantly already for shipping of such a low-value bulk commodity to make economic sense.

We carefully sieved the contents of whole amphoras. This generally consisted of mud, and it was a sweaty, monotonous task to extract it and then wash it through the sieve. Indeed, it took about twice as long to process an amphora in the lab as it did to excavate it, map it for the site plan, and raise it to the surface. In addition to the occasional octopus's shell collection, the mud almost always contained organic remains, usually grape pips, sometimes by the hundreds. This wine would appeal to the sort of person who likes pulp in his orange juice. In addition to the pips, there were other seeds and plant remains, as well as fragments of fish bones. Dylan Gorham, who analyzed the contents, reported that we were looking at red wine flavored with spices and fish paste. This kind of wine is still drunk in the Black Sea region, including the northern coast of Turkey, but it is an acquired taste.

We found about 60 jars that still had their pine-bark stoppers in place, sealed with pitch. The mud had got past the seal on most of these, but 15 jars contained only liquid, usually seawater. In two instances, when we removed the stoppers, our noses were greeted by the unmistakable stench of decomposed organic material, and when we emptied the contents into the sieve, it was a dark red liquid. Yes, we tasted it (who could resist?) but AD 874 was not a very good year.

About a quarter of the amphoras had letters carved into them. Such graffiti have been common on amphoras since Classical times, and usually are owners' initials. In our ship, we have many different people represented, each with a few jars, but two owners had more than 30 jars each. AN (Anastasios?) owned most of the jars in the still-stacked lower layer, while GE (Georgeos) owned much of the upper layer, including the amphoras jettisoned to save the ship. Another owner signed his jars EPIS or EPISKO, short for *episkopos*, or bishop. The church was a major landowner, and so it is not surprising that a bishop was shipping wine. What is most interesting about the graffiti is how they were distributed. In each case, all of the jars belonging to one owner were together. This tells us that there were a large number of owners of this cargo, even though it all came from the same place, and that they were still involved. It suggests, further, that this particular shipment was a collective venture in private enterprise rather than state-organized requisitioning, providing a vital clue to how long-distance commerce might have resurrected itself after nearly two centuries of depression.

Right Our first glimpse of the ship itself was provided by these three frames with a broken stringer running over the top of them. Although only a small sample of what was to come, these pine and oak timbers showed us that we had much to learn, and that we would have to take special care lifting the last layer of amphoras from the hold.

Below **Conservator Jane Pannell Haldane** holds a mold-blown flask of glass as thin as a light bulb, found in the stern with three glass goblets.

A Final Toast

The ship itself is no less intriguing. After three-and-a-half seasons of lifting clay jars, we were able to dismantle and raise the ship's timbers. The ship was probably about 15 m (50 ft) long, and most of the starboard side of the bottom survives, enough to show how the ship was built. Matthew Harpster's careful recording and analysis has shown that the oak planking and pine frames were assembled with a consistent unit of measurement and that some basic arithmetical proportions were used to lay out the main dimensions. These proportions are similar in concept to the more sophisticated method used to build the Serçe Limanı ship 150 years later, and take our knowledge of systematic methods in ship design back into the first millennium.

As a final surprise, we discovered that the crew did not vanish completely without a trace. In the stern, down between the frames, were three extraordinarily fine glass goblets and a fluted glass bottle, much too delicate for regular shipboard use. The captain or a merchant must have been carrying this drinking set for special occasions or as a gift, and it adds a welcome social note to an otherwise practical story of 9th-century commerce.

Solving a Million-Piece Jigsaw Puzzle:
Serçe Limanı, Turkey

GEORGE F. BASS

Drop a light bulb. Try to put it back together again.

Drop three light bulbs. Stir the pieces. Then try to put them back together again.

Drop six light bulbs, four glass vases, and a dozen wine bottles, stir the pieces, and try to put them all back together, as if they were new.

That is like the problem I faced, starting in 1977 – except I was dealing with between 10,000 and 20,000 smashed glass vessels. But now, after more than two decades of year-round mending, my colleagues and I have assembled by far the largest collection of medieval Islamic glass in the world.

But I am getting ahead of myself.

The Discovery

During INA's initial 1973 survey along the Turkish coast, retired Bozburun sponge-diver Mehmet Aşkın told me that he had seen fellow divers bring handfuls of broken glass from the bottom of a nearby bay called Serçe Limanı ("Sparrow Harbor"), just opposite the Greek island of Rhodes. I was living with two other American and three Turkish divers on *Kardeşler*, a 20-m (66-ft) trawler, our recompression chamber, compressors, and air banks strapped to its sometimes wildly rolling deck. We sailed immediately for Serçe Limanı, where Yüksel Eğdemir, our commissioner from the Turkish Ministry of Culture, soon reported:

"There's glass everywhere! You can't fan the sand without cutting your fingers."

On a single, brief dive on the site, I decided that it would be a significant wreck for INA to excavate. But it was not the glass that interested me. It was the wreck's date.

During excavations described elsewhere in this book, at Kyrenia, Cyprus, and Yassıada, Turkey, my colleagues and I had been tracing for the first time the slow evolution of hull construction, from completely shell-first hulls in Bronze Age and Classical Greek times to Late Roman and Early Byzantine hulls in which frames, or ribs, that helped shape the hull were erected before the hull shell was completed. We wondered when the first "modern" hulls appeared in which frames were erected before construction of the hull shell was even begun. This wreck might provide the answer. An amphora I uncovered by sweeping sand away with my hand was from later in the Byzantine period than those at Yassıada. Amphora expert Virginia Grace soon dated it, from a photograph, to the 11th century AD.

The Excavation

Other projects delayed the onset of full-scale excavation at Serçe Limanı until 1977, when we built a camp of stone, concrete blocks, woven mats, and mosquito netting in

Above **The expedition barge is moored over the wreck, just offshore from the camp. A seemingly safe natural harbor, Serçe Limanı holds at least three other ancient wrecks.**

Right **Fred the octopus lived in an amphora in Fred van Doorninck's excavation square, and constantly tried to pull shiny bits of glass from the excavator's hands.**

Serçe Limanı Glass Wreck

Date *c* 1025
Depth 33 m (110 ft)
Found by Mehmet Aşkın
Excavation 1977–1979
Cargo glass cullet, glazed bowls, wine
Glass vessels *c* 10,000–20,000
Hull 15.6 m (51.2 ft) long
Crew Bulgarian

which as many as 35 people would spend the next three summers.

Excavation was in most respects routine. We put down our underwater telephone booth for safety and covered the site with a metal grid to break it into squares 2 m (6.6 ft) on a side so that each diver, or pair of divers, could be responsible for the excavation of a specific area of the wreck. We mapped the wreck with underwater drawings, photographs, and measurements taken from fixed metal stakes driven into the rock around the site.

Every wreck, however, has its own peculiarities. Soon we were uncovering not only the expected ceramic and metal artifacts, but dozens, then hundreds, then thousands of shards of glass. I don't believe in wearing gloves during underwater excavation. So much depends on touch. But soon our bandaged hands looked like they were excavating razors.

At a depth of 33 m (110 ft) the color red is absorbed from daylight and does not appear. Probably every excavator lost valuable bottom time by squeezing a cut finger or palm in order to watch in fascination the bright emerald blood that spiraled up into the seawater.

Another distraction was Fred, the octopus that lived in an amphora in Fred van Doorninck's square and never tired of trying to pull his watch off, or pull the glittering glass from his hands. On one of my dives I felt a shudder in the metal grid

on which I rested my body, looked for the cause, and saw an octopus, presumably Fred's grandfather or grandmother, coming toward me with tentacles that reached from one side of a square to the other. I decided to end my dive early.

We had to abandon any thoughts of labeling every glass shard, but instead gathered shards from squares 50 cm (20 in) on a side, and placed them into labeled plastic bags.

One day Texas A&M graduate student Donald Keith asked in surprise, when he saw us washing the mud from an amphora: "What in the world are you doing?"

"Cleaning the mud out."

"What about the seeds?" Don asked.

Above **A metal grid placed over the wreck divided the site into squares that were assigned to pairs of divers for excavation. At this early stage, wood, amphoras, ballast stones, millstones, dark chunks of raw glass, and iron anchors had already come to light.**

Right **Much of the broken glass was embedded in rock-hard seabed concretion and had to be extracted with dental tools by Jay Rosloff and other expedition members.**

"There aren't any seeds in here, not after a thousand years."

"Don't be so sure," Don responded. "Let me show you."

We were pioneers. We made mistakes. For years we had casually hosed the sediment out of amphoras. Soon Don was sieving the mud, and followed that with flotation, the method of retrieving seeds and pollen from swirling water that has been used at archaeological sites on land for years. The results, as we shall see, were astonishing.

At the end of three summers, the real archaeology began. Finding, mapping, and raising things represent only the first step. Now we began a process that would last decades.

The Million-Piece Jigsaw Puzzle

Oğuz Alpözen, who had first dived with us at Yassıada in 1963 as an undergraduate archaeology student, was now Director of the Bodrum Museum. He assigned to us as workspace the entire English Tower of the Castle of the Knights of St John of Malta, in which the Museum is housed, and additional space in which to build a conservation laboratory. Fred van Doorninck and his family spent the academic year 1978–1979 organizing the tons of material we had retrieved from the wreck, and the following year Ann and I took our 12- and 9-year-old sons out of school so that we could continue the task.

My first job was to tackle the 3 tons of glass we had raised from the wreck, now separated by Fred into 2 tons of raw glass chunks and 1 ton of broken glass vessels. Much of the broken glass was encased in large lumps of rock-hard concretion, from which we removed the shards with dental picks.

We hoped to start mending the broken vessels. All of us still assumed that we were dealing with vessels that had been broken by the impact of the shipwreck. That meant that the fragments of individual vessels should have been found near one another on the site. So we built wooden tables around the entire bottom floor of the English Tower and, using the labels on the bags, laid out all of the shards from a single 1-m (3.3-ft) square, keeping the glass from each bag still separated from the glass from other bags by wooden strips that acted as dividers. After weeks, we had not found a

Opposite **Texas A&M University graduate student Joy Kitson-Mim Mack spent a year in the Bodrum Museum of Underwater Archaeology studying only one of over a hundred different vessel shapes mended from the broken glass.**

Below **One of over 200 intact and broken scent sprinklers of thin glass with high kicks in their bases.**

single join and gave up, defeated. We began to sketch and catalogue thousands of bases, rims, and handles, an incredibly boring job.

One day it suddenly struck me. How does one work a jigsaw puzzle? Usually by separating out pieces that might join together, putting into separate piles, say, the pieces with green grass or blue sky or red bricks. Might this work with the glass?

None of us was a glass expert, so we invented our own 18 categories of glass: plain glass, green glass, purple glass, dimpled glass, purple dimpled glass, green-threaded rims, purple dimpled glass with green-threaded rims, and so on. Then we were almost ready to begin.

But there was a problem. To put all of the purple glass together into one pile meant taking all of the purple shards out of their labeled bags, losing forever any record of where they had been found on the wreck. Artifact provenience is vital on archaeological excavations. So, we copied each of the four or six-character provenience codes with black ink onto each of between half a million and a million shards, covering each number with clear fingernail polish to prevent its being inadvertently rubbed away. We shanghaied passing tourists to help; one young man, on his way around the world, became so fascinated he stayed on the job for months. I even put my young sons to work, thankful that Charles Dickens was not around to write about it!

Once the shards were individually labeled, we could take all of one category and begin the task. I might sit before a pile of several thousand plain purple shards, dividing them into two piles: lighter purple and darker purple. I would then put one of the piles into storage and start again, dividing the remaining shards into darker and lighter shades, again putting one of the resultant piles into storage. After doing this long enough, I might have left before me on the work table only 18 or 19 shards, but all of exactly the same shade of purple. Then we would find the joins and stick the shards together temporarily with tape (often keeping their shapes in individually cut Styrofoam forms), until our conservators could mend them permanently with special glue.

It was only then, at the end of the first year, that we realized something startling about this part of the ship's cargo. We were dealing with a cargo of broken glass intended to be recycled! All of those millions of digits we had inked onto the shards were meaningless, except they provided the proof that the glass had been shoveled randomly into the ship's hold from some even larger pile of broken glass. In no case were all the pieces of any specific vessel on board, meaning either that all of the pieces of any one vessel had never made it onto the ship, or that some of the glass had already been sold during the ship's final voyage. For a long time we had trouble convincing even authorities on ancient glass that shipping broken glass was economically feasible, but some years later roughly contemporary documents were published that described the shipment of broken glass from the Near East to the glass factories of Venice.

Part of the hold had contained a cargo that left no trace, possibly plant ash used in making glass, a commodity known to have been shipped with broken glass from the Near East.

Some 80 intact glass vessels were not from the ship's hold, but from what we eventually proved were living quarters, at the ship's stern and bow; they were

probably carried in bundles by merchants who were prepared to sell them intact.

Glass mending continued year-round for more than two decades. We saw the local glass menders who joined us right out of school not only become expert, but marry and raise children. At the end, they had assembled by far the largest known collection of medieval Islamic glass.

Almost certainly the broken glass was factory waste from one specific source. Some deformed vessels were clearly factory rejects. Other pieces, such as 11,000 moiles (tops of vessels that are cut off and discarded), could only have been factory waste. Robert Brill, Chief Scientist at the Corning Museum of Glass, showed by chemical analysis of samples that almost all of the glass was chemically homogeneous, as if it came from one factory, or perhaps several closely associated glassworks. Lastly, Spanish archaeologist Berta Lledó, lining up one on top of another of Sema Pulak's incredibly accurate drawings on transparent Mylar, showed that even vessels of completely different shapes had started out in the same few molds, and then been crafted into varied forms by the glassblowers.

Dating the Wreck

It was glass, too, that provided the closest date for the wreck. On board were 16 glass disks that had served as weights for pan balances. Some bore the name of a caliph in Egypt and the year of his reign. Michael Bates of the American Numismatic Society, using casts and photographs, informed us that the latest dated to either AD 1024/25 or possibly 1021/22, dates not contradicted by those on three Islamic gold coins,

Above **Glass menders triumphantly raise examples of vessels they put together during two decades of year-round glass mending.**

Below **When small change was needed, bits of gold were simply cut from Islamic coins and carefully weighed.**

although they were from about a decade earlier. There were also Byzantine copper coins, but without dates.

An Early Example of a Modern Ship

Texas A&M graduate student Sheila Matthews traced each wood fragment at full scale onto clear acetate sheets, marking with various colored pens every tool mark, nail hole, or bolt hole. Back at Texas A&M University, Dick Steffy made a one-tenth scale model of every one of the fragments – twice. He used one set to build a diorama of the site, so that we could see everything together in three dimensions for the first time. Lining up nail holes, tool marks, and other clues, he used the other set to build a research model of the hull, a kind of "dress rehearsal," as he called it, for what Sheila would eventually do in Bodrum.

While Steffy worked in Texas, Robin Piercy, who had worked with Michael and Susan Katzev on the preservation of the earlier Kyrenia hull on Cyprus, undertook the three-year process of soaking every piece of wood from the ship in heat-controlled polyethylene glycol, to prevent its shrinking and warping out of recognition if allowed to dry freely in open air.

When the wood was conserved and dried, Sheila Matthews began another three-year task, piecing together with stainless steel wire more than a thousand fragments of wood in the Bodrum Museum's newly built and humidity-controlled Glass Wreck Building. Only about 15 percent of the hull was preserved, so some of the hull's shape was indicated by curved metal rods, but the resultant display was well worth the effort, allowing visitors from around the world to see the earliest known example of a

Above **Dick Steffy carefully modeled every fragment of raised wood at 1:10 scale in order to produce a diorama that allowed him to study the hull's breakup. With a second set of modeled fragments he assembled a hull that served as a dress rehearsal for the reassembly of the actual hull.**

Right **Sheila Matthews spent three years reassembling the hull, whose timbers had already been chemically treated for three years to preserve them. The temporary strings were replaced by stainless-steel wires invisible to museum visitors.**

Above **Dick Steffy's research revealed a ship about 15.6 m (51.2 ft) long, whose boxy hull would have allowed it to sail up shallow rivers. It probably sported two triangular lateen sails, and was steered by large oars, like that in the foreground.**

modern ship; the more practical, flexible kind of ship that allowed Columbus to sail to a New World, and Magellan to encircle the entire globe.

It was a modest vessel, only 15.6 m (51.2 ft) long, its breadth one third of that, probably sporting two triangular, lateen sails; spare rigging, including pulley blocks, were stored on board. The ship's flat bottom would have allowed her to enter shallow rivers.

Life at Sea

The ship's contents provided more information about how people lived in the 11th century than any site previously excavated, but to interpret it properly took years of detective work. At the end of the first excavation campaign I was asked to write an article about the wreck for *National Geographic* magazine. It was a mistake I never repeated. Almost everything I said was wrong. Because of all the Islamic glass and Islamic pottery we had found, I assumed we had begun excavating a medieval Islamic ship, with Muslim crew and passengers. By the second summer, however, we were finding pork bones from meals, ruling out the possibility that the ship's crew were either Muslims or Jews. Then, while opening some of the 900-plus lead sinkers that had been folded over and crimped onto the edges of fishing nets, we found molded crosses and even the name "Jesus" inside. Finally, we found four lead merchant's seals, exactly like the seals crimped every evening onto wire passed through the lock of every Museum door, to show next morning that it has not been opened. One of the ship's seals had not been used, but the other three bore scenes of Christianity: that which depicted the ecstatic meeting of saints Peter and Paul carried on the opposite side, in Greek: "Guardian of the writing I have been placed, bond of Peter," presumably a seal on one or more written documents.

Because our plans showed with great accuracy the position of every artifact on the site, we could determine the social stratification of those on board. The most prominent people – officers and merchants – lived at the ship's stern, eating pork, goat (and possibly mutton), and fish, along with almonds, various fruits, and

Below **When pressed onto the strings that bound and safeguarded bundles of documents, lead seals were left with Greek inscriptions and religious scenes by the pincers used; the upper left seal is unused.**

Left Hand-carved wooden rook or castle and queen (to the right) represent the oldest known firmly dated chess set. A single backgammon checker (left) shows that the much older game of backgammon was also played on board.

Right This filigree gold earring is of Fatimid workmanship according to Marilyn Jenkins-Madina of the Metropolitan Museum of Art.

olives. To while away the hours they played chess. Here, too, were the gold and copper coins, the jewelry, the weighing devices and sets of balance-pan weights, iron padlocks and keys, and most of the weapons and tools.

A slightly less grand living quarters for the merchants was found at the very bow.

The common sailors, however, lived amidships, unarmed, not sharing the pork and possibly not the fruit, and playing the "less intellectual" game of backgammon.

After years of experimentation, we had perfected the method of replicating iron artifacts by casting them with epoxy inside the natural seabed molds of concretion that had formed over them as the iron inside rusted away. Graduate student Joseph Schwarzer spent two years in Bodrum casting with epoxy. At the end, he had the largest collection of Byzantine tools in existence: a carpenter's set including everything needed to build an entire ship from scratch, including axes, saws, adzes, hammers, bow drills, chisels, files, and even the earliest known caulking irons (earlier hulls, built shell first, were not caulked). For foraging on shore for firewood and water, there were two axes, a billhook, a mattock, and a pick; if there was a shovel, it did not survive due to the thinness of its metal.

At the end, Joe also had the largest collection of Byzantine weapons from any site, not surprising since piracy was rife at this time. He had 11 sets, each with a thrusting

Above A number of iron padlocks and a key were replicated by pouring liquid epoxy into the cavities left in seabed concretion when the original iron corroded away. Once hard, the epoxy casts can hardly be distinguished from iron.

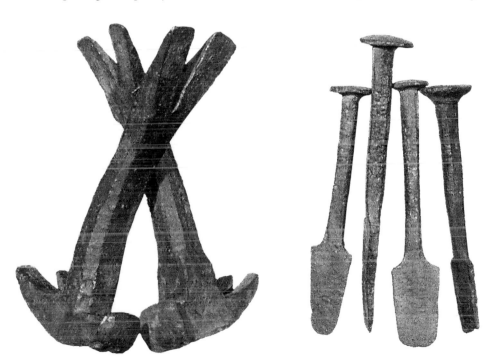

Left All the tools necessary for building a ship were carried on board, including claw hammers (far left) and caulking irons, seen here as epoxy replicas of the original but no longer existent iron tools.

spear and four or five javelins, some still wrapped together in a burlap-like fabric, suggesting 11 armed men in the crew. An iron sword with wooden sheath and a bronze hilt ornately decorated with a plumed bird probably belonged to the captain.

We found one complete grooming kit, with wooden delousing comb, scissors, and razor, and part of another, reminding us of how the sailors under both Columbus and Magellan complained of vermin, and the fact that insect-spread typhus killed more 19th-century transatlantic passengers than shipwrecks. Near these kits were small piles of orpiment, a trisulfide of arsenic that puzzled us until I stumbled on the fact that orpiment mixed with quick lime (which would have dissolved in seawater) has been used for more than a century as a depilatory. Further research revealed that men have, from time to time, used depilatories down the ages.

Over 900 lead net sinkers in three distinct piles revealed that three nets were being mended on deck at the time the ship sank, each estimated to have been about 40 m (132 ft) long, a size matched by an Ottoman net found stored in the Bodrum Museum. Near each was a netting needle, and near one was a bag of spare, unused sinkers. Fish bones reveal that the crew was catching tunny, sea bass, tub gurnard, and drum.

Eight bone spindle whorls at first suggested the presence of women on board. After all, only female spinners are depicted in Greek art, and the excavator of the Viking site at L'Anse aux Meadows, Newfoundland, said that the discovery of a single spindle whorl indicated the presence of women there, proving that it was a Viking colony. However, when I noted that the Serçe Limanı whorls were found where the nets were being mended, I was reminded of pictures of men spinning, from ancient Egyptian tomb paintings to modern photographs of Iranian shepherds. A nearly contemporary Muslim saying expressed the opinion that it was all right for men to spin wool and goat hair, but not flax, which was a woman's job. Even before fibers in some of the net sinkers were identified as being goat hair, I had guessed that the sailors on board were spinning threads to mend their nets! Was L'Anse aux Meadows only a Viking fishing outpost?

Nationality

To emphasize the point that diving and raising artifacts has no more to do with archaeology than randomly collecting arrowheads on land, I must tell the story of how Fred van Doorninck not only determined the nationality of the crew, but revealed a stage in the beginnings of the free enterprise system.

Fred, having taught ancient Greek for years, began a study of the graffiti on the

Above left **The ship was armed with over 60 iron weapons, including javelins (seen here as epoxy replicas), spears, and at least one sword.**

Above **Grooming was important to vermin-infested sailors of the past, as shown by the scissors and fragments of a delousing comb.**

Above **Eight bone spindle whorls found where fishing nets were being mended on deck suggest that the crew were spinning goat-hair threads for their nets.**

Opposite **INA artist Netia Piercy draws Islamic glazed bowls that formed part of the ship's cargo.**

Above **Amphoras for wine and olive oil were scratched with their owners' initials, leading to the realization that merchants on board were Hellenized Bulgarians.**

ship's amphoras. First he noted that all the amphoras marked with "M" (probably "Michael") were found together, as were those marked with "Leon." Eventually Fred identified about a dozen owners. He further noted that many of the amphoras had been damaged but kept in use, sometimes with lips filed smooth after being chipped when a stopper had been pried out, and other times when a handle stump was smoothed down where a handle had been broken away. Unlike the amphoras of the Imperial Roman fleets, which were discarded at voyage's end, these amphoras belonged to individual merchants who prized and protected them, sometimes for many years.

So far, so good. But Fred noticed that one of the amphoras was marked MIR. He couldn't guess what Greek name that represented. His realization that it stood for a Slavic name such as Miroslav, however, led to his teaching himself to read Bulgarian, Rumanian, and Russian, so that he could easily read Slavic and Rumanian excavation reports. He determined that the crew of the ship that sank at Serçe Limanı were Hellenized Bulgarians who lived on the shore of the Sea of Marmara not far from Constantinople. His theory was borne out when Nergis Günsenin excavated some pottery kilns on the shore of the Sea of Marmara that had manufactured amphoras identical in all respects to those on our shipwreck. Nergis, who describes her own shipwreck excavation in this book, had been a non-diving volunteer during the excavation of the Glass Wreck when she was still only a high-school student.

Our ship, it seems, had sailed from near Constantinople to a port on the Syro-Palestinian coast, such as Caesarea, where gold jewelry, glazed bowls, glass jars, and copper buckets like those on the ship have been found. After taking on its Islamic cargo, the ship on its return voyage sought shelter at an anchorage used for millennia inside Serçe Limanı. But then what happened?

The Anchors

Again, Fred van Doorninck's careful detective work provided the answer. After making epoxy replicas of the ship's nine Y-shaped anchors, Fred determined that, as on the 7th-century Yassıada shipwreck, there were two bower anchors on one bulwark near the bow, ready for use, and another on the opposite bulwark. Spare anchors – in this case five – lay stacked on deck near by. But what of the missing bower anchor? It was found where it had been cast, some distance forward of the bow, its shank snapped, presumably from the force of a sudden gust of wind, freeing the ship to be dashed against the rocky shore.

Fred further calculated that the weights of the anchors were multiples of Byzantine pounds, pointing toward the conclusion that laws governing the weights of anchors on ships of various sizes were in force earlier than realized. The unusual Y shape allowed anchors to be of greater weight without being weakened by overly long shanks.

Decades after the diving ended at Serçe Limanı, a 550-page analysis of the ship and its passengers was published, a collaboration of over a dozen scholars on three continents. It is only the first of three volumes of equal size. The second volume will present the Islamic glass and ceramic cargoes. Diving to an underwater site is no more important than driving a jeep to a terrestrial site. It is not the fieldwork, but the years of research, analysis, and interpretation that make it true archaeology.

A 13th-Century Wine Carrier: Çamaltı Burnu, Turkey

NERGİS GÜNSENİN

Çamaltı Burnu

Date early 13th century
Depth 22–35 m (72–115 ft)
Excavation 1998–2004
Dives 4,295
Conservation 2004 onwards
Hull *c* 25 m (82 ft) long, *c* 5–6 m (16.5–20 ft) wide
Cargo *c* 800 amphoras and 37 scrap iron anchors

When I first saw the amphoras on the seabed at Çamaltı Burnu, in 1993, I knew that I had found my "fortune." To understand why, we must go back to the 1980s. I was then developing a typology of late Byzantine amphoras throughout Turkey's museums for my doctoral thesis, which resulted in my finding an important amphora production area at Gaziköy on the northwest coast of the Sea of Marmara. Gaziköy, known as Ganos in ancient and medieval times, was an important monastic center from the 10th century onward. Its monks, along with neighboring villagers, like those of many monasteries, had a virtual monopoly over the production and sale of wine in the area.

My survey of workshop areas at and around Gaziköy, followed by excavation of an amphora kiln, revealed a large amphora production, which indicated an equally large

Below **General view of the amphora cargo during the 2002 excavation campaign. Most of the amphoras, which show a wide range of dimensions and capacities, survived intact and yielded grape seeds.**

production of wine, most of which would have supplied the markets of nearby Constantinople (modern Istanbul). Each time I returned to the region I dreamt of those monasteries and their vineyards – and the thousands of amphoras waiting to be loaded with Ganos wine. Enthusiasm for nautical archaeology, inspired by my meeting George Bass during the summer of 1979, at last led me to search for the ships that sailed from Ganos with those amphoras. My quest began at Marmara Island in the summer of 1992, shortly after completing the excavation of the kiln at Gaziköy. I still search around it and other islands in the Sea of Marmara, and so far have found eight shipwrecks loaded with Ganos amphoras.

The surveys also located a tile wreck, a water-pipe wreck, and, importantly, a marble wreck. The very name of Marmara Island, the site of one of the biggest marble quarries of late antiquity, comes from the Turkish word for marble. Many architectural pieces of the temples, monasteries and churches in Constantinople, throughout Anatolia, and even in Ravenna in Italy came from those quarries, yet this is the only marble wreck ever discovered near the island.

Let's return to the day I first dived at Marmara Island's Çamaltı Burnu (Cape Under the Pine). I was not looking for just any ancient wreck. At that time, the major archaeological material related to Byzantine maritime activities came from three wrecks excavated by INA along the Anatolian coasts: at Yassıada (7th century), Bozburun (9th century), and Serçe Limanı (11th century), all of which are described

Below **Nergis Günsenin with two glazed bowls and a table amphora of recognizable Byzantine origin from the Çamaltı Burnu shipwreck off Marmara Island.**

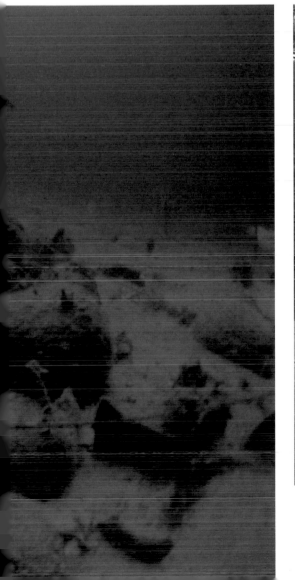

in this book. Chemical analyses by Helen Hatcher of Oxford University on samples from the Serçe Limanı amphoras showed that most had been made in the region around Ganos, and so excavation of another 11th-century shipwreck would break little new ground. I was looking for a younger wreck. The amphoras on the seabed at Çamaltı Burnu were just that, of the 13th century – my "fortune."

These were the last major group of Byzantine ceramic containers used to transport wine in the sea trade, their place soon taken by wooden barrels. Further, little is known of the shipbuilding technology of this period, most of our knowledge being derived from written texts rather than archaeological remains. Thus the excavation of what I called the Çamaltı Burnu I Wreck might well contribute much new information about Byzantine maritime activities, particularly in the region of the Sea of Marmara, during or shortly after the brief period of Latin rule at Constantinople (1204–1261).

Even so, it took courage to decide to excavate the wreck. It would be the first Turkish underwater excavation. I had a very small team and budget. But I remembered George Bass's famous phrase in his book, *Archaeology Beneath The Sea*: "If you don't grab the bull by the horns when you have the chance, you will never get anywhere." So I grabbed the wreck! The day that I raised the first amphora, on 1 October 1998, two dolphins jumped over them. It was unbelievable. Was I liberating some spirit by showing sunlight to those ceramic jars after almost 800 years?

Wine Jars

The amphoras were distributed on a sloping sandy seabed in three principal pockets between 22 and 32 m (72 and 105 ft) deep. At least 30 anchors lay 17 m (56 ft) away from the amphoras, with a group of two-handled, flat-bottomed jars inbetween. We began the excavation by establishing a grid system to divide the site into 160 2-m (6.6-ft) squares and putting datum points around it. Each diver had his own square in which to map every object by taking at least three measurements with meter tapes from four datum points. Using the same computer software as that used by INA during its Bozburun excavation, we recorded extremely accurate three-dimensional locations of all the artifacts on the sea floor. My students had to measure carefully but quickly for at this depth each of us had only 28 minutes for the morning dive and 18 minutes in the afternoon.

Late Byzantine cargo amphoras are not like the Greek or Roman amphoras with which most people are familiar: although thin-walled, they are huge, with large bellies, their size reflecting a need for greater capacity. They represent the transition from clay to wood transport containers.

The amphoras show a wide range of dimensions (41–80 cm (16–31.5 in) high) and capacities (15.5–98.5 liters). The sieved contents of intact amphoras usually yielded grape seeds, which, along with the amphoras' watertight pine-pitch linings, point to a primary cargo of wine. A few amphoras, however, were filled with pine pitch. The large mouths of the flat-bottomed storage jars suggested that they contained some commodity that was not liquid. The ship was carrying around 800 amphoras in total, and we estimate that the weight of the entire cargo of ceramic jars was between 50 and 60 tons.

Amphoras at the excavation house after most had been cleaned of marine growth and desalinated (the process by which salt from seawater is removed from the fabric of artifacts) before being mended.

Raising one of 37 iron anchors found in the cargo and anchor area at the site. The author believes that 13 T-shaped and 18 Y-shaped anchors belonged to the ship.

A Cargo of Anchors?

The large number of anchors was initially very puzzling. Some are Y-shaped and others are T-shaped, but all are Byzantine in design. In addition to the 30 or more anchors lying about 17 m (56 ft) away from the amphoras, four broken anchors were found among the amphoras themselves. Almost all of the anchors have teeth of the same form, set at the same angle to the arms. It is therefore unlikely that even the anchors lying at some distance from the amphoras have to do with an anchorage, since in that case one would expect to find at least a few anchors of earlier or later design. It would seem, then, that all the anchors belong together, probably to our ship. Most are quite small and if the ship had used such small anchors, it could not have been any larger than around 30 tons in capacity – and no ship of such small size would have used anywhere near the number of anchors found. A ship of more like 400–500 tons capacity might have used around 30 anchors, including spares and heavier sheet anchors for use in storms, but they would have been much larger.

One of the smallest anchors at the wreck site would not have worked well, if at all, since the shank (or shaft) is not long enough to permit the stock to easily come to rest flat on the seabed, thereby forcing one side of the stock into the sand (this is known as canting). The shank may have been broken and hastily repaired with a section missing. Some of the other anchors are broken, at least one of them certainly before the time of the shipwreck. It would appear, then, that the ship (or possibly some other vessel) was carrying as one of its cargoes some relatively small, broken anchors, to be repaired or used as scrap iron. A study of the anchors has been undertaken by one of my team, doctoral candidate Ufuk Kocabaş, who helped to raise 31 anchors in the 2003 field season. All were X-rayed at the Nuclear Research Laboratory at Çekmece in Istanbul to make accurate three-dimensional measurements and record all structural features, particularly welds. We plan to conclude the task by replicating the anchors, as was done at Yassıada and Serçe Limanı.

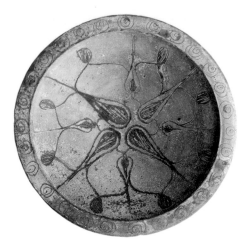

Glazed bowls and other tableware of high quality from the wreck suggest that the captain, passengers, and perhaps some of the crew on board led a relatively affluent life.

Hull Remains

According to Jay Rosloff, the excavation's ship expert, and who was trained at Texas A&M University, no more than 3 percent of the hull is preserved, including a meter of keel, a few frame (rib) segments, and the traceable remains of perhaps 6 strakes (hull planks). Nevertheless, we have deduced that the vessel was a flat-bottomed craft, 5–6 m (16.5–20 ft) wide, built in the modern, frame-first manner with the planks attached to the frame by iron nails. The wood fragments were found within the three pockets of cargo amphoras that extend over a distance of 40 m (131 ft). However, an 8-m (26-ft) empty space between the first two pockets and the third pocket indicates that the ship had broken in two, and we presently estimate that the ship had an overall length of around 25 m (82 ft). From two wood samples identified by Peter Kuniholm of Cornell University, we know that one plank is pine and one frame is elm.

With a tape measure Nergis Günsenin records the coordinates of wooden hull remnants that will be utilized by a computer program to produce an accurate three-dimensional map of the wreck.

Even these sparse facts are important to the documentation of medieval ship types, for this is the only ship of the 13th century excavated in its entirety. The list of comparative materials is short. The remains of the 11th-century Glass Wreck from Serçe Limanı, and a somewhat younger vessel from Contarina, Italy, are the best known examples from the general period. No ship's plans are extant and the building specifications that we know of raise as many questions as they answer.

Merchants and Crew

A concentration of kitchen ware along with roof tiles indicates the presence of a galley at the ship's stern, while other kitchen ware found in the bow indicates a living area designated for the crew.

But what of the origin of our ship? Where was her home port and where was she sailing? How many passengers were on board? Why and how did she sink at Çamaltı Burnu?

The amphoras and daily table wares, including glazed dishes and bowls, are of recognizable Byzantine origin. The monogram stamps on the amphoras are Greek. Similar stamps found on handles of other amphoras from this period are the abbreviations of names, in most cases those of Byzantine emperors or members of their families who were owners of workshops. Presumably, the owners might also include cities, provincial nobility, private citizens, and large cloisters. Besides these stamps, Greek names are carved on some of the table amphoras and pitchers. Another important finding is a stamp mold. Made of an alloy of copper, tin, zinc and lead, it bears abbreviated Greek letters. Could it possibly belong to a "firm"? Unfortunately, the amphoras of the type found can't be linked to any place of production with certainty, which also makes the point of departure for the ship's last voyage uncertain. Also, we found no personal items belonging to the crew.

Early 13th-century written sources indicate that most of the crew, including the captain (*nauklèros*), on many Byzantine ships at that time were monks, since almost all the large monasteries possessed their own ships. These did not form big fleets nor were they involved in large-scale commerce.

In view of the nature of the cargo and the fact that wine was an important monastic commodity at that time, I believe that the cargo lost at Çamaltı Burnu belonged to a monastery in the Marmara region and was being shipped to the markets in Constantinople. The absence of carpentry tools and defensive weapons leads us to believe that our ship was making a journey of relatively short distance. The ship was probably sailing from west to east and then northwest, toward Constantinople, when it ran into some kind of trouble – probably strong winds. The captain tried to shelter in the bay of Çamaltı Burnu and ordered his crew to throw off all the cargo anchors in order to lighten the ship. When they realized that the end was near, they abandoned ship and made their way to the nearby shore, taking their belongings with them.

Ours is an ongoing project. We should soon complete the excavation, but that will end only the first leg of our journey into the Middle Ages. Physical and chemical analyses of the hundreds of amphoras, pitchers, jugs, cooking pots, cups, jars, stoppers, anchors, and hull fragments will have to be completed, but to answer all the questions raised by the ship's discovery will take many years.

Top **A small jar with glazed interior and exterior surfaces reminds the author of a similar jar found on land with 12 coins inside. Did the monks use this jar to store money they removed before abandoning the ship?**

Above **The name Leotēs, carved in Greek on the shoulder of a round table-amphora, indicates the owner of the vessel.**

Below **Further research may reveal if this metal stamp with a combination of Greek and possibly Slavic letters belonged to the monastery which produced the wine on the ship, thereby indicating the origin of the cargo.**

Searching for Deep-Water Ships in the Black Sea

ROBERT D. BALLARD AND CHERYL WARD

Black Sea Shipwreck D

Date 5th or 6th century AD
Depth 320 m (1050 ft)
Exploration Hercules ROV system
Partial excavation 2003
Cargo pine-pitch-lined shipping jars from Sinop
Hull c 13 m (42 ft) long

"Suppose that an ancient wreck can be found on the floor of the Black Sea…Its organic substances should be completely preserved," wrote Willard Bascom in 1976, igniting a spark in many scientists who, since then, have dedicated years to exploring the area. Robert Ballard heard the promise of Bascom's remarks, and in the mid-1990s established a team of archaeologists, oceanographers, and engineers to conduct an integrated land-sea survey of the area near Sinop, Turkey.

People lived on this high peninsula more than 8,000 years ago when the Black Sea was still an enormous freshwater lake, and even then, seem to have established a subsistence pattern that focused on the lake and the rivers around it. When a rising Mediterranean Sea broke through the land barrier that separated the two, the fresh water in the Black Sea mixed with the incoming salt water and became brackish. Wind mixing at the surface formed an upper layer rich in oxygen that supported a variety of life coming in from the Mediterranean Sea, but the water below that layer stagnated and had no continuous supply of oxygen. It soon became anoxic, undergoing chemical changes that resulted in water below 200 m (660 ft) having a high percentage of sulfides and low oxygen content, a cocktail toxic to the usual sea life that devours exposed wood and other organic materials.

Project scientists began to plan a series of underwater archaeological surveys that might reveal ancient farms or camps drowned by the 150-m (495-ft) rise in sea level 7,500 years ago, in addition to expected finds of ships from the thousands of years of maritime trade along the rugged coastline of the southern Black Sea and across its expanse to the Crimea. By working with Fredrik Hiebert, an archaeologist who directed the land surveys that helped identify where the ancient residents of Sinop chose to build their settlements, Ballard predicted the kinds of geological features that specialists in acoustic remote sensing like David Mindell and Dana Yoerger could help to identify.

In the early stages of the project, we used side-scan sonar to pinpoint locations of anomalies, or unusual appearance, on the seabed. Side-scan sonar creates visual images of lumps and bumps on the seabed that might be anything from *Titanic* to a lost anchor or bag of rubbish by calculating how fast the sound travels between the sonar towfish and the seabed and translating those calculations into shadows on a computer screen. Trying to figure out what is "unusual" is a task in itself, and here the extensive experience of everyone on board comes into play. For example, marine geologists recognize certain patterns of sediment deposition as ancient sand dunes, beaches, or landslides. Engineers help screen out "noise" and generate dimensions for anomalies, and archaeologists opine on oval lumps, linear patterns, and other shapes that might be the remains of ancient human enterprise.

Above **Two of the world's best-known maritime scientists, Robert Ballard (left) and George Bass, discuss problems common to archaeological survey in both deep and shallow water during a 1999 visit to the Black Sea by Bass.**

Opposite **In 2000, the ROV *Little Hercules* captured video and still images of Shipwreck B and other targets first identified by side-scan sonar surveys at depths down to 320 m (1,050 ft) in the Black Sea.**

Opposite right **Shipwreck B, the second ancient vessel located by *L'il Herc*, was visited again in 2003. Schooling anchovies swim above transport amphoras lined with pine pitch, an indication of a cargo of wine that sank more than 15 centuries ago.**

While the search for human habitation sites was ultimately unsuccessful, the ancient landscape was visible to us once more through images acquired by specially constructed remotely operated vehicles (ROVs) called *Argus* and *Little Hercules* (*L'il Herc* for short). *L'il Herc* looks like a bright yellow balloon on a black "string" attached to *Argus,* and moves more freely and easily because it is not directly towed by the support ship. The ROVs could send video images back to the ship along the thickly clustered wires in the umbilical cord that allowed pilots to maneuver precisely along the seabed and, we knew, within the archaeological sites there.

The tow-sled *Argus* acts as a platform for lights, a video camera, an electronic still camera, and a 35-mm color still camera. *L'il Herc* carries cameras capable of providing extremely high-quality images; it also has a variety of sensors for pressure, depth, and compass heading, and thrusters for movement both laterally and vertically. It carries obstacle avoidance sonar, which was vital to quickly locating the acoustic anomalies we wanted to investigate.

2000 season   CHERYL WARD

A little before midnight, on my first watch after boarding the ship, I came into the "van" where all the equipment is set up, to serve as nautical archaeologist for the watch. "Slowly, slowly, THERE!" said the ROV pilot as we approached our first target and saw *L'il Herc*'s lights suddenly illuminate a wall of amphoras standing about 2 m (6.6 ft) above the seabed. Shipwreck A, the season's first shipwreck, sank with a cargo of dark orange, carrot-shaped shipping jars typical of the Sinop region and probably dates between the 4th and 6th centuries AD.

We moved to another target location, with a quick stop along the way to check what turned out to be a large rock, and almost immediately to a third anomaly that, like the first on my midnight watch, turned out to be a shipwreck marked by a large pile of Sinopian shipping jars. A few jars with a more oval shape were scattered across the top of the site, and indicate a slightly later date of the 4th to early 7th century.

A third significant target became Shipwreck C after ROV inspection. Buried deeply in the sediments is another lost cargo of the early Byzantine period. In the

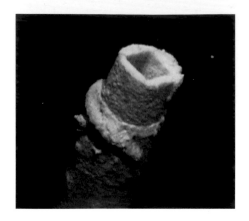

Above **A side-scan sonar survey pass over Shipwreck D showed an upright acoustic shadow more than 10 m (33 ft) long. The ship's mast, its tip illuminated here by *L'il Herc*, heralded the discovery of the best-preserved shipwreck from antiquity.**

Below **The success of the 2000 Black Sea survey provided inspiration and impetus for the construction of *Hercules*, a larger ROV designed and built especially for exploration and testing of archaeological sites in the deep sea.**

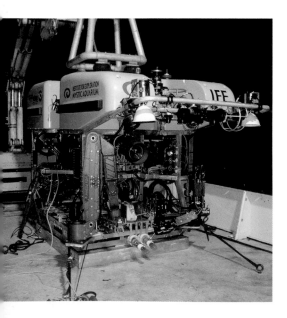

Mediterranean, archaeologists have studied many amphora wrecks, but most are swathed beneath a bed of poseidon grass or other sea growth. The shipwrecks we found at depths of 85–100 m (280–330 ft) are all characterized by piles of amphoras in a mound above the seabed, but without the Mediterranean-style cloak of grass. And the wrecks differed in other ways as well: loose timbers scattered on the surface of the site were relatively well preserved, even if we weren't able to identify any of them as hull components.

The last find of the 2000 season was identified in water 320 m (1,050 ft) deep and was the last target to be visited. Its sonar signature – a long, slender, upright feature – transformed itself into the wooden mast of Shipwreck D, standing about 12–14 m (40–46 ft) above the seabed. The mast lacks any trace of erosion, and is beautifully preserved. Hints as to its rigging exist in a fragment of cordage wrapped around the head of the mast just below a squared cavity that might have supported a separate masthead for attaching rigging.

At deck level, the mast disappears into thick brown sediment topped with a fluffy, whitish organic substance biologists call "marine snow," the remains of tiny organisms that live in the water column. A number of spars, partially covered with drifted sediments, lay along the deck, some between two pairs of stanchions aft of the mast. Frame (rib) ends rise above the sediment, and let me generate a rough tracing of the ship's shape and dimensions that came into startling focus in 2003.

2003 season   ROBERT D. BALLARD

During the years leading up to the Black Sea Project, it became increasingly clear that the modern tools of oceanographers could be used to find and document ancient shipwrecks lying in the deep sea in increasing number. Advanced ROVs could also conduct surface sampling of exposed artifacts should that be desired by the Project Archaeologist, but what was also clear was the fact that ROVs developed by the oceanographic community were not ready to conduct an archaeological excavation effort in the deep sea that met standards of excavation techniques for shallow water sites.

My early attempts using the Navy's research submarine NR-1 and the *Jason* ROV from the Woods Hole Oceanographic Institution to excavate a series of Roman trading ships on Skerki Bank proved that excavating a shipwreck buried in the fine-grain sediments of the deep sea was going to be a truly challenging task.

For that reason, we formed a design team consisting of archaeologists, oceanographers, and engineers that resulted in the *Hercules* ROV system, the first ROV ever built to carry out archaeological excavations in the deep sea. In 2003, *Hercules* joined our robotic team and helped us more thoroughly explore the remains of Shipwrecks B and C. But it was the fourth shipwreck that momentarily silenced the usual chatter in the control van as we watched *Hercules* approach it. In nearly three days of work at the site, *Hercules* excavated sediments, collected shipping jars and their contents, acquired acoustic data, and produced thousands of photographs and hours of tape that will let the archaeologists analyze it more carefully.

Our cruise to the Black Sea was the first field testing of the *Hercules* ROV. Using advanced imaging systems, a force-feed-back manipulator, precise closed-loop

control, and a sophisticated jetting/pumping system, we easily removed the deep-sea muds surrounding Shipwreck D. The excavating system fulfilled its design specifications and maintained visual supervisory control at all times, proving itself fully capable of excavating an ancient shipwreck.

But this was just a test; further time is now needed to carry out a sustained investigation to determine if the full excavation of deep-water shipwrecks is feasible.

I'm a Bronze Age scholar. I'm so ignorant of the medieval and Renaissance periods of Europe that when I was asked to speak on medieval and Renaissance shipwrecks at a national conference of historians, I asked my wife: "When was the medieval period? And when did the Renaissance start?"

"I think the medieval period was when everybody got the plague," she jokingly replied, "and the Renaissance is when they all got well."

These days I'm slightly better informed. The medieval period is also known as the Middle Ages and, more provocatively, the Dark Ages. So as not to confuse you, I will pass over quickly the fact that the Byzantine period we just left in the last section was also part of those Dark Middle Ages!

Although at the end it will return to Yassıada, Turkey, this section will finally take us out of the Mediterranean, with its long and well-recorded history of seafaring, and its long history of marine archaeology, to Southeast Asia and to the Far East – far from medieval Europe. It also takes us to a land excavation, for nautical archaeologists are interested in ships wherever they are found, including those intentionally buried in earlier times, whether by ancient Egyptians or by Vikings, Anglo-Saxons, or other northern Europeans.

The excavation of the 14th-century Shinan wreck was a purely Korean operation, but the Institute of Nautical Archaeology's Donald H. Keith was twice sent to the project by the National Geographic Society, both to offer advice and to recount the story of the excavation to English-speaking readers. More recently, INA Research Associate Jeremy Green visited the National Maritime Museum at Mokpo, which houses the vessel's hull, and talked to those who continue research on the wreck and its valuable cargo.

Although I have twice been to Korea, I have not yet seen the finds from Shinan in the museum at Mokpo. In 2004 in China, however, I was able to see the results of the excavation of a contemporaneous Chinese wreck, equally rich in beautiful, varied, and intact ceramics, excavated opposite the Korean Peninsula under the direction of Zhang Wei of the National Museum of Chinese History in Beijing. Because I knew Zhang Wei when he studied nautical archaeology at Texas A&M University in the spring of 1989, it gave me great pleasure also to visit, in the South China Sea, the diving barges from which he is now excavating an earlier, 12th-century wreck, raising thousands of pieces of intact, glazed ceramics, many of which I saw in the Yangjiang Museum. The publication of these wrecks should be truly extraordinary.

Fred Hocker next takes us to the Zuidersee of the Netherlands, where hundreds, or perhaps thousands of wrecks lie beneath the soil that has been reclaimed from

Two students excavate inside a 2-m (6.6-ft) grid frame on a shallow 16th-century wreck site at Ko Kradat, Thailand. The diver in the foreground, finding himself slightly buoyant, has supplemented his diving weights by placing a rock on his scuba tanks!

the sea. There are so many vessels there that Dutch archaeologists welcome help in recording them, which led to an arrangement whereby graduate students in the Nautical Archaeology Program at Texas A&M University had the opportunity for original research and publication. Fred describes his excavation of a cog, the primary merchant ship of Northern Europe from the 13th through to the 15th century.

Then Jeremy Green transports us to Thailand. The Western Australian Museum, where Jeremy heads the Department of Maritime Archaeology, is perhaps the only institute outside INA that conducts field operations globally, as seen in this book. We are pleased that Jeremy has also worked off and on with us, from the Mediterranean to the Indian Ocean, for nearly four decades. He describes here just one of a number of wrecks he studied during a nautical archaeology training program he conducted for Thai archaeologists.

Lastly, we are introduced to an Ottoman ship of the late 16th or early 17th century. I was personally involved in this one, for when I started tracing timbers going off at an angle from the late 4th- or early 5th-century Byzantine hull I was uncovering at Yassıada, Turkey, in the late 1960s, I thought it was part of the same ship. The Byzantine ship, I assumed, had broken into two pieces, and I was tracing the timbers of one of those pieces. Eventually we realized that this was a later, almost empty ship that had sunk directly onto the Byzantine ship. Cemal Pulak excavated this later ship, dated by a coin to the time of Philip II of Spain, or slightly later, and identified as Ottoman by its contents.

Above **Glazed bowls carried aboard an Ottoman ship that sank in the 16th or early 17th century off Yassıada, Turkey.**

Below **Places mentioned in this section, with the featured wrecks in bold.**

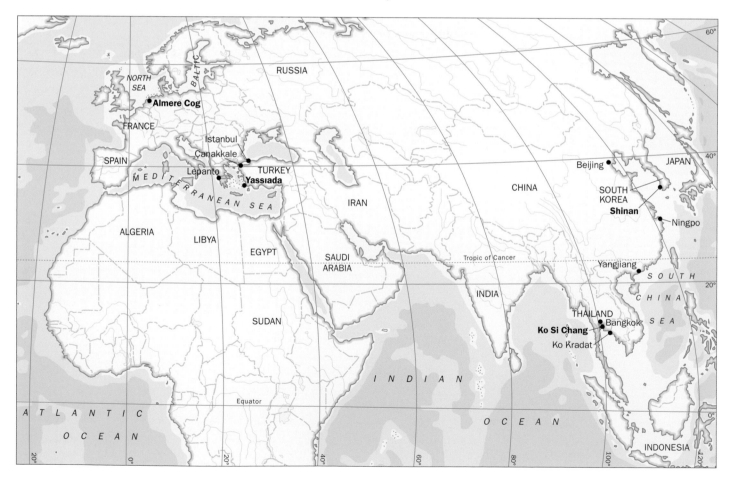

Shinan Wreck

Date   c 1323
Depth   20 m (66 ft)
Found by   Choi Hyung-gun
Celadons   12,359
Coins   7,000,000
Hull   28.4 m (93 ft) long,
6.6 m (21.5 ft) wide

A 14th-Century Chinese Wreck: Shinan, Korea

GEORGE F. BASS

The Institute of Nautical Archaeology's first foray into the Far East, like so many INA adventures, began with a phone call. The year was 1979.

"The Korean Navy is excavating a 14th-century Chinese junk. It's the first real underwater excavation in the Far East. Would you go over as an adviser – and write an article for our magazine?" It was the National Geographic Society.

My hands were already more than full in Turkey.

"I can't make it, but I have the perfect person for you."

I was thinking of Donald H. Keith, who had been with me at Şeytan Deresi and Serçe Limanı, and even on a Revolutionary War wreck in the York River, Virginia. Not only an innovative and brilliant student, Don was one of the finest diver/excavators I knew, uncannily skilled at making beautiful and accurate drawings on the seabed. Don would go on to excavate for INA what was then the oldest known shipwreck in the New World, at Molasses Reef in the Turks and Caicos Islands, where he later established a museum for the display of the finds.

Within days Don was descending a line down 20 m (66 ft) in zero visibility in the Yellow Sea, off the port city of Shinan in southwest Korea. A strong current tugged at him. On the bottom, his dive partner, Lieutenant In Seong-jin, guided Don's hands over what proved to be porcelain and wood protruding from the sediment. Don described what he learned during two trips to Korea in *National Geographic* and, later, *Archaeology* magazines.

The Discovery

The site was found in 1975 by fisherman Choi Hyung-gun, who netted pieces of pottery that were identified by experts as celadons – prized for their resemblance to jade – of the Yuan Dynasty (1260–1386). Choi and his younger brother were rewarded by the South Korean Cultural Properties Preservation Bureau for reporting the discovery, but before a proper excavation could be undertaken, other, less scrupulous fishermen were mining the site for celadons to sell to an antique dealer. Arrests were made, the celadons were recovered, and the Cultural Properties Preservation Bureau, assisted by a Korean Navy squadron commanded by Captain Choi In-sang, began full-scale excavation 2 km (1.2 miles) off shore, sometimes diving in the freezing cold of winter.

In 1982, INA Research Associate Jeremy Green, as part of a research project with Professor Zae Gun Kim of Seoul University, visited the Conservation Laboratory of the National Maritime Museum at Mokpo, and studied a one-fifth scale research model of the ship.

The glazed statuette of the Buddhist deity Kuan-yin, 24 cm (9 in) tall, was found on the Shinan wreck with part of its head cleanly broken away.

The Finds

By 1989, years after the visits by Don and Jeremy, the results of the excavation were astonishing. Seven million coins, weighing 26.8 tons, provided the earliest date the ship could have sunk; although the coins had been minted over six centuries, the latest was from 1310. An even more precise date for the sinking was provided by a wooden cargo tag with the year 1323 written on it. In addition, with thousands of pieces of porcelain, Korea had attained the largest collection of Yuan Dynasty celadons in the world, many found still cushioned by peppercorns in well-preserved wooden crates.

It seems that sailors of all nationalities have passed their time at sea playing games. On the 11th-century Serçe Limanı Glass Wreck, those on board had played both chess and backgammon, and on wrecks of all periods of antiquity in the Mediterranean,

Below **Among the thousands of objects recovered from the Shinan wreck were Chinese ceramics still packed in remarkably preserved wooden crates – that on the right still marked with the words "great luck." One crate was marked on its top with the grid pattern for the Chinese game of Go, presumably played by the mariners on board.**

Right This late 18th-century painting of a Chinese ship by William Alexander is one of the earliest by a westerner. Korean and Chinese archaeological excavations are now adding greatly to our knowledge of still earlier Chinese ships.

Below right This small bronze lion, only 10 cm (4 in) high, was a censer or incense burner whose head could be removed and replaced.

sailors seem to have played knucklebones. On top of one of the crates raised at Shinan someone had carved the board for the Chinese game of Go.

Although the lack of visibility prevented the excavators from making a site plan to the accuracy we are accustomed to in the Mediterranean, they placed a metal grid over the site, dividing it into squares 2 m (6.6 ft) on a side, and recalled just where every object in each square had been found during debriefing sessions immediately following each dive. The hull of this, the first seagoing Chinese vessel ever excavated by divers, was in many respects as expected: flat, with transom ends at bow and stern, its interior divided into eight compartments by seven bulkheads.

An inscription on a counterweight for a balance on board suggests the ship may have sailed from Ningpo in China. But what was her destination? Because the Koreans themselves made celadons in the 14th century, it is less likely that the ship was heading for Korea to unload its wares than that it was on its way to Japan, where Chinese celadons were prized imports. Probably driven onto rocks by a storm *en route*, the ship never reached her intended port.

A 14th-Century Chinese Wreck: Shinan, Korea

A 15th-Century Cog in the Zuidersee: Almere, Netherlands

FRED HOCKER

The landscape is eerie, disorienting. The ground is flat as far as the eye can see, interrupted only by drainage ditches at regular intervals. Trees are all exactly the same height, in even rows under a gray sky that gives no sense of direction or contrast to the land stretching away to the horizon. This is Flevoland, the land the Dutch reclaimed from the Zuidersee. It is an artificial landscape, the world's largest gardening project, and one of its richest repositories of shipwrecks. It was once a busy artery on the most important east-west sea route in northern Europe, and ships were lost here from the 13th century until draining began in the 1920s. Since 1944, Dutch archaeologists have investigated over 400 shipwrecks in this new land. Many are nearly complete, with contents wonderfully preserved by the bottom mud, including medieval clothing, Renaissance mandolins, and Baroque woodcuts.

Among those wrecks are almost a dozen cogs, the heavy ships that carried the commerce of the High Middle Ages and helped make the Hanseatic League the world's first successful, multinational corporation. One was recovered from the frozen ground in the new town of Almere in the spring of 1986, but there were no resources to document it. No cargo survived, only a few small finds, but these included a human skeleton and a curious wooden clapper. The clapper, in the form

Almere Cog

Sunk 1422–1433
Excavation 1986
Recording 1988
Hull 16.4 m (54 ft) long,
4.2 m (14 ft) wide
Cargo capacity *c* 30 tons
Cargo unknown

Left **The substantially complete remains of the cog lie flattened out in the mud where they were discovered in 1986, during construction of a new subdivision in the town of Almere.**

Right **A spade, axe and adze found on board the vessel. They were not worth retrieving when the cargo was salvaged, probably soon after the sinking.**

of St Catherine, was a noisemaker that lepers were required to carry, to warn people of their approach, and the skeleton showed scarring typical of healed lesions. This poor man must have been judged unclean, which may explain why no one saved his life when the ship sank.

I was very interested in cogs, as they formed a major part of the dissertation I was starting at Texas A&M University, and I asked Reinder Reinders, the director of the Dutch Museum for Ship Archaeology, if INA could help with the recording of the Almere cog. Aleydis Van de Moortel had established a precedent of Texas A&M students working on material from Flevoland, and Reinders agreed. So in the summer of 1988, Mike Fitzgerald, Sam Mark, Bob Neyland and I arrived at the museum in Ketelhaven to record the ship in detail. We stayed in one of the nearby holiday houses (called "chicken coops" by the locals), ate badly (none of us could cook), and spent our days attacking a large pile of wet, muddy wood.

There was no diving, no careful sifting of bottom sediments to reveal hidden treasures. Instead, the disassembled timbers were stacked under the steady drizzle of a sprinkler system. We would take an oak timber weighing up to 150 kg (330 lb) to a gridded table and carefully trace the outlines of the piece, the location of each feature, each nail and treenail, as we had been taught by Dick Steffy. Over the course of 12 weeks, we turned the pile of wood into hundreds of drawings. It sounds dreary, but in the intense concentration on details, we began to feel that we were meeting the people who built and sailed the ship. In the pattern of adze strokes we could see that there had been at least two shipwrights building the cog, and that both were right-handed. In the repairs made to the bottom, we could see the long life of the vessel, scraping over the mud flats and sand bars that plague the Zuidersee. In cracks in the planks, we could see the limitations of the wood with which the shipwrights worked and their practical solutions for dealing with them. In the failed joints of the deck beams we could see a bad design decision 600 years before.

Using our drawings, I was able to reconstruct the original appearance of the ship, a vessel about 16 m (52 ft) long that had sailed the Zuidersee in the early 15th century, an unremarkable but essential part of the vast flow of goods and people between the Baltic and the North Sea. Although cogs eventually were replaced by other types, many of the basic features of this small but sturdy ship survived on the inland waterways of northern Europe and can still be seen in steel barges working the lower Rhine or along the canals that still cut through Flevoland.

Above **A full-size replica of the cog, built by the town of Malmö, Sweden, and the Fotevik Museum, launched in 2002.**

Right **The clapper in the form of St Catherine, with the simple prayer "Help me" carved at her feet.**

Pursuing Southeast Asian Wrecks: Ko Si Chang, Thailand

JEREMY GREEN

On the east side of the north end of the Gulf of Thailand lies Ko Si Chang ("Ko" in Thai means island). A famous pilgrimage site for Buddhists, it is also the site of three important Asian shipwrecks. I first heard of wrecks there in 1979, when, with colleagues from the Western Australian Maritime Museum, I was conducting training and exploring sites in the Gulf in a joint project with the Fine Arts Department of Thailand. We had already excavated a wreck at Ko Kradat, near the Cambodian border, and learned exciting new things about Thai ceramics. Many Thai shipwreck sites have Chinese porcelain as cargo, and some, luckily, have the date of the reign of the emperor of China, or even the year of manufacture. At Ko Kradat we had found a Jia Jing (1522–1566) reign date, so we were able for the first time to date accurately Thai ceramics of the kind in that cargo.

Next, in 1982, while inspecting a heavily looted site at Pattaya, about 140 km (84 miles) south of Bangkok, we took a week off to check out the rumors of the wrecks at Ko Si Chang. On arrival at the island's little port, our Thai colleagues quickly found the fisherman who knew one wreck's location. We headed out to sea west of the island and as it receded in the distance we grew increasingly sceptical. We had all been in this situation before! The fisherman was smoking a huge joint and laughing with our Thai colleagues as he accompanied us in his small boat. About 3 km (1.8 miles) off Ko Si Chang, the island almost obscure in the haze, he went unhesitatingly to a spot and pointed down. Here it was, he indicated, in 32 m (106 ft) of water!

Somebody had to dive, just to be polite, but there was no way the fisherman could be so precise this far from land. Several of our crew went down, and surfaced 15

Above **Team member Nick Sander cleans newly recovered ceramics. The larger Southeast Asian storage jar, a trade item, contained lime, which was chewed with betel nut – a mildly narcotic habit.**

Below left **Ceramics were typical of the mixed cargoes of Southeast Asian trading junks: large storage jars from a kiln site in central Thailand; black Southeast Asian kendis, or spouted water containers (left); and Chinese blue and white ceramics (foreground).**

Ko Si Chang Wreck

Date *c* 1600
Depth 32 m (106 ft)
Excavation 1983, 1985
Cargo ceramics, storage jars
Hull *c* 20 m (66 ft) long

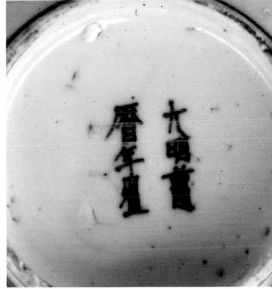

minutes later with two bags. One bag contained two large fish – and the other Chinese blue-and-white ceramics: two large plates and a bowl with a reign date (Wan Li 1573–1620)! They had dived straight into the middle of a wreck with great quantities of ceramics and large storage jars (where they found the fish). Soon we had a surface collection to help identify the site.

The man who showed us the wreck was a line fisherman who said that it had not been found by trawlers. He catches fish that hide in the storage jars. The seabed in this part of the Gulf is a featureless sandy or muddy bottom, and fish are found where there are reefs or wrecks. So how did the fisherman know of this wreck? It cannot be from randomly fishing hundreds of square kilometers of the Gulf and finding such sites by chance. When the ship was lost did local fishermen immediately begin to exploit it, first by grappling for items (it's too deep for free diving), and later simply by fishing there? Did its location then pass by word of mouth over the generations?

We mounted an excavation of the site in 1983 and 1985. The work was difficult because of poor visibility and strong currents, but we learned that the vessel was about 20 m (66 ft) long, with bulkheads dividing it into compartments, and with its planking edge-joined with dowels, a type of construction typical of Southeast Asia. The vessel was carrying a mixed cargo of ceramics, with different types stored in the separate compartments. Of particular interest was the discovery that the bulkheads had waterways in them. Previously, based on Marco Polo's writing of his travels in about 1292, it was thought that such bulkheads were watertight. He wrote that "some ships have 13 holds, or divisions, on the inside, made with strong planks fitted together, so that if by accident the ship is staved in any place, either by striking a rock, or if a whale-fish striking against it in search of food and staves it in, then the water entering through the hole runs to the bilge, which never remains occupied with things. Then the sailors find out where the ship is staved and the hold is emptied into the others, for the water cannot pass from one hold to another, so strongly are they sealed."

Our Ko Si Chang wreck showed once again that Southeast Asian vessels were built along the same lines as Chinese vessels, and our evidence supports the case that Asian ships with bulkheads were not sealed.

Above left **The first items recovered from the wreck. The four shallow plates bear emblems of two of the Eight Daoist Immortals: the fan of Zong li Zhuan, the warrior (left and right) and the gourd of Li Tie Guai, the cripple (center). The bowl on the right was particularly important because of the reign date on its base (*above*). The six Chinese characters starting from the top right read: Great Ming Wan Li Year Made. Wan Li reigned from 1573 to 1620.**

Below **Illustration of a junk from Thailand taken from a Japanese scroll dating from the late Ming period (1368–1644). Such vessels traded throughout Southeast Asia and with China and Japan.**

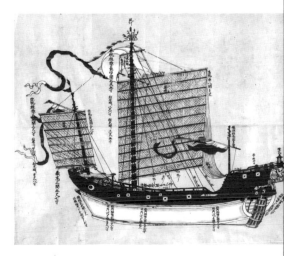

A Rare Ottoman Wreck:
Yassıada, Turkey

CEMAL PULAK

Yassıada Ottoman Wreck

Date late 16th–early 17th century
Depth 39–43 m (128–141 ft)
Found by George Bass
Excavation 1967, 1982–3
Hull c 20 m (66 ft) long,
c 7 m (23 ft) wide
Dives 200 in 1983

For more than six weeks we had been aboard *Virazon* without setting foot ashore. INA's research vessel pitched and rolled laboriously in the roaring waves breaking on the submerged rock reef about 200 m (600 ft) off the ship's bow. The constant howl of the prevailing northwesterly winds, compounded by lack of sleep on the ever-rolling ship, had brought our nerves to the verge of snapping. Yet we labored dutifully to excavate and record the 300-year-old ship that lay 39–43 m (128–141 ft) below us.

Crouched over a drafting table jury-rigged over the double-lock recompression chamber deep in *Virazon*'s hold, and somewhat numbed by the motion-sickness pill I took every few hours, I struggled to focus and steady my hand while drawing on the site plan the timbers I had just measured on the seabed.

The *Virazon* was, in the summer of 1983, moored semi-permanently over the site with its main anchor driven into the submerged reef onto which a late 16th- or early 17th-century ship had struck and sunk. The reef, its shallowest part only 1.5 m (5 ft) below the surface, lies approximately 150 m (500 ft) to the southwest of Yassıada ("Flat Island" in Turkish), a small and uninhabited island approximately 5 km (3 miles) off the western Turkish coast. The same reef had caused the demise of nearly a dozen ancient ships, of which a 7th-century Byzantine ship and a 4th-century late Roman period ship were excavated by George Bass and Frederick van Doorninck in previous years. The watery graves of the wrecks were marked by mounds of two-handled clay jars, or sometimes only by scattered potsherds that bore witness to forgotten tragedies. The seemingly dormant reef still sporadically springs to life to prey on unsuspecting vessels. In 1993, a Lebanese freighter struck the reef and lay suspended on it for months before gradually taking in water and sinking on top of ships that had met their fate millennia earlier.

Puzzling Timbers

In 1967, when George Bass and his team began excavating the 4th-century shipwreck, they were surprised when they uncovered timbers lying at an angle across the stern of the Roman wreck. As more of these timbers were exposed, the excavators realized they belonged to another, larger vessel, of much later date according to the few glazed bowls they found with the timbers. During the second campaign on the Roman wreck, in 1969, they excavated a 6-m (20-ft) section of the bow of the newly discovered wreck, but could not determine the size of the vessel, nor could they identify a poorly preserved silver Spanish coin found near this bow.

Before the next campaign at Yassıada in 1974, this time under the auspices of the newly founded INA, the coin had been tentatively dated to around 1600. With great

Right Conservation of the only coin found on the wreck revealed it to be a silver 4-reale piece issued between 1566 and 1589 by Philip II of Spain.

Below An archaeologist photographs the oak ribs or frame timbers of the Ottoman shipwreck; the bow is at the bottom of the picture. The site is divided into 2-m (6.6-ft) square grids for mapping purposes and the timbers labeled with tags for easy identification.

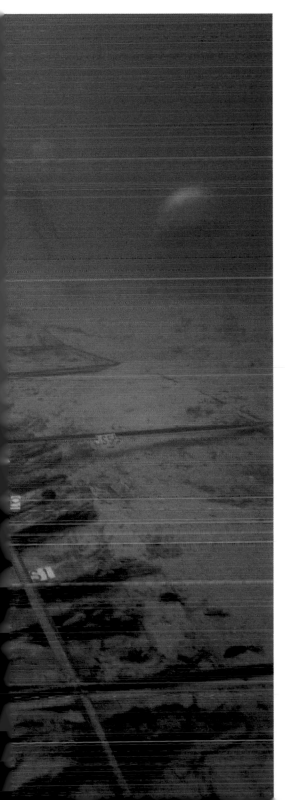

anticipation, INA exposed again the bow section to lift its shroud of mystery. Unfortunately, the campaign was brief, for the outbreak of hostilities between Turkey, Cyprus and Greece that year necessitated immediate evacuation of Yassıada. The waterlogged timbers were abandoned once more.

In 1982, when George Bass decided to re-initiate the excavation of this shipwreck for a Council of Europe field school that INA was hosting in Turkey with the Bodrum Museum of Underwater Archaeology, the coin had been thoroughly cleaned, and identified as a 4-reale piece issued between 1566 and 1589 by Philip II of Spain. My interests lay in 16th-century seafaring, but particularly in ships of the Ottoman Turks – and I suspected this was an Ottoman ship because of its date and location. No intact early Ottoman shipwreck had ever been found and excavated, which meant we knew far more about Classical Greek, Roman, and Byzantine ships than early Ottoman ships. Yet, in the 16th century, the Ottoman Empire had built one of the largest and most formidable navies in the Mediterranean. A major reason for this disparity is that perishable barrels and skins replaced easily detectable and virtually indestructible amphoras in maritime commerce after the 13th century.

At the conclusion of the 1982 campaign we had a fairly good idea about the size of the Ottoman ship and its construction details, but its precise date and function remained a mystery. In hopes of answering these two questions we began our final campaign the following summer. Unlike the previous campaign, conducted from a comfortable camp built on Yassıada for the field school, the 1983 excavation was to take place with only a handful of veteran INA archaeologists and field personnel operating exclusively from *Virazon*.

We again exposed the hull and recorded it on our site plan. The extant timbers suggested that the ship had been at least 20 m (66 ft) in length and about 6 m (20 ft) in beam, of moderate size for its time, but obviously not a rowed war galley of the type used extensively by the Ottoman fleet. With the exception of a few artifacts and a handful of pottery, the ship was empty. Nor was there any indication that it had been carrying perishable cargo, such as grain, that disappeared after the ship sank. This made it all the more puzzling, for how could a ship sink and stay down for three centuries without the weight of heavy cargo or ballast? With its frames and planking of oak, all fastened with iron nails, the ship would have been heavier than a comparable pine-built vessel, but still not sufficiently heavy to sink to the bottom on its own. The answer may be found in the fact the ship was empty, for no ship would sail without taking on some cargo or ballasting to increase its stability during sailing. This meant that after striking the reef, the wounded vessel remained suspended on it for a time before gradually sinking to its watery grave, as had been the fate of the Lebanese freighter that sank in 1993. Evidence for this is found in the ship's badly battered keel, which was broken at three different places. While the ship remained afloat on the reef, there must have been time to salvage everything of value. Nothing of worth, not a single anchor, nor tools or weapons in any quantity, was left on the ship. Even the cargo, whatever it was, had been removed, perhaps transferred to an escort ship or to some vessel that had come to the sinking ship's aid. What remained probably spilled on the reef from the gaping holes in the bottom of the hull. It is impossible to know how long our ship remained suspended on the reef, but it must have been long enough for its oak planking to become waterlogged and sufficiently heavy to sink rather than float off to be smashed apart by pounding waves on some rocky coast.

An Ottoman Naval Vessel?

We wondered if our ship could have played a role in the Battle of Lepanto, one of the greatest sea battles ever fought and the last major battle fought with oared ships. On 7 October 1571, off Lepanto in western Greece, the advancing Ottoman fleet met the most powerful fleet ever launched by Christendom, consisting of Venetian, Spanish, papal, Genoese, Savoy, and Maltese galleys, as well as six large Venetian galleasses. The Christian fleet won a decisive victory, marking the end of unchallenged Ottoman naval supremacy in the eastern Mediterranean. Was our ship a transport or supply vessel that carried marines or provisions at Lepanto? The 4-reale coin indicated that the ship could not have sunk before 1566, but it could have any time after that date. Had the nearly one hundred cannonballs we found spilled on top of the reef come from our ship? Could they and the two stone and one cast iron cannonballs of smaller gauge found aboard indicate that our ship had been a naval supply vessel?

We found two large and ten smaller glazed bowls on the wreck. Aside from differences in size and glazing, they are similar – deep bowls with slightly incurving rims and conical pedestal bases. They are decorated inside with the *sgraffito* technique, the design incised on the top layer of glaze. The bowls correspond in number to the number of crew for a medium-sized naval supply ship with two officers and ten sailors. Duplicate bowls come from excavations at Saraçhane in Istanbul, the Agora of Athens, and Bodrum Castle, all associated with Ottoman military presence (it is fitting that the last location now houses the Bodrum Museum of Underwater Archaeology where the Yassıada Ottoman shipwreck finds are kept). It is likely, therefore, that the bowls represent military consignments. This seems substantiated by the discovery of several bowl fragments of the same type from a pottery workshop on the Dardanelles at Çanakkale, which served as a base for one of the Ottoman fleets. Analysis by Sophie Stos revealed that the lead isotopes in the bowls' glazing is consistent with that mined in the region of Çanakkale, suggesting that all the bowls were made in a single area that produced pottery for Ottoman naval use. But even with an established connection between the Yassıada ship and the Ottoman Navy, what of the battle of Lepanto?

Tree-Ring Detective

We turned to Peter Kuniholm of the Wiener Dendrochronology Laboratory at Cornell University. Since radiocarbon dates were not sufficiently precise, I hoped he could help us accurately date the ship. Matching the growth rings of undated wood with those that have been assembled into a continuous sequence of rings, dendrochronologists are able to determine the date of any well-preserved wood precisely to the year and sometimes to the season during which a tree was felled, providing that the sample has sufficient number of rings present and its bark is preserved. I sent a 5-cm (2-in) thick slice from the ship's keel to Peter, who provided a tentative working date of 1572. However, since an indeterminable number of growth

Below **Illustrator Netia Piercy studies a large glazed bowl for illustration purposes. A total of 12 glazed bowls of three sizes were found on the wreck; examples of medium and small-sized bowls can be seen on the drafting table.**

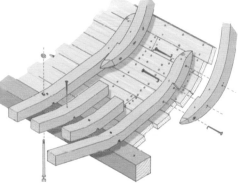

Below Sectional reconstruction of the ship. Each frame, consisting of a futtock fastened to either end of the floor timber with a hook joint and three double-clenched nails, is secured to the keel with a large spike or a forelock bolt. A smaller keel-like timber, called a keelson, that sat atop the frames had completely vanished.

rings had been shaved off during the fashioning of the keel, the tree from which it was made would have been felled well after that date, indicating that the ship was built after Lepanto, although probably not much later.

The Yassıada Ottoman shipwreck nevertheless remains the best-preserved and only completely excavated 16th- or early 17th-century Ottoman period shipwreck. With the exception of part of the ship's planking, all of the timbers have been raised and are in wet storage in the Bodrum Museum of Underwater Archaeology. Even though the full study of the timbers and preliminary reconstruction of the ship is yet to be completed, we have already learned much about a relatively recent but hitherto unknown period in the maritime history of the Mediterranean.

Upon sinking, the Ottoman ship's starboard side came to rest partly on the amphora cargo of a 4th-century merchantman near its bow (left). The ship listed to port, quickly burying that side under sand, preserving it, while the starboard side perished almost completely. The large timber at the right is the ship's sternpost.

NA archaeologists need to keep their passports up to date. For the 17th-century sites they describe here, they excavated in both northern and southern Europe, on two Caribbean islands, and in East Africa, and then conserved an entire ship raised off the coast of Texas!

Robert Neyland, who would go on to salvage and conserve the famous Confederate submarine *Hunley* off Charleston, South Carolina, here describes an excavation he conducted in a hay field for the Netherlands Institute of Ship- and Underwater Archaeology (NISA) when he was still a doctoral candidate in the Nautical Archaeology Program at Texas A&M University. He takes us again to the Zuidersee, where Fred Hocker excavated the medieval Almere cog. Where else are nautical archaeologists photographed with windmills in the background?

In Portugal, as I stood high on Lisbon's São Julião da Barra fortress one day in 1998, I had goose bumps. Francisco Alvez, head of his country's outstanding program of nautical archaeology, was vividly recounting to a group of us the tragic events that had transpired below almost four centuries earlier. The *Nossa Senhora dos Mártires*, returning from India, tried again and again to enter the mouth of the Tagus River during a storm. Failing, the doomed ship was destroyed, with great loss of life, in full view of the families of those on board who were returning home after so many months away.

Filipe Castro, one of Francisco's assistants, whom I met the same day, soon enrolled at Texas A&M University, where he earned a doctorate, and then joined the faculty of the Nautical Archaeology Program. How pleased I was, then, when my new colleague, Filipe, completed the excavation and study of that terrible tragedy, which he describes here.

The role of Peter Throckmorton in the history of nautical archaeology should be clear by now to readers of this book. Not only had he initially involved me in diving on and excavating shipwrecks, but he did the same for Jerome Hall, who later served as president of the Institute of Nautical Archaeology. Jerome was earning a Master's degree in marine biology at Nova University in Florida when he met Peter, then on the university's faculty. It was Peter who directed Jerome to the Dominican Republic and the Monte Cristi wreck, the Pipe Wreck that Jerome describes in the following pages.

One rare wreck I can visit without a passport is that of famous French explorer La Salle's ship *La Belle*. In only 20 minutes I can drive to Texas A&M University's Conservation Research Laboratory, where I am repeatedly awed by the conservation of the ship's hull and contents, under the direction of INA's current president, Donn

A diver raises a decorative wooden cherub from the wreck of *Santo Antonio de Tanna* in Mombasa Harbor, Kenya. Carved wooden wings were found nearby.

Hamilton. Or I can step a few feet away from my office into the office of Barto Arnold, who joined INA shortly after discovering *La Belle* and overseeing construction of a cofferdam around it to enable its excavation in dry air.

Donny seems fated to deal with thousands of artifacts wherever he works. In 1692, the infamous pirate stronghold of Port Royal, Jamaica, at that time the richest English colony in the New World, became the submarine equivalent of Pompeii when it sank beneath the waves in a massive earthquake. In 1980 I was invited to Jamaica, where Prime Minister Edward Seaga asked if INA would undertake the archaeological excavation of the sunken city. Although this was not primarily a ship-wreck excavation – a ship was later found driven into the city by the earthquake's accompanying tsunami – I accepted on the spot, and then asked Donny Hamilton to direct the project, which he did in exemplary fashion for the following decade as a Texas A&M University field school.

INA's involvement in East Africa similarly began with an invitation, this one from Hamo Sassoon, Curator of the Fort Jesus Museum in Mombasa, Kenya. Hamo asked me if INA would examine a wreck located by local divers in Mombasa Harbor, thinking it might be one of the Portuguese ships that had come to the aid of Portuguese Fort Jesus when it was besieged by Omani Arabs at the end of the 17th century. I asked Don Frey and Robin Piercy to undertake the examination, which they did in 1975. Two years later Robin began full-scale excavation of the wreck of the Portuguese *Santo Antonio de Tanna,* which takes him regularly back to Mombasa to study the artifacts for his ultimate publication of the site.

Above **Donny Hamilton gingerly removes concretion from an Amerindian vulture-headed metate (corn grinder) found at Port Royal.** *Below* **Places mentioned in this section, with the featured wrecks in bold.**

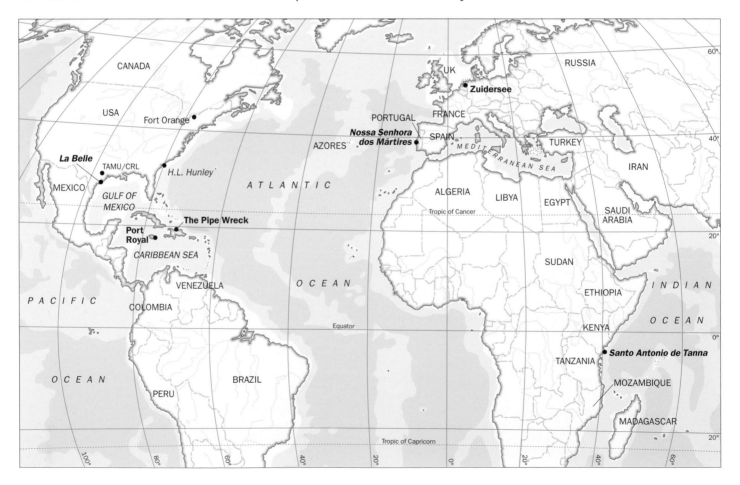

Ship Archaeology in a Hay Field: Zuidersee, Netherlands

ROBERT S. NEYLAND

The wind rippled through the expanse of grass growing over what was once the seabed of the Zuidersee. I imagined an unlucky day for the captain and crew of the newly unearthed boat as the winds began to fill her sails…the breeze starting to blow, building up the waves, and swamping the little freighter. In 1692, or a few years thereafter, these poor souls lost their boat and all their possessions.

OH 107

Our shipwreck lay in agricultural lot "H 107" in the Dutch Province of Flevoland. Named simply "OH 107" when discovered in 1962 by Dutch archaeologists of the Netherlands Institute of Ship- and Underwater Archaeology (NISA), its excavation would wait until I arrived in 1989 with a team of Dutch, German, and Texas A&M University archaeologists. In only three months we unearthed and recorded the 16.5-m (54-ft) long hull and its contents. A similar feat underwater would have taken several field seasons. "We ran an iron-man marathon in archaeology, with events in excavation, hull disassembly and recording, and conservation," commented an exhausted Birgit Schröder, who helped me direct and publish the excavation.

OH 107 is a typical Dutch find in the diked, drained, and reclaimed land called the "IJsselmeerpolder." The wreck was discovered when a machine cutting an agricultural drainage ditch in the newly reclaimed land chewed through ship's wood. Geology revealed to the Dutch NISA staff that the wrecking occurred after AD 1600, when a storm surge increased salinity of the water and deposited salt-laden clay and a thin but distinct layer of marine shells. OH 107 clearly broke through these layers as it sank into the soft seabed. Objects of the crew's everyday life – clay pots, glass bottles, tobacco pipes, and coins – confirmed that the vessel sank no earlier than 1692. Tree rings in the boat's timbers revealed that the trees were harvested between AD 1685 and 1693. An absence of scars from repairs in the unblemished hull suggested that it had only a short career before its owner lost it…and his livelihood.

Excavation

A few shovelfuls of mud made it clear that the bow was the center of life onboard – and the fragile state of the artifacts, which needed to be documented and rescued before being destroyed by the sun, demanded that excavation start there. In the bow was the cabin where the captain slept, managed finances, and took meals. The boat's hearth was a brick and glazed-tile fireplace with wood chimney. A few peat blocks, which provided fuel for the cooking fire, lay scattered among the fireplace bricks. An assortment of glazed ceramic pots, bowls, a pitcher, glass bottles, a cast-iron pot and a

Lucas van Dijk, NISA conservator, prepares a site plan of OH 107 by tracing the hull timbers with a mechanical device called a pantograph. The pantograph uses a series of cables and reduction gears to reduce the original shape of the hull timbers traced to a 1:20 scale.

bronze skillet represented the galley. A single oil lamp provided enough light for the captain to keep his eye on the compass, found here, and to administer the boat's business, evidenced by a pencil and a pair of lead tokens that were carried as proof of payment for tolls on the canals. Clay tobacco pipes, a sewing kit, and even an ice skate were for more leisurely pastimes.

As our excavation moved away toward the middle of the boat, and the cargo hold, recovery of artifacts slowed. No cargo remained, but it was evident from the absence of protective ceiling planking, or flooring, over the frames (or ribs) that the boat was designed to carry a cargo unlikely to damage the hull, perhaps agricultural produce or peat, the indispensable fuel for the fires of both Dutch industry and homes. An amazing find was part of the mast and its supporting framework called a "tabernacle." The weight of a cannon fragment had prevented the mast from floating away, for clever Dutch boat-builders had recycled the fragment for use as a counterweight for the mast, fastening it on with heavy iron straps. This arrangement allowed a small crew to man the boat while frequently raising and lowering the mast as they passed beneath bridges along the rivers and canals of their route.

I anticipated another significant area of finds at the stern. Here would be another cabin, perhaps the mate's lodging or an area for storing the boat's equipment. The excavation quickly revealed that the stern was used differently than the bow. A small and unfurnished cabin was only a humble cuddy containing a caulking iron, clay pot with caulk, chamber pot, and iron scrap. A jumble of bricks proved to be a crude floor. The stern cuddy had the most menial of tools and was too crude to lodge a crewman. A hammer, apparently on the stern deck when the boat careened onto its port side, slid with such force across the deck that it was found still firmly lodged inside the port scupper. "The hammer…used with the caulking iron to drive caulk in the seams… tells the story of our helmsman's hurried struggle to plug a leaking hull," I speculated.

A Working Boat

The captain's possessions told the boat's story. They spoke of a freighter that worked the northern waters of the Netherlands, but also made trips south, plying a route between what are today the Netherlands and Belgium. Most of the artifacts were typical of the northern Dutch provinces, although a few clearly originated in the lower Rhine and show a Flemish connection. One unique find was a green glass bottle wrapped in woven straw, much like a modern Chianti bottle. This type, known as "Fransche Flessen," contained not wine but water from the famous source in Spa in the Southern Provinces. Another surprising discovery was the tureen that served soups prepared in the forward cabin. It was decorated with a stylized "IHS," a Jesuit symbol common in Catholic regions to the south, an exceptional find for the Protestant region where the boat was lost.

OH 107 was a working boat built to ply bulk cargo along the rivers, canals, and over the open waters of the Zuidersee. Built and lost in the last decades of the 17th century, she provides a window into the culture and technology of the time. Despite the boat being 300 years old, its construction shows strong affinities with Dutch boats from the 20th century, perhaps not surprising in a nation of ancient boat-building traditions. It was similar to those built in South Holland, as well as in the provinces of the north, again indicating Dutch and Flemish connections.

Above **A green glass bottle wrapped in woven straw of a type used between 1650 and 1750 for exporting water from the famous source in Spa. They are often referred to as "Fransche Flessen" or French bottles.**

Opposite **The port side and bottom hull planking of OH 107 lies exposed in the hay field. The view is from bow to stern. All of the artifacts, mast and mast step, and frames have been removed. The planking was then recorded and removed.**

Below **Soup was served to the crew in a tureen decorated with a slip glaze that depicts the stylized Jesuit symbol "IHS."**

The Pepper Wreck: Nossa Senhora dos Mártires, *Lisbon, Portugal*

FILIPE CASTRO

Above **The *naus da India* were among the largest ships of their time, designed and built for very long voyages.**

Right **Raising a garboard plank. These massive hull timbers, 11 cm (4.3 in) thick, ensured the sturdiness required to survive the harsh conditions of a six-month trip covering almost 12,000 nautical miles (22,200 km).**

Those on shore, awaiting the return of their loved ones, must have watched in horror at what they saw unfolding in the fury of the storm blowing from the south. The day before, although within sight of Lisbon, Captain Manuel Barreto Rolim had not risked sailing into the Tagus River, but had dropped anchor at Cascais Bay, 33 km (20 miles) to the north. Now, on 14 September 1606, he was willing to try the narrow entry. He almost made it through. But the wind must have fallen for a moment, allowing his ship to be dragged by violent tidal currents running in the channel. And there, at the entrance of the Tagus River mouth, in full view of wives and children, the Portuguese Indiaman *Nossa Senhora dos Mártires*, returning from India, struck a submerged rock and sank.

Witnesses said that within two hours there was such an enormous amount of debris floating around the shipwreck site that it looked more like the loss of an entire fleet than of a single ship. In the fierce storm many did not make it to land, in spite of the scarce 200 m (660 ft) that separated the sinking hull from the fortress of São Julião da Barra. On that very day more than 50 bodies washed ashore on the nearby beaches, and the body count rose to over 200 in the days that followed.

Left **Portuguese merchants as seen by Kano Domi, a Japanese artist in the last decade of the 16th century. Portuguese merchants first arrived in Japan in 1543.**

Pepper Wreck

Sunk   14 September 1606
Depth   10 m (33 ft)
Excavation   1996–2001
Cargo   peppercorns, ceramics, luxury goods
Hull   *c* 40 m (132 ft) long
Crew and passengers   *c* 600
Casualties   over 200

The enormous amount of peppercorns stored in the holds of the *Nossa Senhora dos Mártires* floated to the surface, forming a black tide that drifted up and down the river for many days after the shipwreck. In spite of the dreadful weather the population made it to sea in small boats to salvage as much pepper as they could, and to recover all the boxes, bales, and barrels that washed ashore, as the soldiers patrolling the beaches were unable to stop them.

Arrangements were made in the fortress of São Julião da Barra to accommodate all the peppercorns that were recovered by the king's officers, the pepper was put out to dry, to be sold afterwards, although at a reduced price. The arduous bureaucratic process of identifying bodies and merchandise began immediately.

A Portuguese Indiaman

Indiamen were enormous by early 17th-century standards. Measuring more than 40 m (132 ft) from bow to stern, they sailed annually from Lisbon to Goa or Cochin, on the Indian subcontinent, and returned with heavy loads of rich merchandise from Asia: peppercorns, ginger, and white cotton cloth from India; cinnamon from Ceylon; cloves, nutmeg, and mace from the Moluccas in today's Indonesia; as well as many exotic goods such as precious woods, drugs, gold, diamonds, jewels, exotic animals, and pearls from the Red Sea; furniture, silks, many types of pottery, and stoneware jars from Pegu, in today's Burma; and highly prized Chinese porcelain.

Manned by crews of over 150 sailors and officers, these *naus da India*, as they were called, transported hundreds of soldiers and passengers, sometimes carrying as many as 800 people. It was said that, in spite of the small space, weeks went by after leaving port before first-day acquaintances encountered one another on the crowded decks.

When all went well, these trips lasted six months each way, but the *Nossa Senhora dos Mártires* arrived in Lisbon nine months after leaving Cochin, India, after a stop

Below **Peppercorns, one of the richest cargoes of the Portuguese Asian trade in the 16th century, were transported in the holds of the Indiamen in compartments sealed and caulked to resist the humid environment during the long voyage from India to Portugal.**

over in the Azores. Aires de Saldanha, a former Portuguese viceroy in India returning home on this ship, died during the voyage and the *Nossa Senhora dos Mártires* put up in the Azores to bury him.

We do not know more about the shipwreck or, for that matter, much about these ships and most of their voyages. In 1755 Lisbon was destroyed by an earthquake and its archives and libraries burned for weeks afterwards. A detailed account of this shipwreck was mentioned in an 18th-century inventory of books and documents of Portuguese libraries, but it must have been lost before the second half of the 19th century, since it was not mentioned in a later inventory of Portuguese literature dating from 1860.

A handful of names associated with the voyage survived in Portuguese and Spanish archives. Manuel Barreto Rolim, the captain of the ship, for example, had left Lisbon the previous year, seeking his fortune in the India trade after being disinherited by his father following an unapproved marriage.

Another name we know is that of Francisco Rodrigues, a Jesuit priest from the Japanese mission who was coming to Europe in the company of a young Japanese Catholic called Miguel. Father Rodrigues refused a place in the ship's boat and lost his life when the *Mártires* wrecked. Miguel survived and is known to have sailed back to Asia, dying in China years later, without ever returning to Japan.

A third name related to this voyage is that of cabin boy Cristóvão de Abreu, whose life illustrates well the lives of the adventurers who sailed on such ships as the *Mártires*. He survived another shipwreck a few miles from this one four years later, in 1610, on the way to India aboard the *Nossa Senhora da Oliveira*. Pursuing his career as an apprentice on the India Route he engaged in many other voyages, survived the shipwreck of the *Nossa Senhora de Belém* on the coast of South Africa in 1635, and the 800 km (480 mile) march that followed to the nearest Portuguese trade post in Mozambique. After surviving his fourth shipwreck, on the ship *S. Bento*, in 1642, Cristóvão de Abreu died at sea in 1645, returning from India as boatswain of the *nau S. Lourenço*.

In the summers that followed the shipwreck much of the artillery, anchors, cables, and rigging were salvaged by the king's officers. The shipwreck of the *Nossa Senhora dos Mártires* was forgotten soon afterwards and its remains covered by a layer of white sand. Large rocks found their way over the hull remains, possibly carried by the tidal waves that followed the earthquake of 1755, or by some other storm of which we have no record.

Archaeology of the Wreck

In 1994 the remains of the hull were found, during a survey conducted by a team from Lisbon's National Museum of Archaeology. Nobody had ever excavated a *nau da India*, and the "Pepper Wreck" presented itself as a great opportunity for both archaeologists and naval historians. Although we have several texts, descriptions, and images of these ships, based on the historical data alone it is very difficult to form a good idea of their actual size, how they performed on the sea, and most importantly to nautical archaeologists, how they were designed and built.

In 1996 Francisco Alves, director of the Centro Nacional de Arqueologia Náutica e Subaquática, and I began the archaeological excavation of the site, which we

Below **One of three astrolabes found on the Pepper Wreck, named São Julião da Barra III, bears a maker's mark "G" from the Lisbon Goes atelier, and the date of the departure of the nau *Nossa Senhora dos Mártires* from Lisbon to Goa: 1605.**

Left **Three pots from the south of China dated to the late 16th century. It is not known what they originally contained.**

Below **This late 16th-century porcelain plate of the Wan Li period (1573–1620) was found in a stack in the stern area of the shipwreck.**

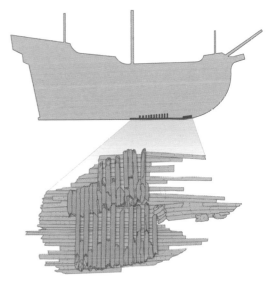

continued through 1998. Soon an impressive collection of artifacts was uncovered, including three astrolabes, nautical dividers, and sounding leads. Gaming pieces, pewter plates and personal jewels illustrated daily life aboard. Most impressive was the collection of artifacts related with trade, the main reason for these voyages. Exotic wood, red coral, a gold bead, and pots from Burma, China and Japan, gave an idea of the geographical span of commerce in which the Portuguese merchants were involved. Chinaware, a luxury possessed by only a few, was also found among an extensive layer of peppercorns that marked in the strata the historic moment in which the shipwreck occurred.

But the most interesting item in the artifact collection was the ship's hull, which I excavated between 1999 and 2001 for the Portuguese authorities and the Institute of Nautical Archaeology. We know so little about these large floating cities, described by their Asian trading partners as tall, black, smelly, and swarming with the activity of its pale, fierce, and long-nosed sailors, soldiers and passengers!

A small portion of the hull survived four centuries of currents and swells, resting between two rocky outcrops, under a layer of peppercorns that was often as much as 35 cm (about 1 ft) thick. It was solidly built of stone pine planks nailed to frames of cork oak with long iron spikes. Using some of its critical dimensions, and applying sets of proportions described in three Portuguese treatises on shipbuilding from the late 16th and early 17th centuries, we tentatively reconstructed the hull. Computer simulation techniques will allow us to test the performance of this hull model under sail, and for different conditions of weather and cargo loads, providing a better understanding of a largely unknown ship type's sailing abilities.

Our archaeological study provides a wonderful opportunity to learn firsthand about the size, strength, and performance of Portuguese Indiamen, and how they offered a living environment for an enormous crowd of sailors, soldiers, merchants, and adventurers – and even to speculate on the hopes and dreams of the inhabitants of "these dark wandering places," as Joseph Conrad describes large oceanic ships, as they saw for the first time the Indian Ocean and the exotic realms of Asia.

Below **The hull remains of the Pepper Wreck preserved only a small portion of the ship, but the existence of carpenters' design marks yielded enough information to allow its reconstruction with a fair degree of certainty.**

A Tobacconist's Dream:
The Pipe Wreck, Monte Cristi, Dominican Republic

JEROME LYNN HALL

When Peter Throckmorton, pioneer of nautical archaeology, shared his excitement late one winter evening about a shipwreck on the north coast of Hispaniola, I sensed a new adventure was unfolding. "Pipes," he whispered as we sat in the Oceanographic Center library. "She's littered with thousands of clay tobacco smoking pipes."

The gleam in his eyes and the way that he nervously studied the people moving about the room befitted someone who had just stumbled upon a cache of gold, not clay pipes. Sensing that I had no idea why such a cargo was considered a prized find, he jumped again into his animated narrative. "They're important tools for dating archaeological sites. If analyzed properly, these pipes will be of great benefit to scholars studying the colonial history of the Americas."

The wreck – little more than a pile of timbers and scattered cargo – forms a small coral reef in the shallow bay of Monte Cristi in the Dominican Republic, only a few miles east of the Haitian border. "She was," he mused quietly, "likely English and contemporary with the *Mayflower*." That alone made it unique since, according to Peter, no English merchant hull from this period had ever been studied. Furthermore, a considerable portion of her timbers remained, making an excavation worthwhile.

Right **Peter Throckmorton, pioneer of nautical archaeology, whose vision and encouragement led to the Monte Cristi Shipwreck Project.**

Monte Cristi Pipe Wreck

Date 1658–1665
Depth 4.4 m (14.4 ft)
Found by Johnny Bigleaguer
Excavation 1991–present
Cargo *c* 500,000 clay pipes
Nationality Dutch

Above **Isla Cabra, home to the Monte Cristi Shipwreck Project. Large salt pans dominate the central portion of the island. The "Pipe Wreck" lies in the shallow water between the shore and the mainland in the foreground.**

Opposite above **Still Life, by 17th-century Dutch artist Pieter Claesz, offers a tantalizing glimpse into the paraphernalia of smoking: a ceramic brazier holds embers from which fire is transferred to the pipe by "spills," or lighting sticks. Note, too, a Rhenish stoneware jug on its side, another artifact type found on the "Pipe Wreck."**

Opposite **Team member Yvonne Broeder works at the dredge screen as the site is uncovered.**

As his tale unfolded, it became clear that in spite of apparent damage from years of extensive looting, this "Pipe Wreck," as it was commonly known, was a remarkable site. What it deserved – and had never been given – was a proper archaeological study.

A few weeks later, Peter surprised me with an invitation to join his survey team. Faced with such an opportunity, everything else in my schedule seemed relatively meaningless. We departed Miami and landed in Santo Domingo, making our way by bus across the island to the barren northern hinterlands. Our summer itinerary dictated that in addition to the "Pipe Wreck," we would survey some of the numerous other shipwrecks to be found in the area. When the season finally ended, we had examined over 30 sunken vessels spanning the 16th to the 19th centuries, yet it was the "Pipe Wreck" that sent Peter home with visions of a full-scale excavation.

The following year, Peter busied himself with myriad other projects while simultaneously trying to raise the funds necessary to return to the Dominican Republic. I joined the INA excavation at Uluburun in Turkey and quickly became "immersed" in the Late Bronze Age. Our dream to return to the "Pipe Wreck" never lost its luster until one afternoon when, immediately after our morning dive on the Bronze Age wreck, a somber Don Frey – then Vice-President of INA – put his arm on my shoulder and told me he had received sad news: Peter had passed quietly in his sleep a few days earlier.

Why it was up to me to pick up the pieces of Peter's dream isn't certain, except, perhaps, that I too had fallen under the spell of the "Pipe Wreck." After days of quiet deliberation, I decided that this odd assortment of broken timbers, ceramic sherds, and clay tobacco pipes would finally get what it deserved: a proper archaeological excavation.

I returned to America and fell on the financial graces of friends, family, and several granting organizations. A new team was assembled and we soon embarked on what clearly would be a multi-year project. Our research was predicated on several important questions: what was a northern European vessel doing on the north coast of Hispaniola? Whence did it come? Where was it headed? When and why did it sink?

Above **Bearded faces decorate the necks of the Bartmannkrüge, Rhenish stoneware jugs excavated from the site.**

Below **Francis Soto Tejeda, Director of the shipwreck conservation laboratory in Santo Domingo, holds a silver ochos reales, one of 28 coins recovered from the site.** *Inset* **Six of these were from the Potosí mint in Peru and were manufactured sometime after 1649. Here, a devaluation counter stamp in the form of a circled crown lies sideways beneath the Jerusalem Cross.**

The Excavation

We arrived at Monte Cristi in the summer of 1991 and set up our base camp on Isla Cabra, a desert island – overrun with rats, scorpions, and a host of biting insects – some 150 m (492 ft) leeward of the site. With the help of Johnny Bigleaguer, the Monte Cristeño fisherman who found the wreck in the early 1960s, we placed our small wooden platform, the R.V. *Rummy Chum*, directly over the reef, 4.4 m (14.4 ft) below, and began working.

What emerged in the following months – and consistently throughout subsequent years – was a cornucopia of 17th-century commercial goods: sherds of blue-and-white glazed earthenware and Rhenish stoneware ceramics, thimbles, combs, straight pins, curtain rings, nested weights, glass beads, iron cooking cauldrons, and assorted brass lighting implements.

And, of course, clay tobacco smoking pipes. Fishermen, salvors, and government officials who worked on the wreck in the early 1960s estimated that they had raised at least several hundred thousand pipes before our team arrived. Some even approximated the total to be over 500,000! Peter's observation that pipes were useful for dating archaeological sites was accurate. Because 17th-century clay pipes were stylish and fragile, they were also popular and disposable. Their ephemeral composition meant that they were constantly broken and replaced, and that their form changed – as most fashions do – on a fairly regular basis. An artifact group that can be distinctly and easily assigned to a specific, but narrow, time frame is nothing short of an archaeologist's dream.

Our collection – meager by comparison – numbers close to 10,000 and yet comprises only two types: pipes with barrel-shaped bowls – accounting for roughly 93 percent of the assemblage – and those with bowls shaped like inverted cones, known as funnel pipes. All are of Dutch manufacture and date to the mid-17th century, but while the former were preferred by Europeans and European-American colonists, funnel pipes are clear imitations of Native American designs and were intended exclusively for the tribal trade.

We know from the silver coins minted in South America that our vessel met her demise sometime after 1651. Exactly why she sank hasn't yet been established, but a small cluster of approximately 800 glass beads may hold a tantalizing clue. Originally strung in hanks, these once spherical beads are now, according to Robert Brill of the Corning Museum of Glass, "slumped and fused" into each other, a phenomenon which occurs with intense heat that lasts for a short period of time. Divers have also uncovered many large "splatters" of melted brass and lead, as well as numerous pieces of charred wood. Interestingly, only 13.9 m (45.6 ft) of outer planking, ceiling, and framing from one side of the keel remained. Do these clues point to an explosion on board?

Interpreting the Evidence

Studies of the ship's timbers by the Dutch Dendrochronology Center in Amsterdam indicate that the hull was constructed from English oak sometime after 1649. Though English-built, our ship apparently flew the Dutch Tricolor, for its typically Dutch cargo compares well with archaeological collections from upstate New York and, specifically, the Dutch-American settlement at Fort Orange (modern-day Albany).

The archaeological record held other important secrets: beef, pork, salted fish, and conch were the foodstuffs that sustained the sailors on board. They weren't the only ones who enjoyed these stores, however, for along with three small rat femurs, many of the bones that we found bore numerous rodent incisor marks.

When applied to our research questions, these critical bits of information reveal a 17th-century merchant vessel that carried a cargo of European-manufactured trading goods, part of which was intended for Native American tribes of the eastern seaboard of North America. Sailing in the middle of a period of volatile competition between the English and Dutch for maritime, mercantile, and military supremacy in both Europe and the Americas, our vermin-infested ship passed along the northern coast of Hispaniola, where it came to rest in Monte Cristi Bay.

The historical record supports the notion that the vessel may have entered the area to engage in illicit trade with the many smugglers known to inhabit the northern coast. Or perhaps she sought a cargo of sea salt. Today, Isla Cabra – as well as the outskirts of the town of Monte Cristi – is home to large, shallow evaporating pans that are harvested regularly for their precious payload of salt. How far back this practice reaches is not known, although Christopher Columbus mentioned at the close of the 15th century that the region held great potential for salt production. Documents note that 17th-century European merchant ships frequently sailed into clandestine bays along the island's northern coast to offload finished goods in exchange for natural resources such as salt, leather, and tobacco, all of which were abundant in the area.

And so it seems that Peter's dream did unfold, after all, into an adventure. The "Pipe Wreck" continues to play a major role in the regional history of the Caribbean Basin. Her cargo – though not yet fully excavated – is still one of the largest and most diverse ever recovered from an inbound merchantman destined for the Americas. This remarkable shipwreck has demonstrated that not all disturbed archaeological sites should be viewed as worthless. They may, if managed properly, yield tremendous information.

Above **Pipes from the Monte Cristi "Pipe Wreck." The funnel pipe (left) was a form manufactured in the Netherlands and exported to the New World for trade with Native Americans. This type comprises 7 percent of the pipe cargo excavated from the site.**

Below **Fort Orange, on the Hudson River, in 1635. This outpost, vital to the expansion of the Dutch empire, was, perhaps, the destination of our ship some three decades later.**

La Salle's Ship Belle: Matagorda Bay, Texas

J. BARTO ARNOLD III AND DONNY L. HAMILTON

La Belle

Built 1684, La Rochelle, France
Sunk January 1686
Depth 3.4 m (11 ft)
Found by Barto Arnold, 1995
Excavation 1996–1997
Conservation 1996–present
Hull 16.5 m (54 ft) long,
4.6 m (15 ft) wide

The Discovery   **J. BARTO ARNOLD III**

It was the first day of testing magnetic anomalies. I had begun this Texas Historical Commission survey a month earlier, my second large-scale effort to find *La Belle*, a small ship lost in 1686 by famed French explorer René Robert Cavelier, Sieur de La Salle. With four ships and 300 men, La Salle was attempting to colonize the lower Mississippi, but missed the great river's mouth by hundreds of miles and ended up in Matagorda Bay in what is now Texas. The loss of *La Belle* to a winter storm cut the expedition off from outside help, dooming the already troubled expedition. There were only a handful of survivors. La Salle himself was murdered by his own men.

In 1978 I'd directed a prior survey in search of this and other historical wrecks in the bay. We found several interesting historic wrecks with our magnetometer, but *La Belle* eluded us. Over the intervening years declining state funding limited our fieldwork, but study continued. Robert Weddle's archival research on La Salle provided more detail on the ship's location, reinforcing my earlier ideas of where, generally, to search. Then, in 1994 and 1995, I was given the time to raise the funds that led to our return to Matagorda Bay for another large-scale search.

That is how, on the morning of 5 July 1995, we relocated the most promising magnetic anomaly I had identified in miles and miles of survey data. It lay just outside the boundary of the 1978 search area and showed tantalizing characteristics of a wreck site. The first dive team located a few artifacts, but nothing of definitive nature. Any wreck up to as late as 1880 or so could have produced them. Then a bronze buckle was handed up to the deck of the dive boat. In form it whispered to me, "I date before 1800."

The second team finished their dive. Chuck Mead, a Florida State University graduate student, and Sara Keys from the University of Texas at Austin climbed on deck. Chuck said, "I think we have a cannon!"

I donned my gear and followed him down to the seabed, 3.4 m (11 ft) below the surface and with visibility at about 15 cm (6 in), retaining with difficulty a skeptical pose of scientific detachment. Chuck put my hand on what was indeed the lifting ring of a cannon. As I put my face mask closer, practically touching it, I saw that, even better, it was a bronze cannon. Not only bronze, but highly decorated. The lifting ring was cast in the form of a leaping dolphin. At that moment I knew that *La Belle* was no longer lost. After 17 years of seeking we had found her before lunch on the very first day of test excavation!

Limited test excavations continued for the rest of July to determine what

Below **Portrait of René-Robert Cavelier, Sieur de La Salle.**

remained of the ship and her contents. At the end of the month we successfully raised the cannon to great fanfare. Then began a year of planning and fund raising. The political leaders of Texas agreed that the wreck and her delicate waterlogged contents deserved the most careful treatment possible. *La Belle* is not just a Texas treasure. She is a nationally and even internationally important heritage icon. We designed and built a cofferdam to enclose the site and pumped out the water so that a Texas Historical Commission team could excavate carefully and effectively rather than blindly. In this way the maximum data was recorded and the delicate, fragile organic remains were preserved for posterity. At that time, I left my position with the State Historical Commission to join the Institute of Nautical Archaeology and my role in fieldwork on *La Belle* ended.

The Conservation DONNY L. HAMILTON

My involvement with *La Belle* began when the Texas Historical Commission contracted the Conservation Research Laboratory (CRL) at Texas A&M University to conserve the ship and her contents, a project that is set to last more than 20 years.

Surrounded by her artifacts, the hull of *La Belle* is to be the central display in the Bob Bullock Museum of Texas History in Austin, the state capital. Together they will tell the story of La Salle's ill-fated attempt to establish a French colony on the coast of the Gulf of Mexico. Although archaeologists spent more than nine months excavating and recovering material from the wreck site, the overall success of the project, as well as the other excavations described in this book, rests with the conservation laboratory and its conservators. Conservation is a continuation of any archaeological excavation, but especially so in nautical archaeology, and is much more than just stabilizing and preserving artifacts. During conservation, additional artifacts are found in encrusted material, and diagnostic features and other details appear that must be thoroughly documented, described, identified, analyzed, and conserved. After more than four decades of experience, Frederick van Doorninck estimates that proper conservation doubles the knowledge gleaned from any shipwreck site, and George Bass has estimated that in general INA spends two years on conservation for every month it dives.

As *La Belle* was excavated, her contents and component parts were shipped to CRL, one of the oldest and best-known laboratories in the United States and an integral part of the Nautical Archaeology Program at Texas A&M University. From the beginning we decided to use the most advanced processes available to treat the material, and to extract as much data as possible. We also decided to share the ongoing hull reassembly and conservation of artifacts with the public by installing cameras and maintaining a web site (http://nautarch.tamu.edu/napcrl.htm).

Above **Among more than 500 personal items from *La Belle* were pewter plates, and a sieve, dipper, and candlestick of brass.**

Opposite **The ship just prior to the final disassembly of the keelson, keel, frames, and outer planking for shipment to Texas A&M University for conservation.**

Below **During the early stages of excavation crosswalks supported archaeologists, under the direction of the Texas Historical Commission's James Bruseth, as they excavated the contents of the heavily laden hold of the ship. The wooden hull was covered with wet burlap bags to prevent its drying out.**

Polearm Conservation

On historic-period archaeological sites in the United States the most commonly found metal artifacts are made of iron, the metal most prone to corrode and the most difficult to conserve. Conservation problems are compounded when the iron is recovered from a marine environment, for the metal is covered with calcareous concretions which hide encapsulated artifacts, and contaminated with corrosive chloride.

Most people, on seeing vats of encrusted iron artifacts, are not impressed. The hafted polearms from *La Belle*, among the most interesting of the ship's iron objects, provide an example. In their encrusted state they were barely identifiable, yet their iron blades included distinctive shapes that eventually identified them as partisans, spontoons, and halberds. As today, when carried by the Pope's Swiss Guard, they served in 1686 more for ceremonial purposes than as weapons.

Before study or display, the polearms required extensive conservation. We photographed them, analyzed radiographs, and traced X-rays carefully, recording every detail. Next we strategically broke the encrustations to expose the voids left by the corroded iron, which we cleaned out before reattaching the fragments and filling the voids with epoxy. After the epoxy set, we removed the encrustation with pneumatic chisels, revealing epoxy casts of the polearm blades, perfect duplicates of the originals. If an epoxy cast contained areas of metal or corrosion products, however, we made a silicone rubber mold of the object and cast that with epoxy to create a permanent replica of the original object.

Electrolytic Cleaning of Iron

Large iron artifacts tend to be in better condition than smaller items like blades because of their mass. A swivel gun, a type of small, breech loading gun used from the 16th to the 18th century, was the only deck gun recovered of the six to eight originally on *La Belle*. When found it was loaded with a cannonball in the barrel, a breech block loaded with black gunpowder, and a breech wedge securing it in the breech chamber. We mechanically removed marine concretion from it with pneumatic chisels, cleaned the bore of the barrel, freed the cannonball, and loosened the breech block and wedge. The chloride corrosion products present in the iron, however, continued to attack it. We effectively removed the chloride compounds by putting the iron through electrolytic reduction over a period of months. This was followed by intensive rinsing in boiling de-ionized water. Then we treated the surface with tannic acid, which converted the surface iron to a black, corrosion-resistant film. Lastly we placed the gun in a vat of molten microcrystalline wax to seal it from atmospheric oxygen and moisture. With proper storage or display, the gun should be stable for years, but being made of iron, it will always remain prone to corrosion.

Right **Conservator John Hamilton uses a pneumatic chisel to remove thick encrustation from the swivel gun, loaded and ready to shoot at the time the ship sank – as revealed by its breech wedge, breech block, and cannonball, shown here above the fully conserved gun.**

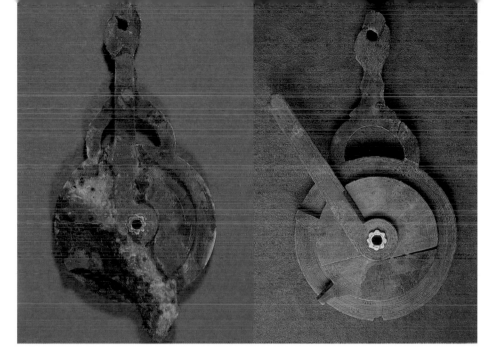

Opposite **Conservator Jason Barrett inspects the X-ray of an encrusted polearm as he devises a plan to conserve it.**

Opposite below **Three different types of polearm were treated in the Conservation Research Laboratory at Texas A&M University. From the left: a halberd, a spontoon, a partisan, and another halberd.**

Right **A rare boxwood nocturnal as it was recovered from the ship and after it was conserved with silicone oil.**

Conservation of a Boxwood Nocturnal

The most difficult artifacts to conserve are those made of wood, leather, rope, and fabric. During centuries in the sea their cellular structures become so degraded that only the water in the cells supports their original shapes. A unique wood device called a nocturnal, of English manufacture, required special treatment. Before clocks, nocturnals were used to determine time at night by the user sighting on the North Star through the center hole and aligning the two arms on two stars in the Little Dipper or the Big Dipper. The measured angle between the stars told the time. The *La Belle* nocturnal is made of four thin sheets of boxwood – a central dial with a front and back piece and a sighting arm on top – attached together with a brass grommet so the four sheets rotated on each other. Because of the thinness of the boxwood, the sheets were prone to warp. This tendency was compounded by the fact that the nocturnal was found in close contact with iron which deposited corrosion products along the top surface and between the top three sheets. The expansion of the iron corrosion products had separated the sheets and caused the center dial to split. Successful conservation required that there be no shrinkage or warping and that the sheets be freed so they might rotate on each other as originally designed. Additionally, the surfaces of the nocturnal have stamped and engraved markings.

Previous experimentation showed that a silicone oil treatment perfected at CRL had the best chance of achieving the conservation objectives. In this treatment, the waterlogged nocturnal was dehydrated through a graduated series of water/ethanol baths and then ethanol/acetone baths until it was in 100 percent acetone. The nocturnal was then placed in a vat of silicone oil mixed with a cross-linker. The vat was placed in a chamber under a low vacuum which allowed the oil to penetrate into the wood as the acetone was pulled out. The nocturnal was then removed and excess oil allowed to drain off over a period of days. It was then placed in a sealed plastic bag with a small amount of liquid catalyst. The fumes of the catalyst started the silicone oil cross-linking with itself, stabilizing the wood. The contrast between the nocturnal

Above **Items of the ship's rigging, including wood blocks, pulleys, deadeyes, parrel trucks, and a mast fid, were conserved with silicone oil.**

before and after conservation is striking. All of its diagnostic features are preserved and it is once more in working condition, although inaccurate if used today because of the shift in the constellations that occurs over time.

Silicone oil treatments result in a dry, natural looking wood that undergoes less shrinkage than in all other treatments. Importantly, artifacts conserved by silicone oils remain as re-treatable as objects conserved by so-called reversible processes. We used variations of the treatment to conserve leather artifacts, rope, glass bottles, trade beads, and small wood artifacts, including blocks and pulleys. However, while extremely effective, its high cost limits its use to small artifacts.

Conservation of the Hull of La Belle

Approximately a third of *La Belle*'s hull survives, weighing just over 12 tons. We did not want it left submerged in a vat, out of sight and out of mind, during conservation. Thus, we sank into the ground a poured concrete wood-conservation vat 18.3 m (60 ft) long by 6.1 m (20 ft) wide by 3.65 m (12 ft) deep, with a platform built inside that can lift 35 tons by means of four winches. The vat, the largest in the world for conservation by immersion, holds 363,400 liters (96,000 gallons) of liquid.

In order to transport the hull to CRL, some 240 km (150 miles) from the Gulf Coast, it was disassembled in the field. At CRL, the wood was stored in a variety of vats as we began removing the original iron fasteners and wood treenails so the fastening holes could be used to reassemble the hull with threaded, reinforced fiberglass rods and stainless steel bolts. The hull was reassembled prior to conservation because if the individual components of the ship were conserved individually, each would undergo some dimensional changes, preventing the fastening holes from lining up.

During its reassembly, the hull has been supported on the platform by means of a preformed, laminated fiberglass and carbon-fiber shoe under the keel and a series of carbon-fiber sheets molded to the underside of each frame (or rib). The platform easily raises the entire hull out of the liquid when desirable for work or viewing.

It is planned that the hull will undergo treatment for eight years in polyethylene glycol, followed by a year of controlled drying. After conservation the ship will be

Below **La Belle** **being reassembled in the wood conservation vat at the Conservation Research Laboratory, Texas A&M University. To prevent its drying, the hull can be raised from and lowered back into the water by four winches capable of lifting 35 tons.**

disassembled again and transported the 160 km (100 miles) to Austin, where it will be reassembled one last time. The same carbon-fiber system used during conservation will support the museum display.

Since only the lower third of the ship remains, Glenn Grieco, by combining data from the actual hull with data from historic records, other ships, and period paintings and drawings, built a scale model of *La Belle* as she appeared in 1686.

Putting a Face on History

During the excavation, a human skeleton was found lying on anchor rope in the bow of the ship. A physical anthropologist determined that it was that of a 28- to 35-year-old male of European descent who had suffered a broken nose, had lower back problems, and had severe dental problems. Astonishingly, brain tissue was preserved in the anaerobic environment of the sealed cranium, but unfortunately, results of DNA samples were inconclusive.

For a facial reconstruction of this crewman, we took the skull to the Scottish Rites Hospital for Children in Dallas, Texas, where a detailed CT scan was made of the skull. From the CT data a resin cast of the skull was made by CyberForm International in Arlington, Texas, using a process known as stereolithography: each CT image slice was projected sequentially via an ultra-violet laser into a vat of light-sensitive resin. When the resin hardened, the resultant cast duplicated every detail of the original skull. Then Professor Denis Lee at the University of Michigan positioned tissue depth markers on the resin cast and, guided by these, molded the facial features in clay. A silicone rubber mold of the clay model allowed a plaster cast to be made and painted for a more realistic effect. He probably would be recognized by his family, although he most likely had a beard and would have been considerably emaciated from the travails he suffered in the New World in the last year of his life.

The bones of the skeleton were thoroughly cleaned to facilitate analysis by the physical anthropologist, but were otherwise not treated since it was known that this crewman would be interred. In 2004 he was buried with due ceremony in the Texas State Cemetery in Austin, his grave becoming the oldest marked grave in the State.

Thousands of other artifacts from *La Belle* have been conserved over a seven-year period in a process that continues. Clearly the conservation phase of any marine archaeology project is as critical as the excavation phase, contributing as much data as the fieldwork – sometimes even more.

Above left **Glenn Grieco, master model builder at Texas A&M University, putting the finishing details on a scaled model of** *La Belle.*

Above **Details of the bow end of** *La Belle* **show the forecastle deck, windlass, main deck, hatch cover, cast iron cannon and carriage in gun port, and a wrought iron swivel gun mounted on the starboard railing.**

Below **Professor Denis Lee shows the facial reconstruction he made from the cast of a sailor's skull found on** *La Belle.*

Resurrecting "The Wickedest City in the World": Port Royal, Jamaica

DONNY L. HAMILTON

Port Royal

Earthquake 11:43 a.m.,
7 June 1692
Destroyed 13 hectares of Port Royal
Population 7,000–8,000
Casualties *c* 5,000
Excavation 1981–1990
Depth 2.7 m (9 ft)

I was preparing to enter Kingston Harbor behind the old Naval Hospital in Port Royal, Jamaica. It was January, 1992. I adjusted my scuba gear, entered the water, and swam northwest down what had once been Lime Street, now carpeted with a layer of eel grass. Then 45 m (135 ft) out, in 2.7 m (9 ft) of water, I could see the low profile of a raised mortar foundation that once supported the walls of a wood frame house (known as Building 3) previously used to store various commodities. Following this foundation, I came upon the corner of what had been a two-story brick row building (Building 1) containing three business establishments. The herringbone pattern of the brick floors, although now covered with moss, was still obvious to the trained eye. I swam along the brick sidewalk of the building, past the entrance of a pipe shop; over 2,000 new pipes once lay on the floor of the first room. I continued on to the doorway of the tavern where numerous corked liquor bottles

Above **Hypothesized reconstruction of Building 1 with its pipe shop, tavern, and cobbler shop.**

Left **Margaret Leshikar-Denton inspects the wood framing of a stairwell on the brick floor of Building 1.**

Right **The partly cleared circular brick walls of a cistern at the back yard corner of Buildings 5, 6, and 7.**

had stood. The occupant of the last premises conducted cobbling, butchering, and wood turning.

I passed over the other front corner of the building and the sand of the 1.2-m (4-ft) wide alley separating it from the corner of a brick foundation that supported another wood timber house (Building 2). Following the front wall, I paused at the plastered brick buttress. From there, I could see the plaster floor and the narrow extension of Queen Street that ran alongside the building.

I continued northwest to the paired, back-to-back hearths used by the occupants of the two halves of a single story, double-roomed building (Building 4). Beyond, I could make out the low brick walls of two hearths used by adjacent buildings (Buildings 5 and 7). I swam to the circular brick wall of a cistern that provided fresh water for three intersecting building lots (Buildings 5, 6, and 7). As I ventured up the brick wall separating the yard of the building from the room housing the large hearth, I could not help but remember the long-handled iron skillets that once rested on the hearth, and reflect on the skeleton of the child lying beneath a fallen wall on the brick floor in front of it. One front room had a plastered floor, while the smaller room had a herringbone brick floor with the wooden beams of a stairwell embedded in it. From the stairwell I could see the front doorway where another small child had lain just outside. Swimming on, I stopped in the hold of a large ship, believed to be the *Swan*, sitting on the brick floor of Building 4. When the city was inundated, it had plowed through the front of the building, shoving both walls and floor forward as it came to rest.

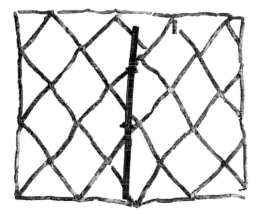

Above **Lead came framing with support rod of a window from Building 5. These grooved bars were used to fasten together small panes of glass.**

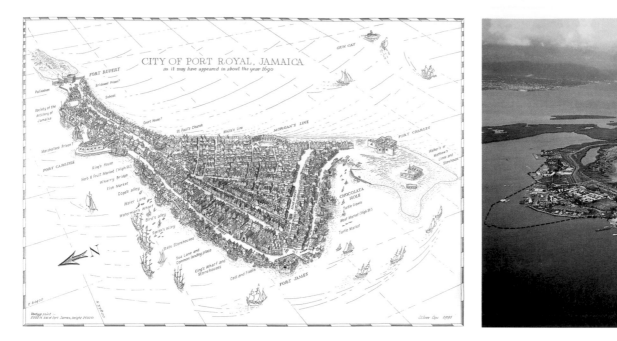

Above **A town plan drawn in 1992 by London architect Oliver Cox shows his version of how Port Royal might have appeared just prior to the 1692 earthquake.**

Above right **A modern view of Port Royal situated at the end of a 29-km (18-mile) long sand spit that separates the Caribbean Sea (right) from Kingston Harbor (left) showing the dotted extent of the sunken city. Kingston can be seen in the background across the harbor.**

Below **Field-school student Janet Mulholland admires an intact, corked bottle she has just excavated.**

The 1992 dive was a nostalgic return to Port Royal 16 months after I had concluded ten years of archaeological excavations (from 1981 to 1990) for INA, the Nautical Archaeology Program at Texas A&M University, and the Jamaican National Heritage Trust. Had it not been for the excavations, none of the features described would have been exposed. They, like the rest of the submerged city, would have been hidden, protected by a carpet of eel grass, underlying sediments, and a thick layer of dead coral. Port Royal's significance as the dominant force in Jamaican politics had ended abruptly when two thirds of the town sank into Kingston Harbor during a catastrophic earthquake; Port Royal became the Pompeii of the New World.

History

How did Jamaica, a Spanish possession, become an English island? And how did Port Royal become the largest, most affluent English town in the New World? In December 1654, Oliver Cromwell, Lord Protector of England, sent an invasion force under the commands of Admiral Penn and General Venables to capture Hispaniola for his Puritan merchant supporters. They wanted to establish trade contacts with the Spanish New World and needed a centrally located English port. However, the Spanish were forewarned of the attack and soundly defeated the English forces attempting to capture the city of Santo Domingo. Fearing Cromwell's wrath, Penn and Venables sailed south to Jamaica, and in May 1655 captured the poorly defended island with little resistance. In short, Jamaica became a consolation prize to appease Cromwell.

Although Port Royal was designed to serve as a defensive fortification, it assumed greater importance since ships could easily be serviced and loaded there within the well-protected harbor. Ships' captains, merchants, and craftsmen established themselves in Port Royal to take advantage of the trading, outfitting, and raiding opportunities, and as Jamaica's economy grew between 1655 and 1692, the town flourished and became the most economically important English port in the Americas.

Port Royal was the mercantile center of the Caribbean and was the principal provider of manufactured commodities and slaves to the Spanish colonies. From its trade contacts and pirating activities, Port Royal was more affluent than towns in other English colonies, and at the time of its destruction was the largest English town in the New World, with a population of 7,000–8,000 inhabitants. Its social milieu was quite different from that of New England, with its religiously ordered towns, or from the tobacco-driven economy of Maryland and Virginia. Port Royal had a tolerant, laissez-faire attitude that allowed for a diversity of religious expression and lifestyles. Mention is made of merchants and a citizenry consisting of Quakers, "Papists," Puritans, Presbyterians, Jews, and Anglicans, practicing their religion openly alongside the free-wheeling sailors and pirates who frequented the port, giving the town its reputation of being the "wickedest city in the world."

Port Royal's heyday came to a sudden and disastrous end shortly before noon on 7 June 1692: the massive earthquake sank 13 hectares of the "storehouse and treasury of the West Indies" into the harbor. A pocket watch made in about 1686 by Paul Blondel, a Frenchman living in the Netherlands, was recovered during underwater excavations; its hands, frozen at 11:43 a.m., serve as an eerie reminder of the catastrophe. It is also the first recorded instance of a stopped watch recording the time of a disaster. An estimated 2,000 persons were killed outright with an additional 3,000 citizens dying of injuries and disease in the following days. Salvage and looting began almost immediately and continued intermittently for years.

As one walks along the narrow streets of the fishing village of Port Royal today, it is hard to imagine that it was once the largest and most economically important English settlement in the Americas. It is now an isolated town at the end of a long sand spit with a population of 2,000 people who view themselves as "Port Royalists," rather than simply Jamaicans. Its unassuming presence belies the unique and unparalleled archaeological record that lies untouched beneath the surface of the adjacent harbor.

It is important to remember that Port Royal is different from most archaeological sites. It belongs to a small group of unique sites that includes Pompeii and Herculaneum in Italy, Akrotiri in the Aegean, Ozette in the State of Washington, and most shipwrecks. All can be termed "catastrophic" sites, for they were created by some disaster in a matter of minutes, preserving the associated material and the all-important archaeological context. In these sites, the archaeologist is not dealing with a situation where, over time, houses, shops, churches, and other buildings were constructed, expanded, neglected, abandoned, razed, and rebuilt. In these cases, archaeologists are mostly studying the refuse that has been left behind. At catastrophic sites, in contrast, the archaeologist is dealing with material left exactly in its place of use. Time is frozen, revealing a complete picture of life in the past as it once was.

Archaeological Excavations

In 1981, the three institutes named above began the ten-year underwater excavation of the submerged portion of the 17th-century town. Present evidence indicates that while areas of Port Royal lying along the edge of the harbor slid and jumbled as they sank, destroying most of the archaeological context, the area investigated by INA,

Above **A broadside (newspaper of the day), published in August 1692, reports the news of the Port Royal disaster to its London readership.**

Below **Remains of a 17th-century watch made in 1686 by the French watchmaker Paul Blondel, recovered by Edwin Link in 1960. An X-ray revealed that the watch hands stopped at 11:43 a.m. marking the time of the earthquake.**

located a short distance from the harbor, sank vertically, with minimal horizontal disturbance as a result of a process called liquefaction.

The investigation of Port Royal yielded a vast array of material from each excavated building. A large number of perishable, organic artifacts such as leather shoes, fish baskets, and even textiles were recovered. Together with complementary historical documents, the excavation allows us to reconstruct details of everyday life in this English colonial port city.

The Port Royal Project concentrated on the submerged, 17th-century buildings situated on Lime Street, near its intersection with Queen and High Streets in the commercial center of the town. Working from a support barge anchored over the excavation area, we investigated eight buildings. Our main excavation tool was a water dredge. The divers breathed air delivered from the surface via hoses so that each dive could last hours. This work contributed a more detailed body of data on the buildings and their *in situ* artifacts than any previous excavations at Port Royal. The recovered assemblage is incomparable. Large collections of 17th-century English tools, ceramics, pipes, candlesticks, and miscellaneous household goods were found. There is an impressive array of trade pottery including Chinese porcelain, German stoneware, and Spanish olive jars. Significantly, Port Royal has the largest collection of English pewter in the world from a single site. The pewter utensils are particularly significant for they are invaluable in identifying the occupants of the different buildings.

Above left **An array of pewter items (tankard, baluster, plates, chargers, spoons, syringes), brass candlesticks, and glass liquor bottles from the INA excavations at Port Royal.**

Above **Margaret Leshikar-Denton records a remarkably preserved wicker fish basket, still in situ.**

Opposite **An excavator uncovers a layer of clay smoking pipes, liquor bottle fragments, and a pewter baluster on the brick floor of Building 1.**

Below left **Items of Chinese export porcelain include blue-on-white medallion cups, Batavia and blanc de Chine tea cups, and a Fo dog.**

Below **English Delftware flower vase with the surface glaze flaked off.**

Above **A cameraman documents the exposed child's skeleton found at the front door of Building 5. The main excavation tool, a water dredge, lies at the lower left.**

Documentary Evidence

Historical archaeology is an intimate marriage of the archaeological record and historic records and documents. At Port Royal we are fortunate to have an unparalleled archaeological record. But, equally important, Jamaica has the best-preserved archives and public records in the Caribbean. Using the archaeological and documentary record together it is possible to interpret accurately the excavated areas and learn a great deal about the occupants of the town.

The relevant historical documents for 17th-century Port Royal, housed in the Jamaica Public Archives and the Island Records Office in Spanish Town, were microfilmed for reference. The land patents, wills, and probate inventories from 1660 to 1720 allowed us to determine the owners of the site's building lots, and compare the contents of households and businesses at Port Royal, and throughout Jamaica. However, while the documentary record was an integral part of our research, it had little direct relevance to our investigation until we could tie the excavated buildings to specific individuals. Once this was done, we could focus our documentary research.

Below **A pineapple flanked by the initials "S" and "B" within an oval braid was the maker's mark of Simon Benning, the only known pewterer of Port Royal, who used it to mark all the wares he made there.**

Simon Benning, Pewterer

One of the first challenges encountered was identifying an unknown maker's mark found on a pewter plate. The small oval mark consisted of a pineapple surrounded by a rope braid, with the initial "S" to the left of the pineapple and the initial "B" to the right. There were no parallels for the mark in the standard references on English pewterers, but we found a reference to a pewter maker by the name of Simon Benning who worked in Port Royal.

Whenever one searches for background on individuals it is always a gamble whether or not the documents recording their activities survived the centuries. Simon Benning turned out to have a well-documented life. Since he was identified as a pewterer, it was logical to assume that he was trained in England and that there would be records on him at the Worshipful Company of Pewterers in London. We

Above **An excavator holds one of 18 complete Chinese porcelain cups found around a window frame in a fallen wall.**

Below **The ownership mark "NCI" of Nathaniel Cook and his wife Jane over Simon Benning's maker's mark.**

Bottom **The ownerships mark "IC" of Jane Cook on a newer set of pewter plates following the death of her husband, Nathaniel, whose initial is now missing.**

found that he was apprenticed in London to John Silk in 1650 before emigrating to Barbados in 1657. There was a reference to a London will that we found in the Prerogative Court of Canterbury which handled the probates of all individuals with property, both in England and in the colonies. Simon's will, written on 19 February 1656, states that he was a pewterer about to embark on a voyage to Barbados.

In the 1660s, many Barbadians moved to the larger island of Jamaica, where there were more opportunities to prosper. A plot of land facing northward on High Street was granted to Benning in 1665 and there he built his pewter shop. Two adjacent lots were acquired in 1667 and in 1670. We next found Simon Benning and the occupants of his home and shop in a census taken at Port Royal in 1680. His Jamaican will was written in 1683 and was entered, soon after his death, into the Island Records Office in Jamaica in 1687. This will provides information on the property that he bequeathed to his wife and each of his children. Simon, the eldest son, inherited the house, shop and tools on High Street and carried on the pewtering trade. The last documentary record of Simon Benning, Jr tells us that he sold the last of his property in 1696. What happened to him remains unanswered, but there is evidence for his death: his married sister, Sarah, returned to Port Royal to settle property claims. Thus there were two Simon Bennings, pewterers, father and son, working in Jamaica in the years between 1663 and 1696.

Identifying the Occupants of Building 5

It was at this stage of research that we asked: "What do the ownership marks found on objects in Building 5 tell us?" The ownership mark "NCI," found on pewter plates, silver forks and silver spoons, and a silver nutmeg grinder, tells us that a family with a surname starting with "C" and a man with the first initial "N" and a wife with the initial "I" or "J" lived in the building (during the 17th century, the letter "I" was commonly used for "J"). But there were two sets of ownership marks on the Benning pewter plates. One set has the pineapple maker's mark and the ownership mark "NCI" on their backs. These plates have numerous knife-cut marks on their interior surfaces and appear very worn. The newer set has considerably fewer cut marks, and has the ownership mark "IC" on interior surfaces and the maker's mark on the backs. The two sets of maker's marks provided the necessary leads to identifying the owners of Building 5.

A search of all the documents (wills, inventories, land plots, and grantor records) found only one family fitting all the required conditions. This was Nathaniel Cook and his wife Jane. The "IC" marks appearing alone on one set of pewter plates indicate that her husband had probably died, after which she had more plates made, with only her initials on them. Later we found a record of Jane married to a different husband. The new "IC" plates were most likely made by Simon Benning, the son, while the older "NCI" plates were probably made by Simon Benning, the father.

This is only one of many stories that can be told by interpreting the archaeological data through documentary records. By the end of the century the buccaneers had left and most of the small planters were also gone. Jamaica, the largest English Caribbean island, which seemingly offered good prospects to ex-servants and small freeholders, had been taken over by the large planters who consolidated the arable land into huge plantations manned by armies of slaves.

The Tragedy of the Santo Antonio de Tanna: *Mombasa, Kenya*

ROBIN PIERCY

Santo Antonio
de Tanna

Built 1681, Bassien near Goa, India
Sunk 20 October 1697
Depth 18 m (59 ft)
Found by Conway Plough
Excavation 1977–1980
Cargo relief supplies
Keel c 30 m (99 ft) long

The train moved slowly through the African night. I lay on my couchette savoring the strange tropical smells that came through the open carriage window. On the bunk below Don Frey leafed through a notebook checking off details of our progress so far.

Tomorrow we would be in Mombasa and work would begin in earnest. We had a fortnight in which to learn everything we could about a ship that was said to have sunk below a reef in the late 17th century. Before we had left our base in Turkey,

Right A detail from the António de Mariz Carneiro map of 1639 showing Fort Jesus and the adjacent small semi-walled Portuguese settlement with surrounding African and Swahili settlements.

Below The seaward end of Mombasa island from the air. Fort Jesus (left of center) guards the approaches to the Old Town and its harbor on the right. The wreck of the *Santo Antonio* lies beneath the excavation lighter, anchored just off shore below the Fort.

MOMBAÇA

George Bass had briefed us, "Hamo tells me that there is a site 60 feet down in the murky waters of Mombasa harbor. He needs help with a survey and advice on the practicalities of an excavation. I can't tell you how big the area is, what can be seen, or indeed if there is anything there." And so in 1976 began an odyssey that has lasted intermittently for nearly 30 years.

Our Institute of Nautical Archaeology had been contacted by Hamo Sassoon, Curator of the National Museums of Kenya's Fort Jesus Museum in Mombasa. Hamo was fascinated by local sport divers' reports of a large wooden shipwreck in the waters below the walls of the Portuguese fort. His predecessor, Dr James Kirkman, had organized an investigation of the area some years earlier which had produced a few late 17th-century Portuguese objects, but was not able to identify the ship.

During the great siege of Fort Jesus by Omani Arabs from 1696 to 1698, a number of Portuguese ships were lost during relief operations, but their precise locations were not known. Hamo's interest had led him to documents in archives in Lisbon and Rio de Janeiro that indicated that the flagship of the relief force might lie close to the Fort.

Shortly after breakfast our train pulled into Mombasa where Hamo greeted us, took charge of our baggage, and guided us through the press of travelers while at the same time energetically describing where we were going, what we were going to do, and whom we were going to meet. An Englishman of boundless energy and enthusiasm, he had thought of everything. We were to stay at the Mombasa Club, conveniently situated next to the Fort, so that we would not have far to walk in the tropical heat. This proved especially convenient, we learned later that day, when Conway Plough, one of the wreck's finders, pointed out that the site was no more than 50 m (165 ft) out from where we stood at the club's shoreline. Correctly anticipating that Don and I would not have brought much heavy equipment by air for a 14-day visit, Conway and his son Angus had brought a car full of diving gear, hoping that we might like to have an exploratory dive right away.

"The tide is right in half an hour for the best conditions," he said. "Let's be quick!"

As we dressed Conway explained that toward high water on spring tides, the last of the flood brought in a great deal of fresh clear Indian Ocean water that often gave visibility of 20 m (66 ft) or more. He said we should not miss this on our first dive even though the current might be a little strong.

Hamo declined to dive, saying that he preferred to wait topside so as to have our reaction when we surfaced.

We entered the water at the seaward end of the site and drifted down over it with the current. It was like being in a warm bath. My partner Angus and I passed over the coral reef and reached the sandy slope below, at a depth of 18 m (60 ft), where we let the current carry us weightlessly over a featureless seabed. Then, as my eyes adjusted to the underwater world, I began to make out formless masses. One looked like a short row of uneven teeth with seaweed swaying on their tops. We swam toward them – the tips of massive wooden frames (ribs) protruding above the seabed – and hung on. My excitement grew as we followed the line for some 7 or 8 m (23 or 26 ft). At this point we met Don and Conway who signaled us to follow them farther down the slope. There the current had undermined part of the hull, revealing heavy ship's timbers. Conway indicated with his hands where he had earlier found objects. And then the dive was over. We broke the surface to see Hamo waiting expectantly.

Suddenly we all began to talk at once. It was then that the Mombasa Wreck Excavation was born. This was clearly a shipwreck of historical significance. Portugal had been one of the greatest of seafaring nations. And if this ship was from the ill-fated relief force sent from Goa in 1696, it would be the first Portuguese vessel ever excavated.

Don and I extended our survey by a week to survey with a magnetometer lent by a local marine salvage company. This added three very large magnetic disturbances to the plans we were making of the wreckage area: "Possibly cannon, but we'll never know unless we excavate."

Fort Jesus Besieged

The great Portuguese voyages of discovery during the late 15th century opened a direct sea route to the East that led to far-reaching historical and political ramifications for Europe, the Far East, and the lands between. Protection of this sea lane, and the expansion of trade that it allowed, led to the establishment of Portuguese forts and colonies along the route around Africa and across the Indian Ocean.

Fort Jesus was built in the last decade of the 16th century on the seaward side of an island in Mombasa's large natural harbor. Its heavy guns guarded

Below **The high seaward wall of Fort Jesus overlooks the entire northeastern arm of Mombasa Harbor and protects the lower outworks through which valuable men and supplies were probably landed during the relief operations.**

the entrance through the reef and provided safety for ships in transit or engaged in trade. Portugal's monopoly in the latter was one of the main reasons for the Arabs' rebellion after nearly a century of exploitation. Toward the end of the 17th century, English and Dutch competition was also cutting into the monopoly. Few Portuguese ships now made the annual round trip, or *carreira da India*, between Lisbon and Goa, Portugal's major colony and trading port on India's west coast.

Early in 1696, when Portugal's decline as a sea power was well advanced, Fort Jesus was attacked by Omani Arabs who were resentful of Portuguese taxes levied on their vessels trading in East Africa. The major part of Portugal's Indian Ocean fleet was in the Persian Gulf, however, engaged in a naval blockade of Arab forces, unable to help the fort's mixed garrison of Portuguese and African defenders.

Ten months later, the situation inside Fort Jesus was desperate. On Christmas Day, General Luis de Mello Sampaio, aboard the frigate *Santo Antonio de Tanna*, led a squadron from Goa to break the Arab siege. However, he did not stay long: after delivering supplies and men from Goa, he sailed with the *Santo Antonio de Tanna* to Mozambique.

Nearly a year later, Sampaio reluctantly returned to the aid of the besieged fort, only to meet with disaster. Eye-witness accounts describe the battering the ship took from enemy fire, severing her mooring cables, before she ran aground on a reef, losing her rudder in the process. On 20 October 1697, due to her precarious position, "the frigate capsized and sank below the reef, leaving only the topsails out of the water." One of only three frigates available for the defense of the whole of Portuguese India was gone.

Above **Silent cannon overlook the wreck site and the Old Town harbor narrows.**

The Excavation

Ten months after our visit in 1976, with an agreement between the National Museums of Kenya and INA, Don Frey and I returned to join forces with Hamo Sassoon for a careful excavation of the wreck we had examined.

Although Portuguese exploration and subsequent commerce, colonization, and defense were all dependent on ships, this would be the first Portuguese shipwreck

Right **At the start of a working day the first team of excavators make a coordinated entry into the water.**

Above **This bronze sail-maker's palm would have been secured to a leather strap around the hand allowing great pressure to be focused on the sewing needle used in the repair of sails.**

Below **At the end of the first season's excavation, project directors Hamo Sassoon and Robin Piercy with excavation artist Netia Piercy look at some of the relief supplies that finally arrived in the fort, 280 years too late.**

scientifically excavated. We had spent the preceding months raising funds and assembling personnel and equipment, but now we started field operations by mooring a 27-m (90-ft) steel lighter over the site as a diving platform, artifact processing center, and overall operations base.

By the end of the first excavation campaign we had clear evidence of the Portuguese origins of the ship, beginning with finds made in the pump well at the base of the main mast: two well-preserved Portuguese faience jars lying undamaged on the ceiling planking. As we enlarged the excavated area toward the stern, we found more faience – and then the wooden bas-relief carving of a cherub carved in a style attributed to Portuguese craftsmanship of the last half of the 17th century! Close by we recovered two wooden wings and a horn or cornucopia.

The wreck's date, presumed nationality, and location by a reef below Fort Jesus all pointed to its being that of the *Santo Antonio de Tanna*. Archival research later showed us that she was built at Bassein, near Goa on the west coast of India, and commissioned in 1681. Between 1693 and 1696 she made only one circuit of the *carreira da India*. Upon her return to Goa she was immediately dispatched to the East African coast with orders to help relieve the siege of Fort Jesus.

Other artifacts raised in that initial year included iron shot, a sword hilt, wooden powder flasks, rigging gear, and a variety of ceramics. Several collapsed barrels in the stern were sandwiched between fallen ship's structures and ballast. Finds here included two compasses, several sail-maker's palms, a wooden bowl, boxes of nails

Right **Among many pieces of jet jewelry found on the wreck were earrings.**

Far right **Only four silver coins were recovered from the wreck, all minted in Goa in the decade preceding the wreck.**

and bolts, a wooden bucket, cannon quoins, and large quantities of rope, all of which suggested a boatswain's store, an idea strengthened the following year, 1978, by the discovery of a mass of sail and rope, caulking tools, and unused caulking. At that time we found Chinese porcelain and many lathe-turned hardwood spindles that were probably furniture fragments or elements of decorative woodwork. Two large concreted boxes adhering to several concreted rigging components were loosened by means of very small explosive charges. Elsewhere on the wreck excavators found wooden combs, shoe leather, many barrel staves, and shell lantern lights.

Excavations in the bow in 1979 produced a stoneware Martaban jar with stamped neck, more Portuguese faience ware, some unusual earthenware Indian flasks, and large quantities of iron shot. Among the small finds were musket shot, Chinese porcelain, brass buckles, and glassware. Once more, a large number of barrel fragments appeared among the ballast stones. At the end of the season, two test trenches down-slope of the wreck yielded many more objects.

A considerable quantity of collapsed hull structure uncovered in the stern area prompted the decision to focus efforts here in 1980, the last year of excavation. Thousands of artifacts came to light, including more pewter ware, a silver-plated candlestick, fine porcelain bowls and plates, jet pendants and earrings, a second bronze swivel gun (dated 1677), a wooden gun port lid, and a coat of arms and figurine of carved wood.

Finds of pottery from Mozambique were evidence of General de Mello Sampaio's voyage to and long stay at Mozambique aboard the *Santo Antonio de Tanna*. The ceramics, published by Hamo Sassoon in the journal *Azania*, constitute a significant comparative collection because they have been assigned a firm *terminus ante quem*, which has already allowed them to date two sites in Mozambique.

At the end, the excavation had yielded nearly 6,000 objects. To cope with this bonanza, the National Museums of Kenya funded the first conservation laboratory in Africa for waterlogged material, which over the decades since has stabilized all but a few pieces.

A representative selection of the artifacts is now included in a display in Fort Jesus that tells the story of its siege, and provides a clear picture of the underwater excavation. Artifacts alone are often of little interest to much of the viewing public, especially if they have no apparent monetary value, but when seen in context, as here, they evoke strong images of life in another time and place.

Below **National Museums of Kenya representative Sayid Mohamed and conservator John Olive clean newly raised objects in the Fort Jesus conservation laboratory.**

The Hull

Careful excavation over the years laid the hull bare. Jeremy Green of the Western Australian Maritime Museum measured sections across it and we recorded it in its entirety with pairs of stereo photographs.

Then we faced a difficult decision. Should we attempt to raise and preserve the hull? We had hoped that it could be the centerpiece for an eventual museum display. Sadly, the sheer size and volume of the 30 by 9.65 m (99 by 32 ft) remains excluded this on economic grounds. We reburied the hull with the mud and sand that had kept it so well preserved for 300 years, to await a future generation with the means to attempt such a huge undertaking. We contented ourselves with the careful records we had made of the finest details of the structure. It certainly deserved the care we gave it.

Despite the importance of the ships that once made Portugal the world's greatest maritime power, our knowledge of Portuguese ships and life aboard them was extremely limited. We did not know to any great extent how the ships were built, nor are we even now certain of the specifics of their terminology. For instance, *nao* and *fragata* as they are used in contemporary Portuguese literature are not clearly understood. Such differences are more distinct for Dutch and British vessels of the time, as known from both archaeological investigations and surviving records. The *Santo Antonio de Tanna* was referred to in contemporary records as a *fragata*, generally translated as a warship, but excavation has revealed a more lightly built hull than would be expected of a warship. An additional research objective was an examination of how her hull differed from those of contemporary Dutch and English vessels, which were more specifically designed for either warfare or trade.

Further, we wanted to determine if the variation between Lisbon-built and India-built vessels was due in any degree to the influence of local shipbuilding traditions. Contemporary Portuguese records show that the average ship built in the dockyards at Lisbon rarely had a life span of more than a decade, whereas ships built in India of Indian teak were expected to have a useful life of at least 20 years. At the time, as the

Above **Archaeologist Ken Potts examines the massive frames toward the stern of the wreck. The keelson appears left of center running from the foreground into the distance.**

Right **This artist's impression of the excavated stern shows the ship's hull preserved up to the lower deck in addition to a substantial part of the pump well that surrounded the pumps and mast step.**

only Portuguese vessel built in India that had been excavated, the *Santo Antonio de Tanna* provided a unique opportunity to ascertain if the high quality of Indian timber was the sole reason for this disparity. A Portuguese student, Tiago Miguel Fraga, is now searching for answers to such questions as part of his Texas A&M University Master of Arts thesis.

Ordnance

Below **Outsize bomb shot dwarf grenades and hand-thrown earthenware incendiary devices.**

Similarly, an analysis of the armaments has yielded insights into the military, financial, and therefore political aspects of Portugal's situation in India, and thus in Portugal itself, at the time the *Santo Antonio de Tanna* was lost.

Examination of the ordnance revealed that the *Santo Antonio de Tanna* was carrying a very light complement for her size and mission. This, and a lack of standardization in the assemblage, appears to reflect the strained circumstances of the Portuguese at this time. That the Portuguese were in economic difficulties is corroborated by Jean-Yves Blot's archival research, which has shown that guns had to be taken from Murmugao Fortress in India to boost the *Santo Antonio de Tanna*'s fire power; apparently there were no other guns available in Goa at the time.

Postscript on the Siege

By cruel fate, almost all of the crew who made it into the safety of Fort Jesus soon died of disease, whilst the remainder chose to die at their posts during the final assault rather than surrender. After 33 months of fighting, the loss of many vessels, and countless lives – more than 3,000 on the Portuguese side alone – only two Indians survived to bring the news to Goa some two years later!

Having been an avid science-fiction fan in my youth, I was thrilled when I received a telephone call from famed author Arthur C. Clarke while I was still a graduate student at the University of Pennsylvania. He was visiting Philadelphia, and invited me to tea. At his hotel, he asked if I would be interested in studying a shipwreck recently found by a friend in Sri Lanka, where he lived. It lay at a place called the Great Basses Reef. As so often has been the case, my continuing work in Turkey prevented my taking on any additional research, and thus it was my mentor in underwater archaeology, Peter Throckmorton, who went to the reef in 1963 to excavate the wreck.

Exactly three decades later, INA Research Associate Jeremy Green was conducting a nautical archaeology training program for Sri Lankan archaeologists when the Sri Lankan Department of Archaeology asked him to undertake an inspection of the early 18th-century site, which he describes here.

Cheryl Ward then transports us from the Indian Ocean to the Red Sea, where she and Douglas Haldane, both former students in the Texas A&M University Nautical Archaeology Program and veterans of INA fieldwork, excavated what was probably a local merchantman that sank soon after 1765.

Any reader jealous of the nautical archaeologists whose photographs show them swimming in the crystal waters of the Red, Mediterranean, and Caribbean Seas, or camped on the bright sands of the Egyptian desert, as was Cheryl Ward, will be in for a surprise when they see the conditions under which Fred Hocker and his team excavated a small sloop lost in the last decades of the 18th century near Savannah, Georgia, in the southern United States. Since Fred has set the scene, we will remain outside clear water for the next two wrecks.

I'm proud that the Institute of Nautical Archaeology undertook the first scientific excavations of both colonial American and British ships of the American War of Independence. The first wreck was reported to me by Captain W. F. Searle, former head of US Navy diving and salvage and a Founding Director of INA. When his students tested a sonar unit during a joint Maine Maritime Academy and Massachusetts Institute of Technology summer training project in Penobscot Bay, Maine, they discovered the wreck, soon identified as that of the *Defence*, a colonial vessel scuttled in 1779. David Switzer, who excavated the site, describes how we were both introduced to it on a January dive, when ice formed on our regulators and we were wearing only neoprene wet suits. As I hit the water it was as if my cheeks had been struck by two sledge hammers! Strangely, the water seemed not much warmer when summer arrived and I helped Dave set up the operation.

Although these large storage jars and 4-m (13-ft) long iron anchors at Sadana Island, Egypt, identify this site as a shipwreck, only its excavation revealed traces of the tons of coffee, coconuts, and incense the ship carried

The *Defence* had provided my first experience of diving with only a few inches of visibility. The visibility was even less in Virginia's York River. There, John Broadwater, who had been with me on INA's 1973 survey of the Turkish coast, instigated serious work on the ships scuttled by General Charles Cornwallis just before his 1781 surrender, which gave independence to the colonies. Soon I was invited by Ivor Noel Hume of Colonial Williamsburg to undertake the excavation of the "Cornwallis Cave Wreck," so named due to its proximity to a landmark near the river. Having solved many of the problems of excavating in clear but deep water in the Mediterranean, I was intrigued by how one might overcome the obstacles of virtually zero visibility and a strong current, and tried building a cofferdam around the site to block the current and allow the water inside to be clarified by industrial filters. John worked with me on those problems during the partial excavation off Cornwallis Cave, and here describes how he vastly improved on that experience during his full-scale excavation of the better-preserved *Betsy*.

We end this section once more in clear water, this time in the Caribbean. Margaret Leshikar-Denton tells us how she located and studied the remains of "the most famous maritime disaster in Cayman Islands history": the Wreck of the Ten Sail in 1794. By combining archaeology, conservation, oral history, and archival research, she has woven a tale that has been commemorated by stamps, a book, a coin, a museum display, and the Wreck of the Ten Sail Park, which overlooks the reefs that sank the ships, and which was dedicated by Queen Elizabeth II during the bicentennial anniversary of the event.

Above **From the cold, murky water of Maine's Penobscot Bay divers raise a rack, still holding cannonballs, that had rested on the deck of the American privateer *Defence*.**
Below **Places mentioned in this section, with the featured wrecks in bold.**

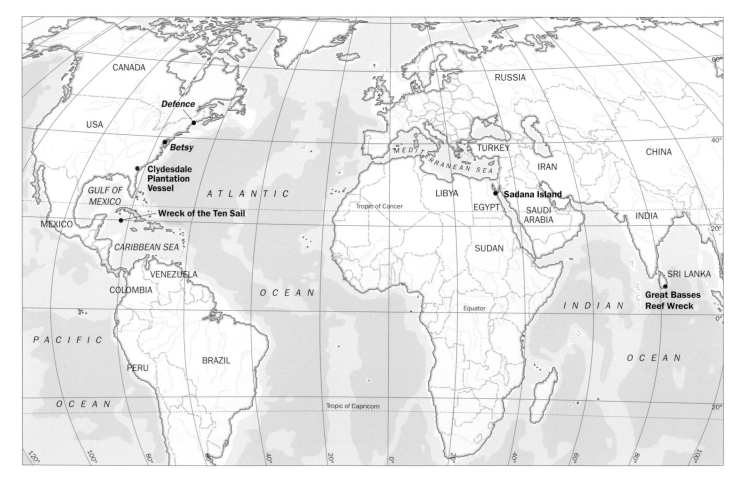

Great Basses
Reef Wreck

Date early 18th century
Dated by over 10,000 coins
Found by Mike Wilson, Bobby
Kriegel, and Mark Smith, 1961
Nationality unknown

Revisiting the Great Basses Reef, Sri Lanka

JEREMY GREEN

The Great Basses Reef lies 20 nautical miles (37 km) off Kirinda on the southeast coast of Sri Lanka. A long and dangerous reef, situated on the direct route between the East and the West, it surely caused countless shipwrecks over the ages. The most famous of the wrecks is the Great Basses Wreck discovered on 22 March 1961 by Mike Wilson, Bobby Kriegel, and Mark Smith. A subsequent expedition, led by Arthur C. Clarke in 1963, included Mike Wilson, Rodney Jonklaas, and Peter Throckmorton.

In Clarke's 1964 book, *The Treasure of the Great Reef,* Throckmorton describes the wreck in his notes as lying in a natural north–south gully, perhaps 9 m (30 ft) wide, between two seabed ridges. He notes that the site is about 18 m (60 ft) long, with two large iron anchors at one end and a series of cannons, jumbled like matchsticks, in the middle. "At about twenty or thirty feet [6–9 m] to the west of the cannons" he continues, "is a smaller brass cannon, about four feet [1.2 m] long by a foot [0.3 m] in diameter – perhaps smaller…and where the brass cannon lies, the bottom is a mass of concreted corrosion products of iron, bits of silver coins, musket balls and so forth, and lying just above the muzzle of the cannon – which lies in [a] north and south direction with its muzzle disappearing into the overgrowth of coral…are two or three pieces of iron, and a mass of generalized corroded mess. I picked out of it the wooden stock of a pistol – still in fairly good condition although just broken off. I tagged the brass cannon. It's got the number 3 on it now. I tagged a couple of the others also."

Clarke's book goes on to tell of the trials and tribulations of that early work, where Peter Throckmorton, fresh from his exploits in the Mediterranean, helped excavate and survey the site. Finds included two small bronze cannon, some copper bars, 20 musket balls, and about 10,000 coins, weighing approximately 160 kg (350 lb), all dated 1113 (Arabic) which equates to AD 1702, except for one dated 1685.

Galle

In 1993 I was in Sri Lanka with a team of maritime archaeologists, mainly from my department at the Western Australian Maritime Museum, conducting a training program for the Sri Lankan Department of Archaeology. The Sri Lankan Government, over the years following the Clarke discoveries, had become concerned about the possibilities of looting and the growing interest from various treasure-hunter groups who wanted to operate in Sri Lanka. Our program, one of many that we had instigated in the Asian region, was designed to train Sri Lankan archaeologists in the techniques of maritime archaeology. To do this it is necessary to make the training practical and apply it to the conditions in the country concerned. The Post Graduate Institute for Archaeology (PGIR) under the direction of Professor Senake

The Great Basses Lighthouse. Designed by Sir J.N. Douglass, the engineer for Trinity House who also built the Eddystone Light, it was prefabricated in Scotland, sent out to Sri Lanka, and erected in 1873 on a small reef top about 200 m (660 ft) from the Great Basses Wreck.

Bandaranayake was our lead institution. Senake had suggested we conduct our training in the World Heritage-listed port city of Galle, and there we set up operations for the program. We found 28 sites, including two 17th-century Dutch East Indiamen, and what is thought to be a pre-European site.

During this exciting and hectic time I was approached by the Department of Archaeology and asked if we could carry out an inspection of the Great Basses Wreck. We were more than happy to take a break from the murky waters of Galle for what we knew to be the crystal clear waters of the Basses.

The Site in 1993

Overnight accommodation was at a rest house at Kataragama. On our first morning we chartered an 8-m (26-ft) fishing boat and a small 5-m (16.5-ft) dingy from the fishing village of Kirinda, following in the footsteps of Clarke and Throckmorton. The trip to the Great Basses took 90 minutes. We anchored our boat on the southern

Below **Archaeologists survey the Great Basses site. The large anchor in the foreground lies alongside an iron cannon. Other iron cannon can be seen in the distance.**

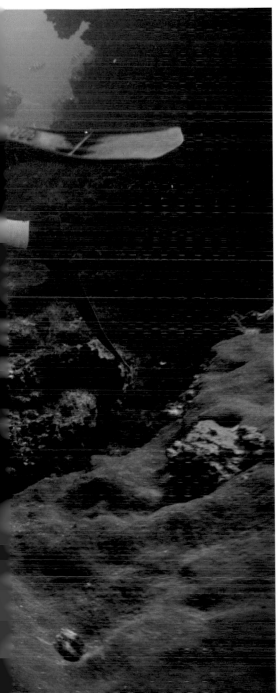

side of the reef, to the west of the lighthouse, the reef running from the lighthouse almost WSW. The site is located against the southern side of the reef between the "Shark's Tooth" rock and a large, flat rock closer to the lighthouse. We found it essentially as described by Clarke and Throckmorton, although there are some discrepancies, the most obvious difference being that there are now only two of the four anchors described by Throckmorton. We assume that the other two have been looted. The main coin area, described by Clarke, is now unrecognizable. Our 1993 team raised a total of 613 coins from this general area together with 56 concretions containing an indeterminate number of coins. We also made a brief tape survey of the site in order to construct a sketch plan.

Obviously the identification of the site is important. The loss of a vessel of this size, carrying such a large cargo of silver, is unlikely to have passed without comment by the colonial administrators. Present indications from the artifacts suggest that the vessel was possibly European. It is thought not to be a Dutch East India Company ship since there were none of the distinctive VOC markings, and since it carried stone ballast rather than the usual brick; the only positive suggestion is the word "Batavia" on a bronze gun said to have been raised from the site later. The vessel could possibly be British from the evidence of guns and ballast. The clustering of the guns strongly suggests that they were in the hold as ballast. This is reinforced by the lack of solid shot on the site. Thus these iron guns could either have been old guns used as permanent ballast, or else they were temporarily placed in the hold as ballast for this trip and the ship was supplied with a small amount of solid iron shot. It is interesting that more grenades were found than solid shot.

The wreck on the Great Basses reef has still a great deal of archaeological potential, although there is now only a small proportion of what was originally on the site. A further archaeological excavation would serve two purposes: to remove the remaining coins and thus make the site reasonably secure; and to recover the remaining artifacts that could help to identify the site. It would be possible, although difficult, to raise one or two of the iron guns; the difficulty being not so much in the recovery operation, but in the ensuing logistical and management problems of conservation.

Chinese Porcelain for the Ottoman Court: Sadana Island, Egypt

CHERYL WARD

Sadana Island Shipwreck

Date c 1765
Depth 30 m (99 ft)
Excavation 1995–1998
Number of dives Over 3,000
Hull 50 m (165 ft) long,
18 m (59 ft) wide
Tonnage c 900

Over a decade before I directed the first Institute of Nautical Archaeology survey in Egypt, George Bass told a group of new graduate students assisting in the Uluburun ship excavation that the easiest way to find a wreck was to have someone show you where it is. Now I was spending months meeting people who dived for much of each year in the Red Sea, talking to them about our intention to do scientific archaeology on underwater sites and to improve the world's knowledge of Egypt's rich maritime heritage. I began to hear about historic ships around the Sinai Peninsula, some visited by archaeologist Avner Raban in the early 1970s, others where visiting sport divers were taken to see pockets of artifacts in the sand.

First Impressions

Our survey began in July of 1994, with Texas A&M nautical archaeology graduate students Peter van Alfen, Elizabeth Greene, and Colin O'Bannon joining Douglas Haldane, Mohamed Mustafa, Mohamed abd el Hamid, Ashraf Hanna, and me in Egypt.

"Land Rovers!" Peter exclaimed as he looked at the two vintage examples Doug had resurrected from junk with the aid of "mechanics alley" in Giza. They carried our tents, water, food, compressors and dive gear, an Egyptian cook, an antiquities inspector, and a representative from the Egyptian Navy. We began at our most southerly point, near the Roman and medieval port of Quseir, and planned to reach Ras Mohamed National Park near Sharm el-Sheikh in the Sinai by mid-August. I checked in with the American Research Center in Egypt one day, and got a phone message: Dr Cheryl was to call a number in Sharm el-Sheikh. No name was attached to the message. As I dialed, I had no inkling of how my life would change in just a few short minutes.

"Hello, this is Dr Cheryl. I have a message to call this number."

"Ah, Dr Cheryl," said a mature male voice with an Egyptian accent. "Sadana Island." Click. And the buzz of an open line was all that remained.

Sadana Island? I remembered seeing the name somewhere, so I consulted our geological survey maps, and my heartbeat quickened. Sadana Island was located in the area that several informants had told me held a huge ship, sunk at the base of a reef and still loaded with a cargo of Chinese porcelain. I had seen several pieces from the wreck, and knew that a dive safari company had spent time at a site like this, but I had not been told exactly where to find it.

After a drive across a bumpy desert road, we arrived at a scooped-out *wadi* where Sadana Island could be seen about 500 m (1650 ft) off shore, but still connected to

Sadana Island probably seemed like an ideal haven, but anchors spread on the seabed northwest of the wreck suggest the ship broke free of a mooring and slammed against the reef edge, here spanned by a metal platform built to move divers and artifacts safely over its razor-sharp topography.

Each morning, as the sun lit up our camp, yawning archaeologists emerged from tents to plan the day's dives to the shipwreck stretching more than 50 m (165 ft) along the base of a vibrantly colored coral reef.

land by a fringing reef. We set up our tents, laid out the dive gear, and paired off for the afternoon's explorations.

Peter and I walked out to the island and began our dive by swimming around its outer edge, continuing to the inner side of the fringing reef, seeing only the explosive beauty of sponges, corals, fish, and even sea turtles that accompanied us. As we looked for a convenient place to mark the extent of our survey, we turned to each other at the same time, eyes wide with excitement, because there below us, stretching more than 50 m (165 ft) along the base of the reef, lay the wreck. The next dive team quickly replaced us. They established the parameters of the wreck, noting a stack of giant iron anchors, hundreds of clay pitchers, and brilliant white, blue, and blue-and-white pieces of broken Chinese porcelain scattered along the ship's massive timbers.

Above **Arabic inscriptions on some of the copper galley wares include names, titles, and even dates. The Arabic date 1178 from the rim of this basin tells us that the ship sank after AD 1765, a time of changing political and economic patterns in the Red Sea.**

Below **Thousands of artifacts excavated at the site include this small cut-glass bottle. Its purpose is unknown, but pilgrims to Mecca often returned home with bottles of water from the spring Zamzam near the Kaaba as a way of sharing the blessings of the pilgrimage.**

Below right **In addition to a valuable porcelain cargo, the ship carried less expensive clay jars called qulal in Arabic. These small jars rapidly cool water and are popular even today throughout the Muslim world.**

The Historical Setting

The ship and its cargo fascinated me from the outset, in part because it was clear that the ship was built in a fashion unlike any I had seen in years of studying ancient ship construction. We knew that the porcelain from the site dated to the 18th century, but it wasn't until the end of 1996, after two seasons of excavation with an international team of archaeologists, students, and skilled volunteers, that Arabic inscriptions on copper cooking pots proved that the ship could not have sunk before 1765.

The ship sank at a time when Ottoman Turks ruled Egypt. The Ottoman Empire, based in Istanbul, had controlled shipping in the Red Sea and Indian Ocean for centuries, but the arrival of Europeans in search of luxury wares from the Far East created a volatile situation. For millennia, Alexandria's warehouses had stocked European and Mediterranean cabinets with spices and luxuries from the East. In the late 1500s, unhappy with paying premium prices and able to reach the Indian Ocean in their own ships, Europeans began trading directly for cinnamon, nutmeg, cloves, and mace. The Dutch take-over of spice-producing islands in about 1600 forever changed world trade. The Ottoman Empire withdrew from the Indian Ocean, and Egypt lost its monopoly on "fine spices" and instead focused on becoming the coffee supplier to Europe and the Ottoman world.

Egypt dominated the coffee market through the 17th century, and even in the later 18th century coffee made up two-thirds of the value of Egypt's imports from the Red Sea. About half of the coffee that reached Cairo was re-exported to the Ottoman world, and this stimulating, and some said, sinful drink, made waves wherever it went. Ottoman sultans periodically ordered all coffee houses shut and trade in coffee halted to prevent the rise of places filled with people doing nothing but sitting about, drinking this dark, bitter beverage and talking to one another, often about politics and government.

When it sank, the Sadana ship was heavily laden with coffee. Longer than the Statue of Liberty is tall and capable of carrying about 900 tons of cargo, this immense ship was sailing north toward Suez when it struck a coral reef and plunged more than 30 m (99 ft) beneath the sea. Its cargo – low-volume, high-value goods – originated in markets stocked with the luxuries of Africa, India, and the Far East. Stacks of porcelain, copper cooking pots and trays, and several thousand large and small clay jars occupied only about a quarter of the site. Egyptian archaeologists cried "Luban!"

Left **Marwa Helmy holds a bi-lobed coconut or coco de mer, an unusual discovery. Found only in the Seychelles Islands, its seed takes ten years to ripen and does not float. Black-lipped pearl oysters, fragrant resins, and coconuts were easily seen, but coffee beans persisted only in the sand inside the qulal.**

Below **Making the site less attractive to visiting sport divers was our first task in 1995, and teams worked to map and then remove artifacts, here using an improvised hammock to carry a single concreted stack of 14 large blue-and-white dishes.**

when they smelled lumps of the golden aromatic resin we call frankincense. In addition to these expensive exotics, we recovered stacks of black-lipped pearl oyster shells, spices, packing materials, foodstuffs, and about a hundred coconuts, originally stuffed into every possible nook and cranny of the ship.

The products of China and other ports remained highly esteemed by the wealthy upper classes of Egypt and other parts of the Ottoman Empire, and reached those customers through an elaborate network of trade contacts across thousands of miles. Near journey's end, one of the last stages of sea transport stretched from Jeddah in Saudi Arabia to Suez, where goods were unloaded from ships like the one resting at the base of the Sadana reef.

Goods like these fed the coffers of the Ottoman Empire through assessed customs duties and also found ready buyers in major cities like Istanbul. The Sultan's palace at Topkapi in Istanbul exhibits one of the world's finest collections of Chinese export porcelain designed for the Middle Eastern market, many pieces from crates that remained unpacked for hundreds of years after arrival. Chinese porcelain factories catered to Muslim customers just as they created special shapes and designs for European or American markets. Cultural injunctions against the representation of human and animal figures meant that most porcelain sold in Islamic markets featured floral or geometric designs. When I first visited the converted kitchens of Topkapi Palace, where 18th-century wares were displayed, it was like looking at a catalogue of some of the finest pieces from our site. The trade was so profitable that even a ship as large as that at Sadana paid for itself after only three voyages between Suez and Jeddah.

The Porcelain

Europeans trading at Mocha in Yemen knew they could bring porcelain from Chinese kilns to trade for coffee. Mocha traders often took the porcelain north to Jeddah with their coffee cargoes, and we suspect that is where the merchants who stocked the Sadana ship obtained the thousands of dishes, cups, and platters originally stowed in the lowest levels of the hull. A quarter of the Sadana porcelain relies on carefully painted underglaze blue designs. The rest, however, is of a popular type called Chinese Imari, which imitates a Japanese style of decoration using red, gold, and other colored enamels over previously fired cobalt blue underglaze patterns. Enameled wares cost at least twice as much as pieces decorated with blue alone. We also excavated dishes, plates, and platters that appeared to be white, but that we suspected had once been highly colored. Our problem lay in discovering the original decoration schemes for the Sadana porcelain because almost all of it had lost its brilliant enamel colors to the unrelenting effects of submersion in the sea.

Luckily, longtime INA artist Netia Piercy possessed the imagination, patience, and recognition of the positive effects of raking light to work wonders. Because the enamel colors lasted long enough to protect the fired white surface beneath them slightly from the effects of salt water, she could trace the designs long vanished from the porcelain.

In addition to beautiful lidded bowls featuring day lilies and chrysanthemums in a framework of underglaze blue leaves with flowering grasses and standard lozenges, Netia's work showed us that we had large bowls with grape-leaf-shaped medallions and spiraling blue panels originally glowing with emerald green, scarlet, and gold like examples at Topkapi. The most brilliant may have been some shallow dishes and plates of three sizes, dull white when excavated. Netia's painstaking work revealed on them a delicate scrolling shell and floral border around a nosegay of spring flowers that originally were hot pink, green, and yellow. In addition to the many enameled bowls and plates, the ship carried thousands of coffee cups, some an intense cobalt blue with now invisible patterns of intricate gilt flowers. Rich brown, pale green, and many blue, red, and gold examples complete the catalogue.

The Ship

The ship, the largest and most technologically informative artifact on the site, has yielded its secrets slowly. Despite a long history of contact between Europeans,

Above **Cheryl Ward and Peter Hitchcock excavate the remains of the largest artifact at the site – the ship itself. Although this ship never left the Red Sea, it probably was built near Suez of oak and pine imported from Mediterranean forests such as those on Rhodes.**

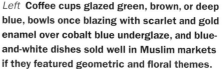

Left **Coffee cups glazed green, brown, or deep blue, bowls once blazing with scarlet and gold enamel over cobalt blue underglaze, and blue-and-white dishes sold well in Muslim markets if they featured geometric and floral themes.**

Above right **About the time the Sadana Island ship sailed, Carsten Niebuhr and a few other disguised Europeans sailed to Mecca on a similarly sized vessel. They mapped the Red Sea, collected botanical and faunal specimens, and sketched their surroundings, including this ship at Tor on the Gulf of Suez.**

Right **Despite the richness of its cargo, the Sadana ship carried few defensive weapons. No cannon or cannon shot existed on the site – only a half dozen lead musket balls, like this one, and a powder flask were found.**

Egyptians, and others who sailed the western Indian Ocean and Red Sea, separate shipbuilding traditions continued. The Sadana Island ship is an example of a type that is non-European, non-Arab, and non Mediterranean. Ribs (frames and floor timbers) joined by iron fastenings are spaced more widely apart than in other contemporary traditions, while stringers that stretch from one end of the hull to the other above the lowest of three decks are unusually robust. Because these timbers are primarily oak for framing and pine for planking, we look to the Mediterranean as their source. But the way the ship is built suggests that it represents an indigenous Red Sea adaptation to working with raw materials that had to be brought to Alexandria, up the Nile to Cairo, and carried 150 km (90 miles) by camel to the shipyards at Suez.

Curiously, there are no cannon on the ship, which tells me that its voyages probably were confined to the Red Sea, within the boundaries of the Ottoman Empire, and its owners had no need to defend themselves from pirates or from European merchant ships with few compunctions against appropriating goods from other vessels in the southern Red Sea. A small gunpowder flask removed by a casual visitor to the site in the early 1990s and fewer than a dozen 1-cm-diameter lead musket balls that couldn't even be loaded into a gun because their casting sprues are still intact comprise the entire armament of this massive ship with its valuable cargo.

The ship, owned and operated by Arabic speakers, carried a crew of 75 men who owned little more than the clothes they wore, but its cargo would have made the owners rich men had it reached port. The north end of the Red Sea was an Ottoman lake in the later 18th century, and the Sadana ship reveals a mini-history of Red Sea trade that dovetails into the greater scheme of international commerce between East and West. Although the last of our 3,000 dives at Sadana Island was in 1998, I sometimes still see the ship in my mind, exposed to the tape measures and cameras of archaeologists, requiring us all to look much closer before it shares its secrets.

The Clydesdale Plantation Vessel: Savannah River, South Carolina

FRED HOCKER

The lightning stopped and the thunderclouds moved off down the river. We loaded the boat with our shovels, notebooks, and cameras and prepared to go home. Everyone clambered in, I put the motor down and turned the key, and was greeted by silence. Not even a click or buzz. The downpour had shorted the electrical system. Our mechanical wizard, Charlie Harris, tried every trick he knew, but the motor was dead. I hate outboards.

If we did not want to spend the night in the swamp, we had to walk down the river to the nearest road, about a mile away. So, with the sun setting and the tide rising, we half-walked and half-swam in the chest-deep water until we could climb out of the river. We were held up near the end by a pair of alligators that disappeared into the sawgrass just ahead of us, but as darkness fell we had reached civilization again and were glad to be out of the mud. The next day, we returned to the boat, pushed it into the water, changed the battery, and started it on the first try. I really hate outboards.

We were excavating a small sailing vessel that had been buried to stabilize a levee near Savannah, Georgia, sometime around 1800. The man-made bank was part of Clydesdale, one of the rice plantations that had dominated the lower Savannah River before the Civil War, and had suffered a blow-out. The hole had to be plugged quickly, or the river would tear away the bank, destroying the valuable rice fields behind. To save the bank, an old boat had been sunk in the gap, and gangs of slaves had shovelled heavy clay into and around the boat until the bank had been built up again.

The boat lay there until the US Army Corps of Engineers changed the flow of the river as a means of naturally dredging the port of Savannah. The boat began to erode out of the bank and was discovered during a survey of the river in 1991. Judy Wood, the Corps archaeologist, invited me to take a look, and after a survey with Kevin Crisman in the winter of 1992, I returned with a crew of six that summer to excavate, document and re-bury the boat.

The Savannah area was developed for rice farming because the Atlantic tide reaches well up the river, with a range of up to 3 m (10 ft). Plantation owners could use the tide to flood and drain the fields, which made rice culture practical, but complicates archaeology. Our choice was to dive at high tide, in zero visibility and with a current, or to dig with shovels at low tide. Either way, we would only have a short window in which we could reach the site by boat. We decided to dig, and so each day we shovelled clay like demons for four hours, then came home to process the day's finds, write up field notes, and rest.

The clay was initially firm, but as we walked around in it, it quickly became softer, until we sank to our hips in the black goo. It had, however, preserved the timbers of

Clydesdale Plantation Vessel

Burial 1780–1810
Excavation 1992
Tons of clay excavated by hand 90
Alligator sightings average 4 per day
Hull 13.4 m (44 ft) long,
5.1 m (16.7 ft) wide
Tonnage 20 tons burthen

Above left **Standing in waist-deep mud, Noreen Doyle clears the port side of the Clydesdale sloop's heavy keel. Not what she expected after years of studying Egyptology!**

Above **Despite its small size, the sloop shows elegant lines and sophisticated craftsmanship. Here excavators clean the remains for photography and begin to record the structure.**

the boat beautifully. It took three weeks to clear a meter (over 3 ft) of clay off the remains, and when we were finished recording, we had to shovel the same 90 tons of clay back into the hole, to protect the boat.

The reward for those sweaty days out in the swamp was a glimpse of an early high point in American shipbuilding. The boat we had excavated was only 13.4 m (44 ft) long, but it had been built with a heavy keel and a sharp bottom, to sail fast under a large press of canvas. It may have been built as a pilot boat, but such vessels were also used for carrying cargoes, and cleared southern ports bound for the Caribbean, Bermuda, and New England. These southern sloops and schooners were popular for high-value cargoes, both legal and illegal, and their reputation for speed and sailing qualities reached across the Atlantic. The little Clydesdale Plantation sloop was an early member of the larger family that included the Baltimore clippers, War of 1812 privateers, slavers, and revenue cutters.

Excavating the Colonial Privateer Defence: *Penobscot Bay, Maine*

DAVID C. SWITZER

Defence

Built 1779, Beverly, Massachusetts
Scuttled 14 August 1779
Depth 8 m (25 ft)
Found by Maine Maritime Academy,
Castine, 1973
Excavation 1975–1981
Weaponry 16 guns
Crew 100

What were the chances that an archaeological undertaking could at least soften the memory of a failed military and naval operation during the American Revolution? An archaeological postscript to the ill-fated Penobscot Expedition of 1779 provided the answer.

The American Revolution was in its third year when that expedition set forth from Massachusetts bound for Maine's Penobscot Bay. It consisted of a fleet of more than 40 vessels, representing the largest American military and naval operation of the Revolution. About half the vessels were warships drafted from the Continental and state navies. A privateer contingent numbered 13. The remainder included unarmed

The arrival of the British Squadron. In the background the vessels of the Penobscot Expedition are retreating towards the Penobscot River where they were soon scuttled to avoid capture.

transports carrying 900 militiamen and a unit of US Marines. The expedition mission was to dislodge a British force from the present-day town of Castine. The arrival of a Royal Navy five-ship squadron, however, put the American armada to flight. By the evening of 14 August the Penobscot River was ablaze with burning and scuttled vessels – a naval disaster rarely mentioned in general histories of the American War of Independence.

Unforeseen Results

One Massachusetts-built privateer mounting 16 guns was not among the self-destructed vessels in the river. Under the command of Captain John Edwards, *Defence* sought to escape by hiding in a small inlet, but was tracked down by a British man-of-war. To avoid certain capture, Captain Edwards issued orders to set explosive charges to sink his ship. Officers and crew, leaving possessions behind, reached the nearby shore. On board the pursuing HMS *Camilla*, the commanding officer noted the explosion in the ship's log. *Defence* had disappeared from history – or had it?

She was indeed forgotten, like the ill-fated Penobscot Expedition – until 1973. That summer students and faculty of Maine Maritime Academy at Castine built a makeshift sonar and tested it across Penobscot Bay, the very inlet where *Defence* was scuttled 193 years earlier. The sonar recorded "something" projecting above the seabed. Exploratory dives by Academy students revealed it was the top of a brick galley stove; test trenches turned up pulleys, bottles, barrel staves, and cannonballs. Later two cannons were recovered.

By the time the discovery was reported to the Maine State Museum, research by Maritime Academy history professor Dean Mayhew had identified the site as that of *Defence*. In 1975, on the eve of the Bicentennial of the Revolution's beginning, the Museum initiated the *Defence* Project, or Project Heritage Restored, which resulted in a seven-summer archaeological excavation. When Captain Edwards saw *Defence* disappear beneath the waters of Stockton Harbor, he could not have realized that he was burying a time capsule.

George Bass asked me to direct the *Defence* Project, which was to last from 1975 to 1981. We were both introduced to the wreck site during a dive on a cold and snowy day in January 1975. As chunks of ice clustered around us, the adrenalin surge counteracted the frigid conditions as I saw the galley stove, the eroded stump of the foremast, and the pristine condition of the inner hull planking.

Opening the Time Capsule

The initial field season of the *Defence* Project in 1975 was a trial period for the task force created by the State Museum. Logistical support was provided by the Maritime Academy, whose Dave Wyman served as associate project director. The recently formed Institute of Nautical Archaeology was given responsibility for conducting the archaeology through field schools. By the end of the seven summers more than 40 students, 25 Earthwatch volunteers, and many non-affiliated assistants had participated. The Museum took responsibility for the conservation and eventual display of artifacts.

The remains of *Defence*, at a depth of 8 m (25 ft), were embedded in a flat, featureless, non-reflective seabed covered by a deep layer of silt, a combination that

A diver/excavator rests on the grid frame above the brick galley cook stove.

sometimes caused blackout conditions; even on the best of days, it was impossible to see more than a few feet. Diver orientation was achieved by means of grids of white PVC pipe, but it was not until we produced a site plan that we could really understand or "see" the entire site.

As we dug, largely by feel, airlifts emptied into constantly monitored floating sieve boxes on the surface.

During that first summer Maritime Academy support included a floating work platform; dormitory living and dining facilities; and our own boat, skippered by Dave Wyman, for the hour-long passage between Castine and the site. During the bicentennial summer of 1976, we were provided with the tugboat *Dirigo* as a research vessel.

At the beginning, we had dreams of raising and preserving the "capsule's" largest artifact, the hull, in the fashion of the Kyrenia ship, dreams quickly dashed for lack of funds, lack of an adequate conservation facility, and lack of interest in a memorial to a naval disaster! The alternate became our motto: preservation through documentation.

Thanks to excellent preservation in the anaerobic environment, fully 40 percent of the hull remained intact, extending some 21 m (70 ft) from bow to stern. This provided a rare opportunity to record the work of the Massachusetts shipwrights. Structural details were photographed when visibility permitted; recorded through the artistic ability of Peter Hentschel; and superbly drafted by Dave Wyman. From the resultant plans and detailed drawings, we concluded that *Defence*'s designer had been innovative in producing a hull configuration similar to that of the fast clipper ships of a later era.

Right **The bow of the privateer. In the foreground are the stem and wishbone-shaped breasthook; farther aft is the brick galley stove with its copper cauldron; just before it stood the foremast.**

Opposite left An excavator descends to the grid frame and the square in which the airlift would be put to work removing bottom sediments.

Opposite As the airlift brings sediments up to the sieve box, a "tender" watches for finds that may have been missed by the excavator below.

As someone who had studied and taught American maritime history, I was thrilled by the ability to touch evidence from the past instead of only reading about it. Rather than the usual museum displays of well-known maritime instruments and other accessories, from *Defence* came the everyday items used by seamen and officers, representing aspects of life and work at sea that were unique.

The contents of a trench across the hull illustrated the variety of items we registered and catalogued daily, ranging from leather shoes, a fragile hat ribbon, and cannon wadding, to the carpenter's and boatswain's tools. Interspersed were artifacts related to the distribution of the daily fare of salt beef or pork. They included wooden bowls, a wooden trencher or plate, ceramic cups, and small wooden buckets or mess kids. Various bottle types suggested that a fair amount of wine and gin was consumed.

Right The leather sail maker's palm was used to push a needle through heavy canvas.
Far right The stave-built mess kid or bucket was used to carry portions of food from the galley to groups of seamen or mess sections who ate their shares from wooden bowls.
Below right What every archaeologist hopes to find at a nautical site, an artifact bearing the initials of a crew member and confirmation of the date of the site, "JL 1779"!

In the galley the cook made edible the salt pork and beef found stored in provision barrels. Portions of meat designated for a group of six or eight seamen, a mess section, were boiled in the copper cauldron to remove the salt. Each portion was identified by a small wooden tag bearing initials or symbols. Matching initials on the mess kids probably identified the "mess captains" who were responsible for doling out the rations.

The seamen ate from wooden trenchers with pewter spoons on which the users or owners had scratched their initials. Tooth marks on the edges of the bowls told us whether each user was right- or left-handed.

A divider in the cauldron suggested that the officers may have been fed a better fare. While eating from pewter plates, officers may have quaffed their drinks from the stave-built tankards. Their items of personal adornment reflected their status: they wore better shoes with fancy buckles, and fastened their coats with metal buttons. One pewter button had the embossed letters USA. One or two officers, perhaps Captain Edwards, drank tea from a fine English Whieldonware tea service.

Traditionally, the captain was responsible for navigating his vessel. *Defence* may also have had a mate with navigation skills. In the galley area where many of the "life and work at sea" items were recovered, navigational instruments included an intact Gunter scale, a rarity among finds from shipwrecks. Made of rosewood, 90 cm (3 ft) long and looking like a yardstick, it was used to solve time and distance problems. Evidence of another instrument was limited to three pieces of a wooden Davis quadrant. A fragment of a slate inscribed with faint lines suggesting navigational use also came to light.

The seamen and the gunners who supervised the operation of six-pounder cannons were well equipped. Wooden tompions sealed the muzzles watertight and wooden crowbars or heavers were used to lever the cannon tubes or wheeled gun carriages. Copper ladles loaded powder, and rammers sent home cannonballs and wadding. To damage enemy rigging or clear his decks, *Defence*'s ammunition stores included both

Left Cannonballs recovered on the shot rack that held them on the deck between the cannons. Once each ball weighed six pounds, but they have lost most of their iron content and now weigh only a fraction of that.

Below Another form of cannon projectile was grapeshot that consisted of a bag of lead balls packed around a wooden spindle. When fired the balls spread out and were a deadly antipersonnel weapon.

grape shot and langrage, in addition to cannonballs in "ready racks" on the deck. Both types of ammunition are described in the works of C.S. Forester and Patrick O'Brien, but intact stands of grape shot or scrap metal fragments that made up langrage are seldom found in museum displays.

Of the 16 guns *Defence* carried on her deck, only two were recovered when the site was discovered. What of the remaining 14? Had they been salvaged sometime after she sank? The historical record is silent. There is the possibility that they rest deeply buried outside the hull structure. Believing that the recording of structural details was a major goal, we did not excavate outside the hull for fear of disturbing the integrity of the site's major artifact.

The fact that the mystery of the missing cannon was not solved did not trouble me. While we know a great deal about cannons – their calibers and techniques of casting – the variety of artifacts we did recover represented life and work at sea in the 18th century as strikingly as their excellent condition. And the proveniences of these finds showed where they were stored or used on board.

The Legacy of Defence

It is time to return to the question posed at the beginning of this account: could the results of an archaeological endeavor expiate a military and naval disaster? I believe the answer is that it could, and has!

From the first moment we first delved into the hull of *Defence* it seemed that we were present at that chaotic moment when the crew were fleeing the privateer, with no time to save either personal items or equipment. Many Revolutionary War battlefields and encampments have been investigated by historical archaeologists, but the "time capsule" aspect has never been as literally evident as was the case with *Defence*.

Maine and national periodicals provided excellent coverage of our seven summers of excavation, never failing to make some analogy between the *Defence* project and the 1779 Penobscot Expedition, stating how present events were offsetting those of the past.

There has been another legacy of the *Defence* excavation. Influenced by their field-school experiences, a number of students and volunteers went on to follow careers in nautical archaeology. In this light, the "second Penobscot Expedition" has indeed overshadowed its predecessor.

From Collier to Troop Transport: The Betsy, Yorktown, Virginia

JOHN D. BROADWATER

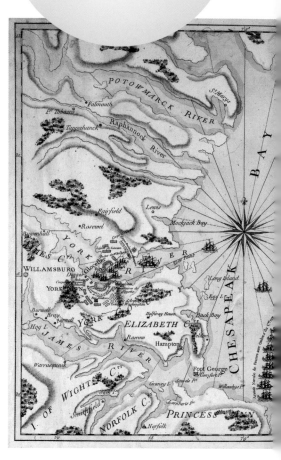

The Betsy

Built 1772, Whitehaven,
Cumbria, England
Sunk October 1781
Depth 7 m (23 ft)
Excavation 1982–1988
Hull 23 m (75 ft) long
Tonnage 176 tons burthen

Events leading to the discovery and excavation of the *Betsy* began in late October 1975, as I sat in a small Yorktown restaurant overlooking the cold, turbid waters of the York River. With me, studiously examining several damp sketches on Mylar, were William Kelso, Virginia State Archaeologist; Gordon Watts, North Carolina State Underwater Archaeologist; and John Sands, Director for Collections at The Mariners' Museum. Gordon and I were explaining the sketches from our day's dive just offshore from where we sat. Gordon reported, "We have a large wooden shipwreck, more than 30 m (99 ft) long. There's every reason to believe that it dates to the American Revolution."

"And there's evidence it's being pilfered by recreational divers," I added.

John Sands was aware of the artifact removal. His recently completed Masters' thesis examined the history of British ships sunk during the Battle of Yorktown, the last major battle of the American War of Independence. He had learned that a shipwreck at Yorktown was being looted and had alerted the Commonwealth of Virginia. Sands reminded the state that this area of the York River had been designated a Historic District on the National Register of Historic Places – the first underwater site to receive this distinction. The state's response was not encouraging, so John and I resolved to organize our own Yorktown survey. The North Carolina Division of Archives and History allowed Watts to assist us, and Bill Kelso, with a limited budget and no nautical archaeologists on his staff, granted us access to the site and provided staff support.

The survey report we submitted to the state verified that a significant 18th-century shipwreck lay in state-owned waters off Yorktown and was threatened both by looting and shoreline erosion. We recommended an intensive assessment of the site along with its protection from further unauthorized disturbance. Press coverage of our survey had an unexpected result. The Virginia General Assembly, concerned about the looting, passed an emergency bill that resulted in the Virginia Underwater Historic Properties Act of 1976. With no formal state support and no funds, our private survey team had done all it could. At that time, archaeology was an avocation for me, and I could volunteer only during weekends and annual leave.

Not long after we submitted our report, the Virginia Historic Landmarks Commission invited George Bass to conduct a formal investigation of the shipwreck. George, in the process of relocating his Institute of Nautical Archaeology to new quarters at Texas A&M University, agreed to organize a Yorktown field school for the following summer. I was elated. I had worked as sonar operator and diver with George in Turkey in 1973, on INA's very first survey, and thought that Virginia could do no better than to collaborate with the Institute.

Opposite **Major General Charles Cornwallis, commander of the Southern British Army, in a portrait by Thomas Gainsborough. Shortly before he surrendered his forces at Yorktown on 19 October, 1781, he scuttled at least a dozen vessels in the York River as beach obstructions to thwart a French amphibious attack.**

1976: The "Cornwallis Cave Shipwreck"

Thus, in July 1976, the bicentenary of the American Revolution, excavation began on the "Cornwallis Cave Shipwreck," named after a local landmark on the adjacent Yorktown shore. The site proved to be the lower hull of a large wooden ship whose nautical and military artifacts confirmed that it was a British vessel of the late 18th century – almost guaranteeing that it was associated with the British fleet sunk during the Battle of Yorktown in 1781. There was ample evidence of recent disturbance and artifact removal, but George converted and enlisted the help of some of the local divers who had been collecting souvenirs. The local press became fascinated with the wreck and the historic artifacts brought daily to the surface.

While the field school continued, George and Bill Kelso prepared a grant application requesting funds from the National Endowment for the Humanities (NEH) for additional research at Yorktown. His field school concluded that the "Cornwallis Cave Shipwreck" was historically and archaeologically significant and should be documented before divers and erosion destroyed it. I was certain the proposal would be funded, but for a variety of reasons George had to return to Turkey in order to concentrate on other promising projects for his fledgling INA. Bill Kelso then turned to me. Would I consider being designated project director for the Yorktown grant application? As project director, I could apply my expertise in marine survey to the location of additional shipwrecks while Kelso, as principal investigator, would provide his academic skills for a detailed archaeological plan. I was overwhelmed by the offer and asked for time to consider the opportunity. The first person I consulted was my wife, the second was George Bass. George said that if I accepted the position, he would continue to mentor me as he had done since 1973.

The 1978 Shipwreck Survey

I accepted the state's offer, recommending that we amend the grant application to propose a one-year survey to locate and assess as many Yorktown wrecks as possible. Sands' research had revealed that 26 British ships were unaccounted for after the Battle of Yorktown. Thus, if successful, our survey would allow us to evaluate numerous shipwrecks before committing to a full-scale excavation. The grant was approved in May 1978 and I was hired as Virginia's first underwater archaeologist. Kelso immediately assigned a member of his staff to the Yorktown Project on a temporary basis. But we needed a larger team. Turning to INA, I hired two of their recent M.A. graduates to assist me.

The 1978 survey was more successful than we dared hope. We located nine shipwrecks from the Battle of Yorktown, seven along the Yorktown shore and two on the opposite bank. With these results, we were granted NEH funds for survey, assessment, and excavation planning.

The 1980 HMS Charon Field School

In 1980, with excavation planning still underway, INA again collaborated with Virginia for a Yorktown field school, this time investigating a wreck on the north shore, at Gloucester Point, believed to be the remains of HMS *Charon*, the largest British warship at Yorktown. The team, directed by Dick Steffy, confirmed the

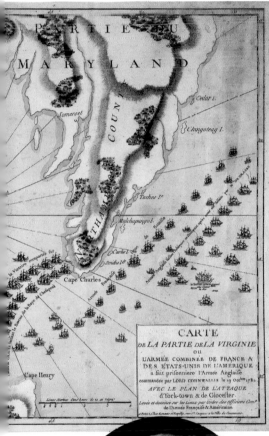

Below **A French map, published soon after the Battle of Yorktown, depicts several events that took place in September–October 1781, including the "Battle of the Virginia Capes," the subsequent French blockade of the mouth of the Chesapeake Bay, followed by the entrapment of British forces at Yorktown (far left).**

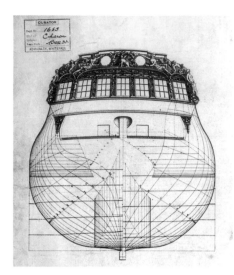

Above **A stern plan of HMS *Charon*, the largest British warship at Yorktown. *Charon*, set afire by red-hot shot from a French battery, sank on the night of 10 October, 1781, the first major casualty of the French-American siege of the British position.**

Below **The cofferdam built to facilitate the excavation of the *Betsy* at Yorktown.**

identity of *Charon* while recovering a variety of artifacts. I had the pleasure of sharing office space with Dick Steffy while he assimilated the daily site data and compared them to surviving plans of the *Charon*. One day I heard Dick chuckling to himself which meant, I had learned, that he had discovered something interesting in the data. Curious, I went to his drafting table. He glanced up with a satisfied grin and said, "Just look at what that shipwright did during the construction of *Charon*. See these site drawings from yesterday? There's a mortise in the keelson that's been plugged and there are three stanchions – instead of two, as shown on the plans – to support the capstan. That shipwright said to himself, 'I don't care what those fancy Admiralty architects drew, I know that capstan needs three stanchions to support it!' And three stanchions he installed!" Although an electrical engineer by training, Dick could get into the minds of long-dead shipwrights better than any anthropologist I've ever met.

The Betsy *Cofferdam Excavation*

Our survey results, the INA excavations, and the resultant press coverage helped us obtain federal, state, and private funds for the excavation of the Yorktown shipwreck that offered the most research potential, a well-preserved wreck known only by its official site number, 44YO88. Although the vessel was buried, we could tell that it sat on an even keel and that approximately half of its hull was intact.

Because the visibility in the York River rarely exceeded a few inches, and because strong currents and choppy waves made diving difficult, we built a steel enclosure, or cofferdam, around the wreck to eliminate currents, and then filtered the enclosed water to improve visibility. Usually, water is pumped out of cofferdams, but we proposed retaining the water to protect the ship's fragile timbers and artifacts from exposure to air, which would accelerate decomposition. This idea had been proposed previously but never implemented.

The cofferdam was completed in 1982. A pier between the cofferdam and shore provided access for staff and utilities – and allowed thousands of visitors to watch our excavation in progress, possibly the world's first publicly accessible underwater archaeology project. The filtration system improved visibility to an average 7.6–9.1 m (25–30 ft), increasing excavation efficiency and allowing us to document the site photographically. Excavation continued through 1988, providing training opportunities for scores of students; more than a dozen field schools and an equal number of internships were conducted at the cofferdam.

Research and Analysis

As excavation progressed, we developed a better picture of 44YO88: she was relatively small, approximately 23 m (75 ft) from stem to stern and a maximum beam of 7.3 m (24 ft); her hull was boxlike, suggesting a merchant ship; she had two masts; she had a large central cargo hold, with a bulkhead well forward and another aft. In the stern we recovered cabin furnishings and personal effects, several of which provided important clues. The head of a small barrel was carved with the initials "JY" and there were several uniform buttons from the British 43rd Regiment of Foot. The bow contained an assortment of boatswain's stores

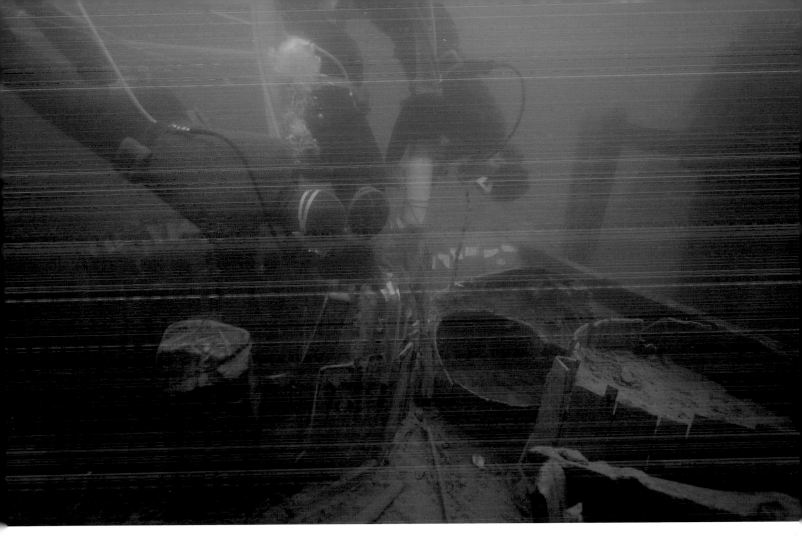

Above **Archaeologists encountered a variety of cooperage in the *Betsy*'s hold, including many with markings identifying contents and packing locations.**
Below **The *Betsy* yielded an assortment of buttons, including several from the 43rd Regiment of Foot; regimental records eventually led to the identification of the *Betsy*.**

and large and small barrels, many with markings identifying contents and shipping points. Amidships, on the starboard side, we learned how the ship sank. A hole had been cut through her hull, just below the waterline. The barrels, buttons, and hole supported our hypothesis that 44YO88 was serving as a British transport when she was purposely scuttled during the Battle of Yorktown.

As we had hoped, the buttons proved to be critical clues. John William Morris III and I learned that soldiers from the 43rd Regiment were transported to Yorktown aboard three vessels, one of which, the *Betsy*, was the same size as 44YO88. Investigating further, we found a listing for a *Betsy* of the same size and same type of rig – and its captain and owner was Joseph Younghusband, whose initials matched those on the barrel. Over a period of several years, this identity was confirmed and a detailed picture of *Betsy* began to form.

An Image of the Betsy

Betsy was built in 1772 in Whitehaven on the northwest coast of England. We feel certain that Younghusband, the captain and owner, named *Betsy* for his wife, Elizabeth. *Betsy* was a collier, a vessel built to carry coal. English colliers were known for their sturdy, bluff-bowed hulls, ideally suited to the transport of bulk cargo. Like the majority of her contemporaries, *Betsy* was rigged as a brig. While colliers were not noted for speed or beauty, their reliability and strength were legendary. Captain James Cook, one of England's greatest explorers, chose British colliers for his round-the-world voyages. Bligh's *Bounty* was a collier.

Every six to eight weeks during spring through fall, *Betsy* delivered coal from Whitehaven to Dublin, Ireland. Then, in 1780, she was leased to the Royal Navy for use as a transport in the war in America. Late the following summer *Betsy*, with her original captain and crew, joined a fleet of nearly 60 warships and transports under the command of General Cornwallis, who moved the fleet to Yorktown, Virginia, along with his army of about 10,000 men. In September, he found his army surrounded by French and American troops, with French warships blocking his escape to the sea.

Above **The *Betsy*'s bow proved to be unique, without a traditional apron structure; the horizontal interior bow framing and radial cant frames suggest possible Dutch influence.**

Left **A wooden gun carriage, intact but for a missing truck, was discovered in *Betsy*'s hold. Examination showed that the carriage had never been used.**

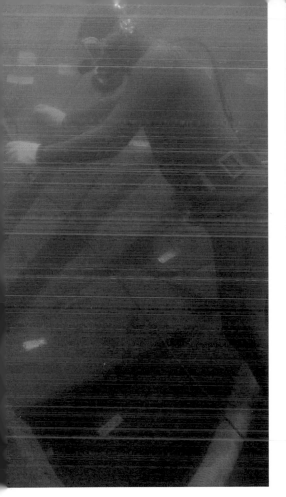

To prevent a French assault from the river, Cornwallis ordered more than a dozen transports, including *Betsy*, scuttled as beach obstructions. Not long afterward, surrounded, outnumbered, and with no hope of reinforcements, Cornwallis asked for terms of surrender. After the British surrender on 19 October 1781 the French conducted limited salvage operations, soon abandoned. The Yorktown ships passed out of memory as they settled into the protective riverbed sediments.

The End and a New Beginning

As the excavation was ending and efforts were shifting to conservation and analysis, Virginia's governor cancelled the underwater archaeology program and abolished our jobs. I could not, however, abandon this ship. Throughout the Yorktown Project I received much good advice from George Bass, including: "Always remember, an unpublished site is a looted site!" After several years, with the assistance of another NEH grant and nearly a dozen collaborators, I was able to produce a final project report.

I made numerous trips to England, frequently at my own expense, where new discoveries provided tremendous personal satisfaction. In Whitehaven, I stood before the tombstone of Joseph and Elizabeth Younghusband, and later held the family Bible bearing an entry describing Joseph's death in Charleston, South Carolina, in 1782, presumably from disease while in a prison camp. *Betsy* taught us a great deal about the construction of 18th-century British merchant vessels, but there is more to be learned. Research never seems to end on a project of this scale.

Top The *Betsy* was purposely sunk by a single hole cut in her starboard side, amidships.

Above The hole that scuttled the *Betsy* had been cut below the main deck by someone who chiseled a neat opening in an inner starboard plank, as if he knew his work would someday be inspected.

Tracing the Wreck of the Ten Sail: Grand Cayman, Cayman Islands

MARGARET LESHIKAR-DENTON

Wreck of the Ten Sail

Date 8 February 1794
Ships lost HMS *Convert*, Captain John Lawford; *William and Elizabeth*, Goodwin; *Moorhall*, Nicholson; *Ludlow*, McLure; *Britannia*, Martin; *Richard*, Hughes; *Nancy*, Leary; *Eagle*, Ainsworth; *Sally*, Watson; and *Fortune*, Love

A cannon shot roared from the darkness. "Breakers ahead! Close to us!" cried a seaman from a topsail yard of His Majesty's Ship *Convert*, on an 18th-century passage to Europe from the Caribbean. Captain Lawford bounded up on deck as Grand Cayman's jagged eastern reefs appeared in every direction. To his surprise and dismay, the ship firing distress was ahead of its escort, as were several others – not collected, as they should have been, with the Jamaica fleet sailing under *Convert*'s protection. Fifty-eight merchant ships were in peril – but not from the French, from whom *Convert*, formerly *l'Inconstante*, was a recent prize. Royal Navy gunners signaled the convoy, laden with West Indian wood, cotton, sugar, and rum, to disperse and save themselves. A merchantman on the opposite tack crashed into *Convert*'s bow, foiling her escape. As the crews of the two wooden ships disentangled their rigging, *Convert* struck and bilged. It was three o'clock in the morning, 8 February 1794.

"The dawning of the day presented a most melancholy scene. Seven ships and two Brigs on the same reef with the *Convert*, a heavy sea running and the wind blowing directly on shore," wrote John Lawford in a dispatch to the Admiralty. Eight people drowned. The loss of the well-armed frigate during wartime – the French

Below **HMS *Convert* and nine merchant ships sailing under the frigate's protection wrecked on 8 February 1794, on the windward reefs of Grand Cayman. A 20th-century wreck attests to the ever-present danger of this fringing coral barrier.**

Revolutionary Wars (1792–1802) – presented a hardship to Great Britain and agony to her newly appointed captain, though he was honorably acquitted by court martial. So did the catastrophic loss of nine merchant ships, returning to Europe with much-needed supplies from the colonies. The small island population, for its part, recovering from an October hurricane, had much to gain in salvageable goods.

Archives

Details of this remarkable tale were revealed in original documents that I discovered in the early 1990s. Clues emerged from the ink on weathered pages in English, French, and Jamaican archives. *L'Inconstante*'s papers and those of her first commander, Captain Riouffe, are in various national and military archives in France. Engravings of frigates and official cannon regulations are in French naval scholar Jean Boudriot's collection. In Jamaica, the Public Archives and National Library hold *l'Inconstante*'s prize papers, Council of Jamaica Minutes on the convoy and impressment of seamen, and periodicals containing advertisements for convoy ships. David Lyon helped acquire draughts of *l'Unité*, *Convert*'s sister ship, at London's National Maritime Museum. Lloyd's Register of Shipping provided merchant ship details, while the College of Arms illuminated a chronology of Captain Lawford's career. The Public Record Office (PRO) in Kew, London, houses the greatest wealth of documents: Admiralty and Secretariat Papers, Captain Lawford's letters and court-martial proceedings, convoy registers and instructions, *Convert*'s muster table and salvage account, related captains' and masters' logs, merchant ship registers, periodicals, and miscellaneous original correspondence.

There was a remarkable moment at the PRO when new discoveries had become infrequent. I found the *Royal Gazette* of early 1794; no prior volumes were listed, and none again until 1813. I turned the pages, hardly breathing, until I read, "Thursday night arrived from the Grand Caymanas, Lieutenant Bogue, of His Majesty's Ship

Above **Captain Lawford survived the Wreck of the Ten Sail, which occurred when he was 38 years old, without any major effect on his reputation. He went on commanding ships until 1811. With a career spanning the American War of Independence, the French Revolutionary Wars and the Napoleonic Wars, Lawford attained the rank of Admiral by the time of his death in 1842, aged 86.**

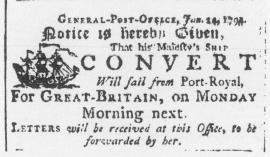

Above **A General Post Office notice regarding HMS *Convert* appeared in the Jamaica Royal Gazette of 18–25 January 1794, only days before *Convert*'s loss.**

Right **HMS *Convert*, formerly *l'Inconstante*, was a French-built 12-pounder frigate, as illustrated by Pierre Ozanne in an 18th-century engraving, "view of a frigate seen from abeam close-hauled on the port tack."**

Convert, with the melancholy intelligence of the loss of that frigate, with nine vessels of the fleet under her convoy, on the North-east end of that island…names of the merchant vessels lost are the *William and Elizabeth*, Goodwin; *Moorhall*, Nicholson; *Ludlow*, McLure; *Britannia*, Martin; *Richard*, Hughes; *Nancy*, Leary; *Eagle*, Ainsworth; *Sally*, Watson; and *Fortune*, Love." This discovery alone was worth the trip to England. Suddenly I knew the precise wreck location, and the name of every ship and captain.

Oral History

The Wreck of the Ten Sail is the most famous maritime disaster in Cayman Islands history. R. Tulloh Coe remembered a story – correct in many details – told by his grandfather, who assisted the survivors. Upon hearing Coe's account, Cayman Islands Commissioner George Hirst, writing in 1910, dismissed hearsay that cannons on the Gun Bay reef were remains of a fort and affirmed that "on this spot, the 'wreck of the ten sail' took place." Hirst was on target, but his words, like the names of the wrecked ships, faded. The Wreck of the Ten Sail became a legend.

Archaeology

I had seen artifacts, thought to be from the Wreck of the Ten Sail, on the seabed in 1980 while participating in an INA shipwreck survey with Roger Smith. Ten years later, as an INA research associate, funded in part by a Texas A&M dissertation fellowship and the Cayman Islands National Museum, I combined archaeology, archival research, and oral history to piece together the truth. The strategy was to locate, document, and assess sites associated with the *Convert* convoy, to make recommendations for further investigation and future management, and to recover, conserve, and analyze samples of artifacts.

A search for cannons adorning public and private places on land was a priority. My team of volunteers documented over 30 guns; ten had come from a sandbar inside the East End reef. They are 12-pounder cannons cast in 1781 at Forge-Neuve, an ironworks near Angoulême in Charente, France. The long-pattern cannons, cast according to the French Navy's "Regulations of 1778–1779", are part of the original ordnance placed on board *l'Inconstante*, which was lost when *Convert* wrecked.

Offshore work relied on visual survey with metal detectors over a 3-mile (5-km) tropical reef zone. This method is effective in the clear waters off Grand Cayman, especially in shallow areas that are inaccessible to boats. Test-excavations on the sandbar where the French cannon had been found suggest that 13 cannons remain buried here, most likely the final resting place of *Convert*'s gundeck, carried up and over the reef.

Crumpled copper sheathing at the nearby Frigate Spillage Site testifies to the *Convert*'s grinding over the reef, while 12-pounder cannonballs and barshot match

Below left **Ten *Convert* cannons, raised to adorn public and private places years before our project, were located and documented. This gun, like most antiquities raised by non-archaeologists, has suffered from corrosion due to lack of professional conservation.**

Below **Inscriptions on one of HMS *Convert*'s cannons reveal that it was a 12-pounder cast in 1781 at Forge-Neuve, a French ironworks.**

the calibre of the French guns. Pig-iron ballast, standing rigging, and ship's fittings lie encrusted but exposed on the seabed. The trained eye will recognize their shapes, so we mapped their locations over a 12,000-square-meter area, leaving most *in situ*. We mapped and collected copper ships' nails, galley bricks, ceramics, glass, cutlery, personal items, and samples of shingle ballast.

Anchors, ships' fittings, and concentrations of ballast mark sites along the reefline where hulls of the merchantmen once appeared. Directly ashore is the Salvage Campsite, containing many 18th-century artifact fragments. On this spot, near a place where fresh water percolates into shallow seawater, Captain Lawford camped for six weeks with his officers and 30 chosen seamen, salvaging what they could from the wrecked frigate while they waited for a Royal Navy ship to carry them back to Jamaica.

Above **Offshore work relied on visual survey with metal detectors over a 3-mile (5-km) tropical reef zone. Here, in shallows inaccessible to boats, the author examines a chain-plate without its wooden deadeye, part of *Convert*'s standing rigging, found encrusted to a living coral formation.**

Above right **Wreck of the Ten Sail artifacts, including ships' equipment like this 18th-century anchor, lie encrusted but exposed on the seabed.**

Right **The author explains a 1994 exhibition commemorating the 200th anniversary of the Wreck of the Ten Sail, in the Cayman Islands National Museum, to Britain's Queen Elizabeth II and Prince Philip. During her visit, the Queen dedicated the Wreck of the Ten Sail Park, which includes a view of Grand Cayman's windward reefs.**

WRECKS OF
MODERN TIMES

Our coverage of modern times, from the beginning of the 19th century, begins with the rather bizarre story of the first deepwater yacht built in the United States, a yacht sold in 1820 to King Kamehameha II of Hawaii. Paul Johnston describes the history of the yacht and his excavation of its remains.

We then move to boats that were not propelled by wind or steam, but by horses. This might seem like the lead-in to a joke about how many horse-power any given boat had, but horse-powered ferries were surprisingly common in North America in the early decades of the 19th century, at the very time that steam propulsion was gaining popularity. Kevin Crisman had the good fortune to excavate what today would be considered a most exotic craft. As this is written, Kevin is excavating the earliest known steam-powered western riverboat yet found in the United States, the *Heroine*, which sank in 1838 in the Red River, which now separates Oklahoma from Texas.

It is little appreciated that when the mass production of large steamboats began, they had a more profound effect on the western movement of people across North America than did the railroad – my great-grandfather, as a young man, wrote letters home about his trip from Virginia to Texas by river steamers in the 1850s.

Within a quarter century of the *Heroine's* sinking, steamships were serving other purposes in North America. The battle between the famed Civil War ironclads *Merrimack* and *Monitor* may have marked, according to Winston Churchill, "the greatest change in sea-fighting since cannon fired by gunpowder had been mounted on ships," but fast, wooden steamships that evaded the blockade of the Confederate States proclaimed by President Lincoln were equally important at the time. Barto Arnold describes his work on one of the most successful of these blockade-runners, the *Denbigh*.

Art Cohn, who calls canal boats "the 19th-century equivalent of the modern tractor-trailer," describes the discovery of a type of canal boat that was not thought to have existed in North America. Such discoveries keep nautical archaeology constantly exciting.

At last we enter the 20th century. I crossed the Atlantic Ocean 28 times by ship before ever I flew across, something I now do several times a year. Three times I passed through hurricanes, and once traveled from France to New York in a full December gale on the *Queen Mary*, before she was stabilized, in waves the size of mountains. These were unforgettable experiences. There were daily sailings from New York. "Do you want to go to northern Europe or to the Mediterranean on Tuesday?" the agent would ask. It is hard to realize, then, that to future historians of

One of *Titanic's* huge bronze propellers, more than 7 m (23 ft) in diameter, rests in a bed of rusticles that have fallen from the ship's deteriorating hull.

seafaring, the entire history of transoceanic passenger steamships will be but a tiny blip, only slightly more pronounced than the history of transoceanic travel by propeller-driven airplanes, which lasted only decades. Transatlantic passenger steamships operated regularly for but a century and a half after their introduction in 1830. That is not much time to an ancient historian.

Yet that short era produced the most famous ship, and the most famous shipwreck, in history – the *Titanic*. Even before the blockbuster film "Titanic," the story of the "unsinkable" ship, the iceberg, and how 1,500 people died in freezing water in April of 1912 was known around the world. Certainly, no other wreck could have tempted me to descend two and a half miles below the surface of the North Atlantic. What nautical archaeologist could resist? Would you have done it?

World War II saw the most powerful military fleets ever assembled. Yet the military vessels that are the subjects of the last two contributions to this book were not victims of giant naval battles between warships. All of the losses date to 1944. The Japanese ships that now make Truk Lagoon one of the most favored diving spots in the world were sunk by American warplanes while at anchor. Jeremy Green describes how he located one that had earlier escaped detection, and the immediate aftermath of his discovery.

The American vessels studied by Brett Phaneuf off the coast of Normandy were not battleships, cruisers, or destroyers, but the more modest landing craft that ferried thousands of troops across the English Channel to Normandy on 6 June 1944 – modest in size, perhaps, but not in their monumental contribution to eventual allied victory in Europe.

Above **J. Barto Arnold with the 250-kg (550-lb) connecting rod of the blockade-runner** *Denbigh*'s **port engine before it was cleaned of encrustation.**
Below **Places mentioned in this section, with the featured wrecks in bold.**

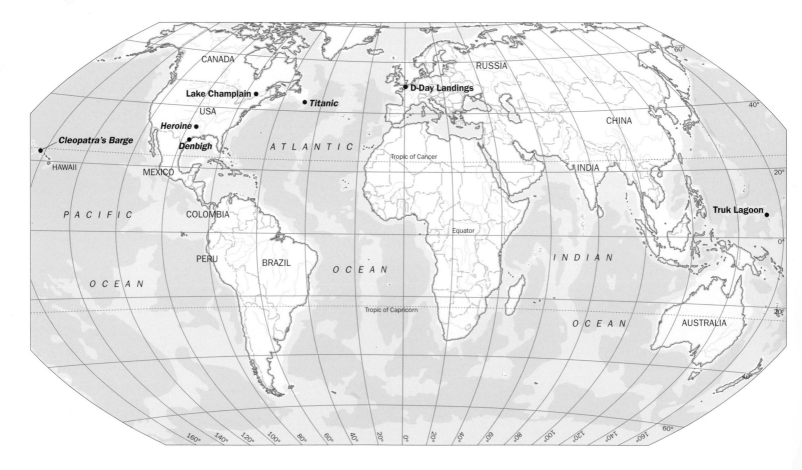

Cleopatra's Barge:
Kauai, Hawaii

PAUL F. JOHNSTON

I first heard the story of *Cleopatra's Barge*, America's first ocean-going yacht, on the first day of my first real job after graduate school. Newly hired as Maritime Curator at the Peabody Museum in Salem, Massachusetts, I was ushered into a small period room decorated with exotic woods, red velvet, and gold leaf. Cabinets were filled with ancient curiosities, and the room itself was a replica of the main salon of the *Barge*, based upon descriptions contemporary with the vessel's construction in 1816 in Salem. Adjacent rooms held ship models, rare furniture, log books from old ships, memorabilia, and watercolor portraits of those same ships – all related to George Crowninshield Jr (1766–1817) of Salem, owner of the fabled yacht.

Objects from the *Barge* had been removed before the ship's public auction in 1818, then passed down to family members or sold off. Over the next 163 years they made their way into the Peabody's collections, helped largely by two proud Crowninshield descendants who had cleared out their attics, browbeaten relatives, and followed marine art auctions for more than 50 years, snatching up anything to do with their famous ancestors and their large fleet of deepwater trading ships.

As I learned the story of the famous ship – one of the most bizarre in America's maritime heritage – it sent chills down my spine. It seemed an authentic tall tale, but

Below **The eldest of five sons, George Crowninshield Jr worked for his family's shipping company in Salem, Massachusetts. By the age of 20, he had served as a ship captain, but he preferred shore duty and took over the construction, fitting out, and maintenance of his family's sizable fleet of merchant ships.**

Below right **Deaf-and-dumb artist George Ropes painted this extraordinary portrait of *Cleopatra's Barge* in August 1818, the same month the famous yacht was auctioned after her owner's death. Every sail is bent, and the hermaphrodite brig is tearing along in a stiff breeze.**

it was true, involving such diverse elements as an American president, a pair of Emperor Napoleon's boots, seven lines of Shakespeare, British explorer Captain James Cook's entrails, the respective kings of England and Hawaii, and the first elephant in America.

But although much was published about the first half of the ship's life, mostly in and out of New England, the second half of her short, eight-year career prior to her violent loss in 1824 was totally unknown.

It was this uncharted and unexplored later phase, which took place in the Pacific island kingdom of Hawaii, that appealed so strongly to me. Almost nothing is preserved from early 19th-century Hawaii (or earlier periods), due to both the tropical environment and the organic origins of most objects prior to the "discovery" of the Sandwich Islands by British Captain James Cook in 1778. What might be left of the wreck of the famous ship, and what could it tell us about the material culture of the early Hawaiian monarchy – America's only authentic royalty?

Research revealed that a pipe was the only surviving possession of the Hawaiian king who had bought *Cleopatra's Barge*: Kamehameha II, nicknamed Liholiho. Son of Kamehameha the Great, who had united the Hawaiian Islands, Liholiho was responsible for the breakup of the royal system of taboos in Hawaii, and for allowing Christian missionaries in, changing Old Hawaiian culture forever.

Purchased from Boston China traders for $80,000-worth of sandalwood only ten days after her arrival in Hawaii in 1820, Liholiho's royal yacht and her contents promised to amplify the sparse story of his brief, five-year reign, a story written almost exclusively by *haoles*, or foreigners.

Search and Discovery

I contacted the State of Hawaii regarding a survey for the wreck of *Cleopatra's Barge* in early 1994. On the basis of experience elsewhere, I expected to obtain a permit through the State Historic Preservation Office and begin diving that summer in Hanalei Bay, where the *Barge* had sunk. But my permit application was the first ever

Above **King Kamehameha II inherited both a love of western ships from his father, as well as an appreciation for their social and political value. In an 1821 letter, local American merchant Charles Bullard wrote, "All sects are tolerated but the King worships the *Barge*." He always captained the ship when aboard.**

Below **Hanalei Bay, Kauai, where the royal yacht sank in 1824. On the ship's first visit to this island in 1821, King Kamehameha II used her to kidnap the local ruler, thus cementing his rule over all Hawaii. The wreck site is in the water to the right, very near the shoreline.**

Below **The "W&G" stamp on the corner of this piece of copper hull sheathing refers to Williams & Grenfell, the early 19th-century Liverpool copper merchants. The "G24" represents 24-gauge copper, which weighed 24 oz per sq. ft.**

received by the state for a scientific underwater archaeological survey, and consequently there was no process for such an application. As a result, I needed to submit a formal Environmental Assessment for review by 26 state and federal agencies as well as the general public, and found out that a separate permit would be required by the US Army Corps of Engineers. Moreover, one of the state agencies reserved a year's review period "after receipt of a complete application," and informed me that there were 60–70 applications ahead of mine!

A year later I held five different state and federal permits, one non-permit, and a total of 44 discrete conditions for the survey. And this was only for permission to *search* for the wreck – what might be required if we actually *found* something and it warranted fuller investigation?

Written in May 1824, Boston missionary Hiram Bingham's eyewitness account of the *Barge*'s partial salvage by Kauai islanders stated that she had struck a shallow reef and sunk off the mouth of the Waioli River, near the beach in Hanalei Bay, on 6 April 1824. The wreck had occurred as the result of a storm, a parted anchor cable, and an intoxicated crew. This information, combined with the use of a magnetometer and metal detector, resulted in test trenches that quickly yielded early 19th-century artifacts. A piece of copper hull sheathing stamped "W&G/G 24" was traced to the early 19th-century British copper dealers Williams & Grenfell. Other 1995 finds verified the wreck's identity and indicated that there was enough left to justify excavation before storm-driven waves finally destroyed what remained.

Finds

Over the next four excavation seasons, more than 1,250 artifacts were found on the site, including a 12.2-m (40-ft) section of the stern nestled against the reef that had wrecked the ship. Among the most significant small finds were 18 fragments of olive-green square case bottles, so-called because they packed easily into wooden cases. The presence of these alcoholic spirit containers aboard the royal yacht lent weight to

Below **These fragmentary square-sided case bottles from the early 19th century most commonly held alcoholic spirits, such as gin. Their presence aboard the royal yacht supports contemporary accounts that alcoholic beverages were a factor in the ship's loss.**

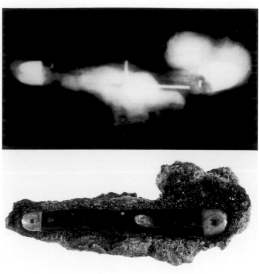

contemporary missionary accounts that one of the reasons the ship had sunk was due to an inebriated native Hawaiian crew.

The discovery of five human bones was unexpected. Historical accounts indicated that no one was injured during the 1824 wrecking, much less killed. The distribution of bone types and ages from the site did not match the bodies of unrecovered victims of recorded drownings in Hanalei Bay. Stronger possibilities were bones washed out of a Japanese cemetery just up the Waioli River, or bones from shallow Hawaiian beach burials from the pre-contact period. However, there is no Hawaiian DNA database from which to derive concrete answers, so a definitive source for the bones remains a mystery.

Personal items included unfinished carved sperm whale teeth, an ivory finger ring, a pair of nail scissors, a pen (folding) knife, and a table knife and fork. Among maritime tools were a leather belt holster containing a sailmaker's heaver; a sail needle; a sand glass for measuring the speed of the boat; and a meat fork whose identical twin was illustrated in a late 18th-century marine dictionary.

In October 1822, King Liholiho sold ten cannon from his yacht – now renamed *Haʻaheo o Hawaiʻi* (*Pride of Hawaii*) – in exchange for the timber from a condemned ship; according to contemporary missionary accounts, he retained at least one as a signal gun to announce his comings and goings from local ports. Two guns were recovered in an 1857 salvage of the yacht's wreck, but we found none. Nevertheless, evidence for their presence was recovered, in the form of a lead cannon apron; part of a wooden gun carriage wheel; a wooden tompion (plug for a gun muzzle to prevent moisture or contamination); and a large, hollow iron shell that would have been packed with powder and plugged with a fuse before firing. Other firearms were confirmed by a wooden musket forestock; three sizes of lead shot; a small patent powder flask made of copper; and remains of a small powder keg filled to the brim with gunpowder.

Hawaiian Finds

Relatively few native Hawaiian objects appeared, but the highlight was a *pu*, or conch shell horn, complete with a tonal hole knocked into its side. In Old Hawaii, these were

Above left **Tom Ormsby and Rick Rogers record details of the royal yacht's teredo-ridden bow timbers, found hard against the reef that sank the ship.**

Above **Artifacts containing iron bond with the surrounding sand and form shapeless lumps, called concretions, as they deteriorate over time underwater. Here, an X-ray of such a concretion reveals a folding knife, which has then been partly exposed as the hard crust is carefully removed in the conservation process.**

Below **A copper musket (or "pocket") powder flask attests to the presence of modern western weapons aboard King Liholiho's yacht. The type was patented in 1814 by Briton Thomas Sykes; this example may be an American copy of the English patent.**

Above **Clockwise from the bottom, Hawaiian artifacts include two canoe breakers, a pounder, a sharpening stone, a canoe rubber, an ulu maika (bowling stone), and another pounder. In the center is a *pu*, or conch horn.**

Below **In contrast to the two large Hawaiian grindstones found in the wreck is this delicate bronze furniture mount, originally gilded. It depicts Cupid sharpening an arrow on a western circular grindstone, operated by a foot treadle. Originally the artifact would have adorned the corner of an elegant English or French table.**

used as horns signaling an event or arrival, not as musical instruments. Dozens of iron adze heads, made from sections of straight and slightly curved barrel hooping, were paralleled by two Hawaiian stone examples. Iron adzes were highly prized in the early contact period, and the royal yacht has yielded the largest known hoard, dated far later than historical sources would indicate. Pointed tools included two picks or awls of bone, and two made from copper hull spikes. Two large, heavy grindstones served to sharpen a variety of Hawaiian tools; they are joined by a remarkable French or English copper furniture mount, originally gilded, depicting a cupid sharpening his arrow on a foot-treadle-operated circular grindstone. Two large pounders and a small oil lamp made of local, rough-surfaced lava are relatively crude, not what one would expect aboard the yacht of a monarch. A few other stone tools for sharpening or burnishing complete the Hawaiian tool kit left behind by the vessel's original salvors. Thin walled gourd fragments attested to organic liquid containers aboard the vessel; these and two cowrie shells pierced for octopus lures were the only evidence for Hawaiian food gathering, preparation, or consumption.

Three large, ovoid lava stones, with grooves cut around their short sides for ropes, were known as canoe breakers, swung and flung at enemy canoes, and then hauled back for another broadside. With Western firearms, powder, and ammunition on board, it is hard to believe that they were anything but anachronisms – or perhaps a nod to tradition.

What was not found is as telling as what we recovered. Of course, delicate organic objects had not survived the dynamic surf zone in which the ship had been cradled. However, not a sherd of Chinese export porcelain was found, nor remnants of any other luxury items that would be expected to adorn a king's yacht. The overall picture that emerges from the five-year archaeological investigations of the vessel that served as the royal Hawaiian yacht from 1820 to 1824 is one of extreme modesty, excepting only parts of the hardware that were almost certainly part of the original Crowninshield fitting out.

Aftermath

Perhaps the absence of any royal trappings can be explained by their removal and storage when the king left the islands in November 1823 to meet and consult with King George IV in England. Whatever was left aboard could also have been removed during the 1824 salvage, broken up in the surf-lashed reef environment, consumed by voracious teredo worms, or further broken down during the 1857 salvage. These sorts of unknowns embody the old adage that archaeology always poses more questions than it answers.

King Kamehameha never learned of *Ha'aheo*'s loss. He and his favorite queen were still at sea when the ship wrecked in Hanalei Bay. Before news of the tragedy could reach him, they both died in London, on the other side of the world, victims of measles, a western disease to which their Pacific island kingdom had never been exposed. Today, around a quarter of *Ha'aheo*'s hull structure below the water line remains buried in the shallow sands of Hanalei Bay, one of the most beautiful spots in Hawaii. It and the artifacts recovered from five seasons of excavations are all that remain of the fabled ship, one New Englander's dream and a Hawaiian king's most cherished possession.

A Horse-Powered Ferry: Burlington Bay, Lake Champlain

KEVIN CRISMAN

Horse Ferry

Built	1820–1840
Sunk	1840s
Depth	15 m (50 ft)
Hull	18 m (59 ft) long, 4.6 m (15 ft) wide
Deck	7.2 m (23.5 ft) wide
Crew	2–4 men, 2 horses

There's an old saying: "You can lead a horse to water but you cannot make him drink." True, perhaps, but you could make him walk on water if you lived in the 19th century and owned the latest in maritime technology: a horse-powered boat. Hundreds of these ingenious craft once plied ferry crossings throughout the North American continent, whisking people, livestock, and wagons over the rivers and lakes that were a barrier to overland travel. In their day "horseboats" (also known as "teamboats") were a common sight, but their story was largely forgotten until the discovery of a horseboat wreck in Burlington Bay, Lake Champlain.

The wreck first appeared on a side-scan sonar printout, sitting upright in 15 m (50 ft) of water, listing over slightly to port, its deck extending out beyond the sides of the hull in the manner of a steamboat. A pair of sidewheels were visible slightly forward of amidships. Only 18 m (59 ft) long, the wreck looked like a small steamboat, but when my colleague Arthur Cohn and I dived into the cold, greenish depths, we saw no signs of a boiler or steam engine. There was machinery, however: a giant spoked wheel beneath the after deck, connected to the sidewheel axle by iron gear wheels and an iron transmission shaft. This was surely one of the lake's mysterious horse-powered ferries, but how did it work?

Answering that question and many others took four years of measuring timbers and digging out the fine mud that filled the wreck. Inside the bow were artifacts that told part of the story: broken horse shoes (for relatively small horses); pieces of discarded leather horse harness; gear wheels and a bearing from the machinery, all heavily worn; a shattered, cheaply made teapot; a caulking iron; and the extensively repaired rudder. The ferry had obviously seen many years of service on the lake and was scuttled in Burlington Bay when no longer worthy of repair.

The other part of the story was found in libraries and archives, where much time was spent researching the history and technology of horseboats. We learned that the idea of harnessing animals to simple machines and to power boats went back as far as the Roman era, and that working versions were made in the 17th and 18th centuries. The idea really caught on when steamboats began paddling over North American waters after 1807. Paddle-wheel propulsion was a gigantic leap forward in transportation, but steam engines and boilers were not always economical for smaller craft like ferryboats. Horses were a cheaper alternative, and unlike early boilers, they did not explode. The first teamboat ferry began service in New York City in 1814, starting a craze for these boats that continued for many decades.

Horse machinery changed over time. The earliest type forced the horses to walk in a circle, much like an animated merry-go-round. It worked, but the contraption took

Above **Texas A&M University graduate students Gail Erwin and Joseph Cozzi record the horse ferry wreck's heavily repaired rudder.**

Below **A photomosaic of the wreck as it was found on the bottom of the lake. The fore deck was missing, and the planking of the after deck was in sad shape, but the hull and its unusual machinery were nearly complete.**

up too much deck space and the horses got dizzy. The second type, patented in 1819 and widely employed over the next two decades, had a flat treadwheel under the after deck with openings cut through on each side to allow the horses to walk in place on the wheel. The third and final type, the treadmill, looked and worked much like the modern version used for exercising people: the horse stood in a narrow stall and walked upon an "endless floor" that revolved under its hooves. This machinery, having the advantage of being lightweight and easily repaired, caught on in the 1840s. The wreck in Burlington Bay was outfitted with a horizontal treadwheel, and was therefore built sometime between 1820 and 1840 when this mechanism was popular.

Historical records suggested that Lake Champlain entered the horse ferry era in the mid 1820s, and that about ten such ferries were employed over the next 40 years. *Experiment* was the first horseboat on the lake. *Eagle* rescued the crew of a sinking steamboat in 1841 and was in service for at least 12 years. *Eclipse* was a six-horse boat that also enjoyed a long career, but had to be abandoned after a heavy cargo of cattle collapsed the deck onto the treadwheel. *Gypsey*, a treadmill-equipped boat, was probably the last horse ferry on the lake.

And what was the name of the vessel sunk in Burlington Bay? Neither the wreck nor the historical record could tell us. What is certain is that the ferry had a long and honorable career carrying people and goods over the waters of Lake Champlain. Listen closely and you may still hear the clop of hooves, the splash of paddle wheels, and the snorts of the ferry's engines.

Above **A diver inspects the corroded but intact gear shift system of the Lake Champlain horse ferry.**

Below **An interior profile view of the horse-powered ferry, reconstructed to show one of the horses on the treadwheel. The ferry was equipped with hinged ramps at the bow and stern (not shown) to facilitate loading and unloading passengers, livestock, and wagons.**

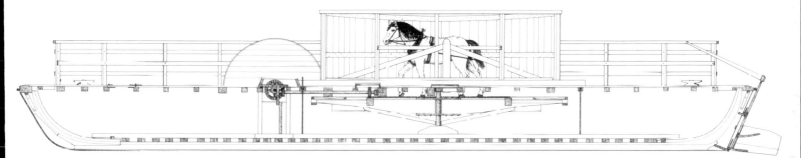

The Sidewheel Steamer Heroine: Red River, Oklahoma

KEVIN CRISMAN

In March, 1838, the river steamboat *Heroine* loaded provisions and stores in Vicksburg, Mississippi, to supply the US Army garrison at Fort Towson in the Oklahoma Territory. Shortly after leaving Vicksburg, *Heroine* began the hazardous 600-mile (965-km) voyage up the winding Red River. Submerged logs – "snags" – lurked beneath the surface and had already sunk two steamers that spring, but *Heroine*'s pilot was skilled – or perhaps just lucky. Near the fort, however, the luck ran out, and with a crash the boat ran headlong into a snag. Water poured in and the steamboat settled to the bottom. No lives were endangered – the upper decks still protruded above the river – but *Heroine*'s career was over. Much of the cargo was ruined, but the crew unbolted the engine and loaded it onto a steamboat bound for New Orleans. A sudden rise in the river a few days later filled the hold with sand and ended salvage operations. Abandoned by all, the steamboat was forgotten for the next 150 years.

"They don't call it the Red River for nothing." The words of INA President Donny Hamilton came back to me as, in September 2002, I dipped my face into the river for a first "look" at the unknown steamboat below. Once on the wreck I could feel the structure around me, but its timbers were nearly invisible in the swirls of reddish-brown water. However, if the river was turbid, the wreck's potential was clear.

Amidships, a center-mounted flywheel for a single piston poked above the surface of the water. Single-piston sidewheelers were largely obsolete by the 1840s, making this vessel the earliest western river steamboat yet discovered. Test excavations inside the hull in 2001 and 2002 turned up tools and barrels of provisions, while probing in 2002 showed that the hull was complete to the main deck and stretched for 43 m

Heroine

Sunk May 1838
Excavation 2001–present
Cargo military provisions and stores for Fort Towson
Hull 42.7 m (140 ft) long, 7.3 m (24 ft) wide
Tonnage 160 tons
Crew *c* 20
Casualties none

Below left **A contemporary watercolor of the steamboat *Ouishita* on the Red River, similar to *Heroine* in its age and tonnage. Cargo, livestock, and steerage passengers occupied the main deck, while cabins on the upper deck provided comfort for first-class passengers.**

Below **The iron hub and support timbers for *Heroine*'s flywheel protrude from the river during a time of low water. The cast iron used for the machinery shattered easily, as evidenced by signs of both damage and repairs on *Heroine*'s surviving sidewheel.**

(140 ft) under the sand. All in all, it was a spectacular discovery in an unusual location – the only known historical shipwreck in the state of Oklahoma.

In 2003 and 2004, we were back to excavate the steamboat's stern, braving strong currents in the shallowest and most exposed part of the wreck. With small headlamps to illuminate the area directly in front of our masks, it was just possible to read measuring tapes. Despite the buffeting, three teams excavating with dredges recovered scores of artifacts and exposed the hull structure.

One of our first discoveries was a small hatchway through the main deck at the stern, an opening once secured by a long iron hasp. Digging under the deck revealed a cramped space filled with mundane objects: a giant C-clamp, a pair of can hooks for lifting barrels, a broken iron fire grating, and personal possessions such as a boot and shoes, an iron stirrup, and a silver spoon handle with the owner's initials scratched into the surface. The compartment, we later learned, was known as the "run" and commonly held the crew's belongings. On this vessel it was also a catch-all for tools, ship's stores, and worn-out equipment.

The adjacent cargo hold held barrels of pickled pork intended to feed the garrison at Fort Towson. Several barrels were recovered for treatment at Texas A&M University's Conservation Research Laboratory. The pork flesh had congealed – "saponified" is the technical term – into waxy, pungent blocks of fat and bones that included halved pig skulls. From an 1830s perspective, modern military rations look quite appetizing.

The largest artifact yet recovered is the steamboat's rudder. A massive assembly of oak timbers, the rudder had many cracks and repairs. These and other clues suggested that the steamboat had seen much service before it was fatally snagged – a suggestion that was proved when the steamboat was later identified.

For a time the name of the wreck eluded us, although we were able to narrow the likely date of its sinking to the late 1830s. Research turned up letters from Fort Towson's commander describing the loss of an unnamed supply boat in May of 1838. New Orleans newspapers finally provided the name: *Heroine*. Western river steamers fundamentally changed concepts of time and distance, and forever changed the interior of North America, yet our knowledge of their architecture and steam machinery has been sketchy at best. The *Heroine* is helping to reveal these secrets, while its equipment, personal effects, and cargo tell us about river navigation, river life, and river trade. More exciting discoveries surely lie ahead.

Above left **Rafts and boats moored over the steamboat *Heroine* support divers studying the wreck. The placid surface of the Red River belies the turbulent conditions encountered by divers beneath its waters.**

Above **Pierre Laroque, Arthur Cohn, and Jim Lee remove lifting slings used to recover the rudder of the *Heroine*. Despite 165 years under water the rudder still retained traces of its original paint.**

Below **A computer-generated image of *Heroine*'s stern as it appears today. A shallow draft hull was necessary for successful navigation of the western rivers, and *Heroine* was therefore lightly built in comparison with seagoing ships.**

The Denbigh, *A Civil War Blockade Runner: Galveston, Texas*

J. BARTO ARNOLD III

Denbigh

Built 1860 in Birkenhead, England
Sunk 23 or 24 May 1865
Excavation 1998–2002
Hull 55.5 m (182 ft) long,
6.7 m (22 ft) wide
Trips as runner 13 successful
round trips
Cargo capacity *c* 500 bales, or
225,000 lb cotton
Crew 21

I looked at Tom Oertling, he looked at me, and we both looked back at the buoy we had just dropped. "Oh, no," I said, "somebody sank a shrimp boat in the middle of our search area." The buoy floated just 10 m (33 ft) from the large iron wreckage that barely broke the surface of Galveston Bay's entrance from the Gulf of Mexico.

We were in a small boat with four dedicated avocational archaeologists from the Southwest Underwater Archaeological Society (SUAS). Our purpose on that December day in 1997 was to scout the general area where the famous and successful Civil War blockade runner *Denbigh* had been sunk. On a dark night in May 1865, this speedy and elusive vessel was sneaking through the Union Navy's cordon around the bay entrance. The vessel was carrying military supplies and manufactured goods urgently needed by the Confederate Department of the Trans-Mississippi, where Rebels still held out after General Robert E. Lee's surrender at Appomattox in April – and even after President Lincoln's assassination. In fact, the next morning, as the *Denbigh* burned furiously after being shelled by the blockading fleet, Sherman's army was holding a victory parade down Pennsylvania Avenue in Washington, DC.

Surely, we thought, modern wreckage was the most likely identity of the debris the INA preliminary survey party viewed that day, since, in Texas waters as in most

Below **Thomas C. Healy's portrait of the *Denbigh* dated 29 July, 1864, at Mobile, Alabama. The painting shows the *Denbigh* running out of Mobile with a full cargo of cotton.**

Above **High-resolution side-scan sonar image of the portions of the *Denbigh* that protrude above the bottom of the bay. The twin paddle-wheel frames of iron appear at top and bottom, the boiler at the right, and, in the center, the eccentrics and disconnecting mechanisms on the axle or shaft.**

Below **The covered paddle wheel with its feathering mechanism was mounted outboard of the hull, supported by the sponson on which the man stands. This computer-generated reconstruction shows the feathering paddle wheel that greatly increased efficiency by keeping the wooden paddle blades near vertical while in the water.**

places, historic wrecks are usually buried in the muddy bottom. We continued to circle the debris lying exactly where the *Denbigh* appeared on an 1880s map Tom had turned up by chance in the course of other research. Slowly it dawned on me that the cluster of broken pipes exposed by an unusually low tide combined with the effects of strong offshore winds must be steam machinery! Tom and I snorkeled the next day in the frigid but clearer than normal water, locating the paddle wheels and measuring what we later learned was the ship's boiler. The *Denbigh* was found, though we said to ourselves: "This can't be it. It's never this easy!"

The Paddler

The *Denbigh* was a distinctive type of ship known as a British coastal paddle steamer. She served for a few years as a passenger ship plying the short run from Liverpool to Rhyl, a resort in Wales. At the time the *Denbigh* was built, at a cost of £10,250 (approximately $1 million today), the coastal paddle steamer was something of a test case for the development of maritime technology.

In building this type of vessel, the prominent shipyards experimented, participating in a virtual race to improve speed and efficiency. At her launch and time trials in 1860, the *Denbigh* was recognized as a shining example of her kind, and she became one of the most successful blockade runners of the Civil War.

Running military supplies and manufactured goods into the South and, especially, running cotton out was an astoundingly lucrative trade. Just one round trip would buy the ship outright, pay for inbound and outbound cargo, handsomely pay the crew – and still turn a profit. The average runner survived four trips, but the *Denbigh*, capable of carrying approximately 500 bales, or 102,273 kg (225,000 lb) of cotton at a speed of 13.7 knots (15.75 mph), racked up a near-record 13 successful round trips.

Skillful and daring masters and pilots were indispensable in a blockade-runner's success. Captain Godfrey of the *Denbigh* had these qualities. He earned a small fortune, and after the war bought the finest hotel in Mobile, Alabama, the port that was the *Denbigh*'s first Confederate terminus. Sadly, Captain Godfrey then promptly drank himself to death.

Not only were coastal paddle steamers perhaps the most successful vessels used for blockade running, the Union Navy similarly found that captured runners of this type were the most effective cruisers for offshore patrol against blockade running.

The more general type, the side-wheel steamer, was the progenitor of modern marine engineering. Although paddles were eventually replaced by screw propulsion, and reciprocating engines were replaced by steam turbines and then internal combustion engines, the story of marine engineering began with the paddle wheel. All of which underscores the importance of the *Denbigh* as a rare surviving example of a side-wheel coastal steamer.

Speed was the overriding consideration for a blockade-runner. Shallow draft was also important in order that runners could use secondary shore channels for entering Southern ports, and in keeping their distance from deeper-drafted Union vessels. Improving speed by increasing length in proportion to the beam of a vessel reduced cargo space, as did shallow drafts, but for cargo of sufficiently high value, the ability simply to get through outweighed the reduction in cargo-carrying ability.

Despite its shallow-draft advantages, the *Denbigh* ran aground at the entrance of Galveston Bay, and was then shelled and burned by the Union blockading fleet.

INA's Denbigh *Shipwreck Project*

The goals of the INA *Denbigh* Project are research, education, and public outreach. Archaeological research at the *Denbigh* site is particularly important because, although there is historical evidence for her operations, the historic record preserves almost nothing of her construction details. For example, plans of the ship have not survived, although descriptive information on the dimensions, cargo capacity, operational history, and other aspects of the vessel exist.

The 1998 field season's pre-excavation mapping of the *Denbigh* included recording the remains of the vessel's machinery that protruded above the 2-m (6.6-ft) deep floor of the bay to a height usually just below the water surface. In addition to mapping exposed remains, the first season's working phase included remote sensing surveys using magnetometer, side-scan sonar, sub-bottom sonar, and fathometer. The exposed remains consisted of portions of the *Denbigh*'s boiler, paddle wheels, and the very upper parts of the twin steam engines. The deck level was just below the muddy sand bottom.

The 1999 season consisted of three units of test excavations: one centrally located in the engine room, one in the forward area thought to be a cargo hold, and one toward the stern in an area thought to lie beneath the crew quarters. The engine room revealed that the major components of the *Denbigh*'s machinery were intact. This was a welcome but somewhat unexpected discovery, since engines and other machinery were often salvaged. The finding was particularly important because the ship's technology was a major aspect of interest for further investigation. The test excavation unit in the forward area found the port side of the

Below **Computer reconstruction of the ship's boiler based on details recorded under water in near zero visibility, and on plans for a similar Laird's boiler from archival sources.**

ship had broken and collapsed outward. The aft test excavation unit found the stern area of the hull intact. Beneath about 3 m (10 ft) of overburden, a few artifacts were found, hinting at the presence of cargo and crew possessions. Only the first 60 cm (2 ft) above the hull's bottom yielded relatively undisturbed archaeological deposits, a pattern that seems to be usual at this site.

Three summers of full-scale excavation from 2000 to 2002 allowed us to record the hull construction, the complex paddlewheel and drive train, and the port engine together with the condenser, air pump, hot well, and boiler. Another excavation unit in the stern half of the hull helped confirm the location of the crew quarters, but excavations were mainly concentrated in the engine room and just outboard of the engine room.

Small artifacts were generally scarce, but a remote corner of the engine room contained a storage area for engineering department tools and a private stash of liquor. Some bottles were sealed with intact contents, which we will soon analyze and identify.

Our excavation strategy was to study the wreck in place rather than raise the hull. The cost of completely excavating, recovering, and then conserving, restoring, and exhibiting a 55.5-m (182-ft) long by 6.7-m (22-ft) wide iron hull are beyond practical contemplation. The expense would run into many tens of millions of dollars.

The *Denbigh* Project now enters a phase of conservation, analysis, and publication. We plan at least two more books to join W. Watson's *The Civil War Adventures of a Blockade Runner* (2001) in a series: first, the main excavation report and history of the ship, and second, a collection of documentary sources about the *Denbigh*. Historical research continues, and the archaeological potential of the site is far from exhausted. The bow and the stern need attention as the next areas for excavation and study. Very likely there are further areas in the hull where important and intact archaeological deposits remain. When the present reporting phase is complete, INA's *Denbigh* Project excavations will continue.

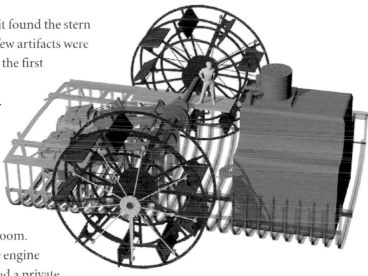

Above **Computer generated reconstruction of the *Denbigh*'s engine room and machinery without the iron hull plates and wooden deck. The stern and the twin inclined engines are to the left. Each engine had a single 40-inch-diameter cylinder and a high-tech cutoff valve.**

Opposite **Exposed remains of the *Denbigh*'s machinery in a computer-generated image. The ship's buried deck level is just inches below the paddle shaft. Beyond the boiler at top right, the bow lies buried.**

Far right **Helen Dewolf and Amy Borgens prepare *Denbigh*'s calcareous encrusted superheater top for X-ray at Texas A&M University's Conservation Research Laboratory where the *Denbigh* artifacts are being cleaned and preserved. The X-ray (*right*) reveals the construction details of its connection to the pipes through which smoke and hot air from the burning coal entered the smoke stack. Steam surrounded the pipes after exiting the boiler, gaining heat and expansive force. The superheater was an advanced feature helping produce superior speed and efficiency.**

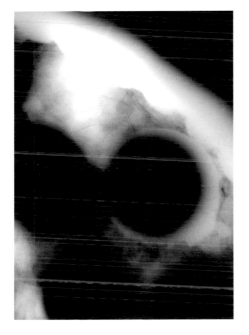

The Sailing Canal Boats of Lake Champlain

ARTHUR COHN

Lake Champlain Canal Boats

Depth of lake   122 m (400 ft) max
Length of the Champlain Canal
103 km (64 miles)
Sailing canal boats   250 built
General Butler *built*   1862
General Butler *sunk*   1876

After three decades working in Lake Champlain's cold, dark waters, it may have been the most extraordinary sight I had ever seen. The Lake Champlain Maritime Museum's side-sonar survey team of Fred Fayette, Peter Barranco, and Tom and Pat Manley of Middlebury College had located an intriguing anomaly in the lake's deep water. Our instruments told us the object rose more than 9 m (30 ft) off the bottom, far too tall for any of Lake Champlain's wooden shipwrecks. It must be geological, perhaps an oddly shaped boulder dropped 10,000 years ago by a receding glacier, we agreed. Although it did not look like a shipwreck, we still needed to identify what lay more than 30 m (100 ft) below us. As I descended slowly into darkness I was left with only my dive light to illuminate a narrow channel of water in front of me. I could scarcely believe it as the sodden timbers of a boat's transom appeared, towering above the lake bottom. At that moment I knew I had solved a 175-year-old tragic mystery with the discovery of the canal schooner *Troy of Westport*.

To some observers Lake Champlain may seem an unlikely place to study shipwrecks. The lake lies far from the ocean, nestled between Vermont's Green Mountains and New York's Adirondacks. However, geography favored this inland lake as it provided a 193-km (120-mile) long north–south navigable waterway. During the historic period when roads were awful, if they existed at all, travel by water was the best option. Today, the lake's collection of some 300 shipwrecks (and still counting) attest to the rich and layered history that took place around and over Lake Champlain.

Sailing Canal Boats

The disappearance of the *Troy* is wrapped within a larger mystery that began with the discovery in 1980 of the *General Butler*, an intact shipwreck a stone's throw from the shoreline of Burlington, Vermont. Old timers had told me about a boat that sank in 1876 after running headlong into Burlington's massive timber-cribbed, stone-filled breakwater. When the *General Butler* was discovered its dimensions suggested it was one of the region's typical wooden canal boats. Canal boats were the 19th-century equivalent of the modern tractor-trailer, carrying freight throughout the communities located along the region's waterways. The canal boom engulfed Lake Champlain in 1823 when the Champlain Canal opened. The canal connected Lake Champlain to the Hudson River, and in 1825 to the Erie Canal; commercial shipping on Lake Champlain prospered like never before. Canal boats had a distinctive long, narrow shape designed to maximize their cargo capacity while still allowing them to fit through the canal locks. They were towed by steamboats or tugboats when in open

Below **The canal schooner *General Butler* as she looks on the bottom of Lake Champlain.**

water, such as Lake Champlain, or pulled by horses or mules when in the canals. As we examined the remarkably intact remains of the *General Butler* we noted rigging elements and two mast tabernacles, three-sided boxes used for stepping a mast on the deck, all suggesting that this canal boat was designed to sail.

"Not so!" was the universal response from canal historians we approached for information. According to these experts, while sailing barges had been part of European maritime history, they had never been built in North America. Never. Happily, we can now report that the discovery of the *General Butler* has opened up a new branch on the North American naval architecture tree. Research over the past two decades with my partner, INA's Kevin Crisman, has determined that sailing canal boats appeared on Lake Champlain simultaneously with the opening of the Champlain Canal in 1823. The very first boat to transit the new canal was the *Gleaner* from St. Albans Bay, Vermont. The *Gleaner* was celebrated at Hudson River ports all the way to New York City where she received a 24-gun salute. In the New York newspaper *Mercantile Advertiser*, she was described as a vessel "built as an experiment and is found to all the uses intended. She sails as fast and bears the changes in weather in the lake and river as well as ordinary sloops and is constructed properly for passing through the canal." The *Gleaner* was a Lake Champlain sailing canal boat!

Sailing canal boats were the practical response of Lake Champlain merchants and mariners who wanted a vessel that could be loaded with cargo and then have the independent ability to sail to the canal entrance at Whitehall, New York. Once arrived, they lowered their masts, which stepped on the deck, and raised their centerboards for the trip by mule through the canal. Once on the Hudson River, they would raise their masts, lower their centerboards and sail south, all without having to handle their cargo until they reached their final destinations. As the 19th century progressed, steam towboats on the Hudson River became more reliable, so few sailing canal boat captains found it economical to sail on the Hudson. Most left their masts and sails in storage at Whitehall to be re-stepped on the northbound journey.

Lake Champlain's sailing canal boats evolved over time. The first generation of sailing canal boats, known as the 1823-class, were 24 m (79 ft) long and 4.1 m (13.5 ft) wide. The earliest boats of the 1823-class were built as experiments, and it was not until 1841 that a more standardized design was adopted by the region's shipwrights. In 1862, the first expansion of the Champlain Canal locks was

Above left **Rigging elements such as this deadeye on the *General Butler*'s bow were the first clues that this was no ordinary canal boat.**

Above center **The *General Butler* was lost, in part, because its steering mechanism broke. The captain rigged the rudderpost with a makeshift tiller, but it was still not enough to save the boat.**

Above **Toy model of a sloop-rigged sailing canal boat found aboard the *General Butler*.**

Below **Sailing canal boat *P.E. Havens*, circa 1900.**

Above **The still intact wheel of the *O.J. Walker* attests to the excellent shipwreck preservation conditions in Lake Champlain.**

Above right **The stock of an anchor hangs over the *O.J. Walker*'s bow.**

Below **Drawing of the canal schooner *Troy* as it looks today.**

completed giving rise to the 1862-class of boats. These were 26.8 m (88 ft) long and 4.4 m (14.5 ft) in beam. The 1873 expansion of the canal gave rise to boats that were 29.6 m (97 ft) long and 5.3 m (17.5 ft) in beam. These 97-footers were the last of the line. The sailing canal boat was becoming obsolete, a victim to the year-round and expanding railroads.

Historian Scott McLaughlin estimates that only 250 sailing canal boats were built on Lake Champlain during their century of operations as compared to 4,000 towed canal boats. During our sonar surveys we have located more than 50 standard canal boat shipwrecks, as compared to only five intact sailing canal boat shipwrecks. The *General Butler*, built in 1862 in Essex, New York, lies within a half-mile of the *O.J. Walker*, built in Burlington, also in 1862. The *Butler* carries marble blocks and the *Walker* bricks and tile. Two intact but still nameless 1841-class sailing canal boats have been located, one with a load of marble and one with a load of iron ore. Both have the standardized look expected of boats built in the 1840s or later. Missing from this collection was an archaeological example of an early experimental 1823-class vessel – until the discovery of the *Troy*.

Troy of Westport

We knew from historical research that the canal schooner *Troy of Westport* had been lost in 1825 in a November gale. Her crew of five young men and boys were never found and her loss devastated the community. Details of the tragedy became evident as I descended along the hull. Unbelievably, the transom hung in the water, while the rest of the hull plummeted perilously downward. As I reached the bow, a tangle of spars and cargo lay strewn before me on the otherwise featureless bottom. It was clear

Right **The schooner *Lois McClure* under construction in 2003.**

Right The schooner *Lois McClure* under construction in 2003.

Below **The Lake Champlain Maritime Museum's replica canal schooner *Lois McClure* under sail in August 2004.**

that the heavy cargo of iron ore had rushed into the bow as the boat sank, pulling it rapidly toward the bottom. The steep descent was halted when the bow slammed into the soft mud of the bottom, those tons of iron ore acting as a massive anchor, which ensured that the rest of the hulk would continue to hang in the water column, precariously reaching for the surface.

An Underwater Preserve and the Canal Schooner Lois McClure

We left the *Troy* exactly as we found it, as the Lake Champlain Maritime Museum has done with the vast majority of Lake Champlain's shipwrecks. Its deep-water location and the probability that it contains human remains make management of the site a complicated matter. The sailing canal boats *O.J. Walker* and *General Butler*, however, are seasonally visited by hundreds of recreational divers. These vessels are part of the Lake Champlain Underwater Historic Preserve – a program that began in 1985 as a tool for giving recreational divers reasonable access to appropriate shipwreck sites. Of course, most of the public does not dive, so the Lake Champlain Maritime Museum was founded, in part to allow the public access to Lake Champlain's extraordinary shipwreck collection. As a museum, we are always looking for new and effective ways to share the shipwrecks and their stories. In the 1980s we built, launched and operated a Colonial era bateau (1758) and a replica of the *Philadelphia*, one of Benedict Arnold's gunboats at the Battle of Valcour Island (1776). On 3 July 2004 we launched a full-sized, working reproduction of an 1862-class sailing Lake Champlain canal boat. The new schooner, christened *Lois McClure,* will serve as an ambassador from her time and to the fragile and irreplaceable shipwrecks on the bottom of Lake Champlain.

Mapping the "Unsinkable" Titanic

GEORGE F. BASS

Many events in my career as a nautical archaeologist have resulted from a single piece of mail. It was a letter from Peter Throckmorton to the University of Pennsylvania Museum in 1959 that led to my even learning to dive. Forty-four years later, on 22 May 2003, another letter arrived, this one by e-mail from Captain Craig McLean, Director of the Office of Ocean Exploration for the National Oceanic and Atmospheric Administration (NOAA):

> "Hello George.
> "I have an opportunity for you, if I can tear you away from Turkey. NOAA's exploration program is using the Russian vessel *Keldysh* and the two *Mir* submersibles to visit some mid-Atlantic ridge areas for biological and geological inventory. Shortly thereafter, we are able to make some dives on *Titanic*….We will make a brief excursion for some photomosaic work….Would you like to join us and make a dive? Your views and expertise on the matter would render a respected voice to be heard as this subject further develops. Craig"

Below **For a brief few days, until sent to a watery grave two-and-a-half miles deep by an iceberg, RMS *Titanic* was the largest and most luxurious liner on the Atlantic Ocean.**

Above **At the very tip of the bow, one of** *Titanic*'s **spare anchors rests under the anchor crane, still secured to the deck. Rusticles on the railing were produced by iron-eating microbes.**

Anyone, nautical archaeologist or not, would jump at the opportunity of visiting the most famous shipwreck anywhere – and since I had designed the first method of making shipwreck photomosaics from a submersible back in 1964, I might be helpful. But I was hesitant. It was not just that the deepest I had ever been was 90 m (300 ft), and *Titanic* lies two-and-a-half miles – that's 12,460 ft or almost 4 km – beneath the North Atlantic. I'm a little superstitious. In 2003, after more than four decades of fieldwork, being responsible for tens of thousands of deep decompression dives, and dives in various types of experimental submersibles, I had just decided to end it, without announcement, to simply stop while I was ahead – the news item about an aging stuntman who was killed when making one last jump with his car, after announcing his plan to retire, has long stayed with me.

Why would I go to a place where rescue was out of the question if any piece of equipment failed? What if a spark started an electrical fire? Or my *Mir* became trapped by wreckage? The pressure on the submersible at that depth would be 3 tons per square inch! Small wonder that more people have been in outer space than have ever visited *Titanic*. In fact, more people have been to the top of Mount Everest in a single month than have ever seen first hand those spectacular remains.

I turned to the ultimate authorities: my family. In less than 24 hours my writer son, Gordon, e-mailed me in Turkey: "Come on, you HAVE to do it!" Alan, my younger son, said by telephone that I'd be crazy not to go. I assumed that my wife, Ann, would talk me out of it. I was wrong.

R/V Akademik Mstislav Keldysh

With no more excuses, I sailed out of St. John's, Newfoundland, on 20 June, aboard the Russian R/V *Akademik Mstislav Keldysh*, the world's largest research ship. Icebergs in the distance reminded me of why I was there.

I represented INA among a seven-person team headed by NOAA marine archaeologist Jeremy Weirich. Others were National Park Service archaeologist Larry Murphy, whose continuing study of the battleship *Arizona* at Pearl Harbor has made him especially knowledgeable about the long-term stability of iron hulls, and Drs. Roy Cullimore and Lori Johnston, microbiologists who specialize in the study of the microbes that eat iron and form, at *Titanic*'s depth, huge brown things like stalactites that were dubbed "rusticles" by Robert Ballard when he located the wreck. Both Roy and Lori were returning to *Titanic*, Lori for her fifth visit. Rounding out the team were NOAA's Laura Rear, who had taken care of the logistics of the mission, and Craig McLean himself, whose impressive background includes not only degrees in zoology and law, but two years as a professional helmet diver.

The *Keldysh* carries *Mir 1* and *Mir 2*, two of only four submersibles in the world capable of diving as deep as *Titanic*, the subs used by James Cameron in his epic film "Titanic." Each cost $20 million. They usually dive together, about an hour apart. No one said it explicitly, but I think part of the reason for this is safety, for one sub, with its manipulators, could help untangle the other should it become snared by cables or twisted metal.

Dr Anatoly Sagalevitch is the driving force behind *Keldysh* and the *Mirs*. Since the collapse of the Soviet Union, under which all three vessels were built, he has had to depend on private sources to fund their operation – indeed, to fund all of the

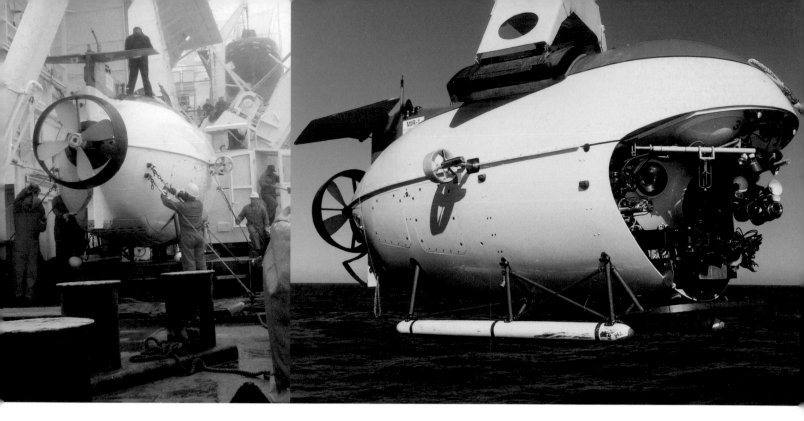

Above **The crew of R/V *Akademik Mstislav Keldysh* unloosen the restraining cables of *Mir 2* in preparation for the submersible's dive. The great protective hangar for the two *Mirs* has already been raised up and out of the way on its hinges.**

Above right **Mir 2 is lowered into the sea from the deck of R/V *Akademik Mstislav Keldysh*. Once in the water, it will be towed farther to sea by a launch before beginning its descent.**

Opposite above **During the dive, the two submersibles took turns at the widely separated parts of *Titanic*. Here, in this reconstruction painting, those in *Mir 2* map the bow section while those in *Mir 1*, in the distance, study rusticles at the stern.**

oceanographic research conducted from *Keldysh*. He thus often uses them for projects like the one I was on, or for filming, or even for taking paying passengers to *Titanic* for $36,000 a dive. I became highly impressed by Anatoly's entrepreneurship and his humanity.

On our first morning over the wreck, the crew of *Keldysh*, using GPS coordinates, dropped four transponders around *Titanic*. Every other day for the next ten days the *Mir*s dived and navigated with seeming ease within this "sonic box." I was scheduled to be on the last dive.

There were many books and videos about *Titanic* on board, so I spent the time before my dive becoming completely familiar with the story of the ship and what has happened to her since she was discovered. Early one morning I stood alone on deck, staring at the calm sea, thinking about the fact that one night in 1912, exactly at this place, over 1,500 people in life jackets were calling for help, drowning, or freezing to death.

Down in Mir 2

On the day of my dive, 29 June, I felt like an astronaut as I walked the corridor to the *Mir* laboratory in my blue, fireproof jump suit. Then, up the ladder, off with shoes, and down inside a steel sphere about 2 m (7 ft) in diameter.

Craig McLean had preceded me into *Mir 2*. I was followed by Victor Nischcheta, our Russian pilot. A technician closed the hatch, which would soon be held tight by mounting pressure, and we were attached to the ship's crane and lowered over the side, all 18 tons of us, barely swinging from side to side. We were blessed by smooth seas for the entire voyage, as today, when it was calm but foggy. The instant we hit the water, a Russian "cowboy" leapt from a Zodiac onto the top of the *Mir* to unhook us from the crane and hook us to a launch, which towed us clear of the *Keldysh*. We were

in a near dead calm, but I have seen films of these cowboys performing the same maneuver in large waves that washed completely over them as they held on for dear life like aquatic broncobusters.

Mir 1, with Anatoly Sagalevitch at the controls, had descended about an hour earlier. Now we began our two-and-a-half-hour descent. I glanced often at our depth gauge. Two miles down, Victor pulled out box lunches for the three of us. When we eventually reached 3,790 m (12,434 ft), the incredibly bright exterior lights went on, flooding the seabed. Almost immediately I spotted a large soup tureen, and then dozens or hundreds of wine bottles in the positions they had held in wooden cases

Below **INA's George Bass, Russian pilot Victor Nischcheta, and Captain Craig McLean, Director of the National Oceanic and Atmospheric Administration's Offioo of Ocean Exploration, assemble in front of *Mir 2* just before it takes them down to *Titanic*.**

nine decades ago, followed by a bathtub. I was moved emotionally when I saw a woman's lonely, high-topped shoe.

Our exact position within the four seabed transponders was being carefully monitored in the navigation room on *Keldysh*, which remained in contact with Victor over transceivers, so we knew that we would soon reach *Titanic*'s badly mangled stern. Once there, we began a four-hour program of videotaping the wreckage for a photomosaic that should serve as a database against which future damage from age, visitors, and remotely operated salvage equipment can be measured. Kneeling before a central port about 20 cm (8 in) in diameter, Victor operated the *Mir* with intense concentration, often glancing quickly at a compass to be sure we were on line. Craig, using coordinates from the sonic transponder "box" in which we operated, guided

Below left **Titanic**'s great bow remains an awe-inspiring sight, approached either from below or, as here, from above. Without the dangling rusticles, the railing would appear as new.
Below **A photomosaic shows Titanic's anchor crane extending up and over the bow. A spare anchor, still secured to the deck, rests at the crane's base, and the port anchor is seen in the lower right corner of the image.**
Bottom **Looking from port to starboard, this photomosaic of Titanic's bow depicts the aft portion of the forecastle where the forward mast had fallen back, collapsing over deck winches and the #1 hold.**

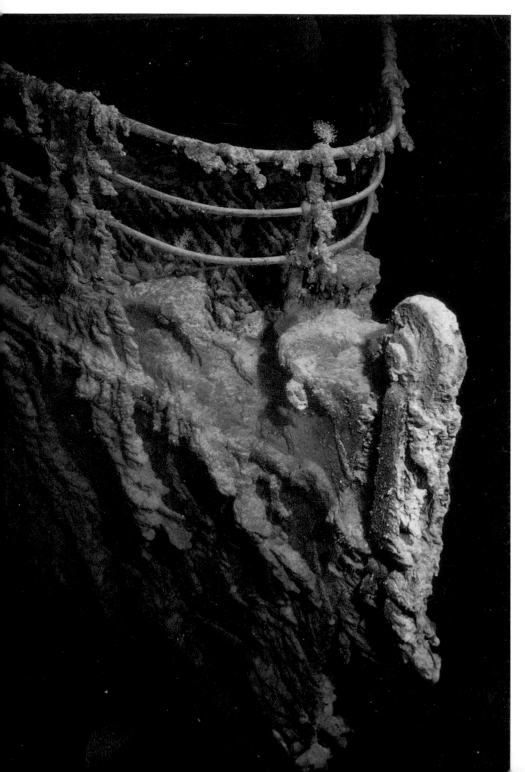

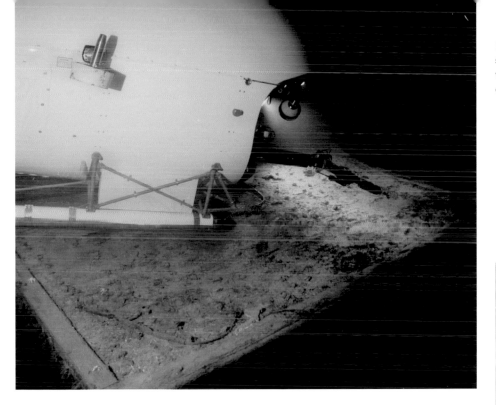

Above NOAA Captain Craig McLean, inside *Mir 2*, studies the submersible's position inside a "box" delineated by sonic transponders while directing the pilot to the starting point for another photographic pass over *Titanic*.

Victor to the starting point for each of the 16 parallel passes, and then, reading from a digital monitor, recorded on paper at timed intervals our exact position. Similarly, so that Victor would not be distracted by keeping track of too many gauges, Craig routinely read aloud our depth from another monitor, letting us know that we were staying exactly 3,783 m (12,411 ft) deep. Sometimes I relieved Craig by reading our depth aloud. At other times I lay on my stomach on my bench to follow our progress, occasionally photographing through my smaller, starboard port.

After nearly four hours, we saw a startling sight: traffic! Two-and-a-half miles down in the sea! *Mir 1*, with Lori Johnston and Jeremy Weirich inside, was coming to take our place at the stern. Although I often could not identify what I was seeing on the wreck, Roy and Lori must have had a field day studying the rusticles. They estimate, I believe, that the ship is disintegrating more quickly than previously supposed.

It was time for us to move about 600 m (2,000 ft) to *Titanic*'s better-preserved bow. The great ship broke into two immense pieces, which landed nearly half a mile apart. The vast debris field between the two halves of *Titanic* has been legally picked over by RMST Inc., which holds salvage rights to the ship, and which has raised and conserved several thousand artifacts that have been seen by millions of people. Still, many plates and other objects remain in this area. The salvors are forbidden by law to sell anything, I am told, or to take anything from inside the ship, itself.

14 April 1912

Then we arrived at the bow, which is magnificent, stunning – and unimaginably huge. More than 15 m (50 ft) of it are buried in the seabed into which the ship plowed with tremendous force when it landed, but its towering height remains awesome.

We rose slowly until we reached the railing. Here the ship is so well preserved I wondered if I would see Jack and Rose standing at the rail, with Jack proclaiming himself "King of the World." We soon began to move slowly over the seemingly solid

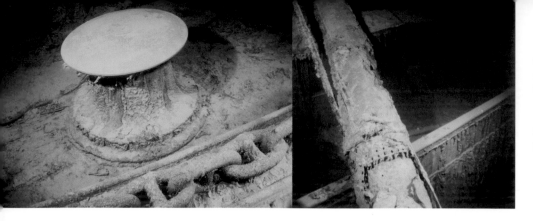

deck in controlled and carefully navigated passes, at a fixed depth, making a mosaic of the shipwreck from above with the submersible's external video camera. Deck winches looked as if they could be oiled and put back to work. I spotted a davit from which one of the far-too-few lifeboats was lowered.

We reached the mast, which has toppled backward. As we moved along its length, we saw clearly the opening through which lookout Frederick Fleet stepped out into the crow's nest from which, not long before midnight on 14 April 1912, he rang the warning bell three times and called down to the bridge those immortal words, "Iceberg, right ahead!" The crow's nest was still in place when Robert Ballard found the *Titanic* in 1985, but we saw no sign of it. There are rumors of illegal and clandestine salvors visiting the wreck during winter months, with remotely operated vehicles to remove more objects, but we do not know if the crow's nest has simply fallen.

On the bridge, First Officer William Murdock made a fatal mistake when he received Fleet's warning. He ordered the ship turned hard to port, which meant *Titanic* scraped the iceberg, tearing a long gash in her starboard side that allowed too many watertight compartments to flood. A head-on collision would not have been so devastating.

Below ***Titanic*'s bronze telemotor, on which the ship's wooden wheel was once mounted, still stands on the bridge where First Officer Murdock made his fatal mistake. Modern memorial plaques have been placed at its base by previous submersible visitors.**

The ship's brass telemotor, on which the great wooden wheel was mounted, stands as a silent reminder of the moment the helmsman spun it as far as he could. Memorial plaques have been placed at its base by past submersible visits.

But we did not linger. There was more work ahead. We began to make a video mosaic of the starboard side of this part of the wreck, often drifting with the current at a fixed depth. The lights of the submersible were so bright I could see from the top of the ship to the seabed far below, and could imagine passengers promenading just inside on some of the open-air decks. Most of the portholes still have their glass in place. Several were open. Did a passenger look out of that open window, nearly a century ago, to see what all the commotion was about?

As excited as we were by our dive, we knew that on a cold night just over 90 years before, more than 1,500 passengers and crew perished in this ship or in the sea around it. There were only 705 survivors. Stories of bravery and cowardice have become legend. It is true that all the members of the ship's band played until the end, and all perished. One of the objects raised by the salvors is a clarinet. It is true that Captain Smith went down with his ship, and it is true that Mrs Isador Straus, on being urged to climb into a lifeboat, returned to her husband's side, saying: "We have been living together for many years. Where you go, I go." When offered space in a lifeboat so he could accompany his wife, Straus refused, saying there were still women

Right The rusticle-framed window of an officer's cabin remains open, as if someone had just leaned out to see what was causing the commotion on board. Such features are identified from photographs of the *Titanic* before she sank.

Below A Russian "cowboy" rides *Mir 2* to attach a lifting cable so the sub can be raised back onto the deck of the R/V *Akademik Mstislav Keldysh* at the end of a long day.

to be saved. They were last seen sitting side by side in deck chairs. Benjamin Guggenheim and his valet went below and returned in their evening clothes, prepared, as Guggenheim said, to "go down like gentlemen."

Ascent

We had been in *Mir 2* for seven-and-a-half hours, with two-and-a-half hours of ascent still ahead. It was time to leave *Titanic*. Victor had been deep in concentration for every second during our mapping program. Now he could relax. As we started up, he offered Craig and me hot tea and biscuits. Later, in various positions, the three of us used the large plastic bottles that were under Craig's seat for their special purpose.

We came up after dark in a dense fog. After ten hours in the *Mir*, we flopped around for about half an hour more before we felt that we were being towed back to *Keldysh* by the launch. Soon the cowboy, balanced like a circus bareback rider, attached the crane's heavy lifting cable, which would bring us back on board *Keldysh*. Then he leapt back onto his Zodiac. We were quickly on deck and outside our *Mir*, with hugs all around (especially from Anatoly, who had preceded us up in *Mir 1*), followed by dinner that had been saved for Craig and me in the dining room. With most of the NOAA team around us, we toasted with Russian vodka our successful dives.

Then two full days back to St. Pierre (how many people know that there are two tiny, tiny French islands only a few miles south of Newfoundland?), an overnight stay, and on to St. John's by small charter jet.

On our way back from Turkey in August 2003, Ann and I visited Cobh, Ireland, *Titanic*'s last port of call – then called Queenstown – on the great ship's only voyage. In just one summer I had been to the beginning and end of one of the most famous ocean trips in history.

The Japanese Fleet in Truk Lagoon, Micronesia

JEREMY GREEN

Sapporo Maru

Built 1930, Japan
Sunk April 1944
Original use deep-sea fishing trawler
Wartime use auxiliary provisions storeship
Tonnage 361 tons
Casualties unknown

Following World War I, Japan was awarded German Micronesia, including the Truk Islands, and secured a mandate from the League of Nations following the Treaty of Versailles. In the inter-war years Japanese interest was to make the South Sea Islands profitable, and in the late 1930s the base at Truk was expanded with new airfields and military installations. By 1941, the Japanese, aware of the looming prospect of war with the United States, started to fortify the islands. After the outbreak of the war, the island maintained its strategic position, but by late 1943 the writing was on the wall that the Americans were coming.

Truk in World War II

In February 1944 two Catalina photo-reconnaissance aircraft overflew Truk and photographed the assembled Japanese fleet of over 60 vessels, including the fabled *Musashi* and *Yamato* battleships. The Americans had been planning a naval offensive against Truk, and this was an opportune moment. The ensuing operation, designated "Hailstone," was under the command of Pacific Fleet Commander Admiral Chester Nimitz, with Task Force 50 totalling over 53 vessels, including nine aircraft carriers able to send up over 500 combat aircraft that included fighters, bombers, and torpedo aircraft.

On 17 February the task force approached Truk undetected. The attack that followed caught the Japanese completely unaware. The first wave of fighter aircraft began what has been described as the greatest all-fighter-plane battle of history. The initial waves destroyed most of the Japanese air opposition. Then installations and

Below left **Marine reconnaissance photograph taken prior to the first attack on Truk. The photograph shows numerous warships and merchantmen at anchor. Etan Island is in the center with Dublon Island to the left and Fefan Island in the lower right.**

Below **Dublon Island during an attack on 17 February 1944 by aircraft from USS *Enterprise*. The crippled *Seiko Maru* is on fire and sinking at the center. To the right is the undamaged *Hokuyo Maru*. Two attacking aircraft can be seen above center.**

Right **Inside the Betty bomber lying in shallow water off Etan Island. The view looks forward toward the now missing cockpit, which was probably demolished in the crash. The aluminum fuselage is slowly corroding, as seen at the upper left.**

shipping were targeted. Luckily for the Japanese, the earlier reconnaissance aircraft had been spotted and some of the fleet had already escaped, but the Americans still found over 60 vessels within the lagoon and managed to sink 45 of them, including two light cruisers, four destroyers, and 26 naval and army auxiliaries, totalling over 220,000 tons. During the two-day operation, 270 aircraft were destroyed. A second strike, on 29 and 30 April, further reduced the effectiveness of Truk as a Japanese base. For the rest of the war Truk was effectively bypassed and neutralized, and a land-based invasion became unnecessary as Truk was no longer a threat. This was probably a relief to the Americans, as landing on islands with considerable elevation and heavily fortified gun emplacements would have been costly.

By October 1944, Truk was so irrelevant it was being used as a training area by the Allies to provide battle experience to new units; aircraft used the island for bombing exercises and fleets stood off to sea and bombarded the island as they passed on their way to Japan.

Side-Scan Sonar Survey

In late 2001, I was involved with a local documentary company to produce three television programs about the work of my Department of Maritime Archaeology at the Western Australian Maritime Museum. The series, called *Shipwreck Detectives*, was being produced by Ed Punchard, a colleague and former student of mine. We were having problems with a program about remote sensing, for the story simply was not interesting enough. Ed was wringing his hands and wondering aloud what else we might film. A few months earlier I had been asked by another old colleague, Bill Jeffery, if I could help with a project he was undertaking for the Federated States of Micronesia, providing a management plan for the ships and aircraft lost in Truk Lagoon. He wanted me to bring our side-scan sonar to accurately pinpoint known sites and to look for some missing sites, but there were money problems and it looked impossible for him.

I said to Ed: "How about Truk Lagoon?"

"Fantastic! When can we go?"

So in February 2002 we joined Bill Jeffery in Truk.

These sites are now a major tourist destination and the Government of the Federated States of Micronesia is concerned that they are properly managed and preserved. The objective of the survey was to relocate as many of the known wrecks as possible and produce detailed sonar images that could be placed on a GIS (Geographical Information System) plan of Chuuk, the modern name for Truk. Most of the sites are known to dive tour operators, but their precise locations are not recorded, nor are their orientations, sizes and conditions. For two weeks we steamed around the atoll locating sites and creating side-scan sonar images of the wrecks. With these images Bill was able to list and record all the sites known only anecdotally.

The Sapporo Maru

In addition Bill wanted us to find one of the last undiscovered shipwrecks in Truk Lagoon, the *Sapporo Maru*. Dan Bailey's definitive book *World War II Wrecks of the Truk Lagoon* provides a background to the vessel: "The *Sapporo Maru* had been built in 1930 as a trawler…[in] January 1944, the *Sapporo Maru* was attached to the 4th Fleet at Truk as part of the Replenishment Force and categorized as an Auxiliary Transport (provision ship) or Special Transport (provision)….Japanese sources indicated that the vessel went down north of Fefan Island….The wreck of the *Sapporo Maru* is one of the few that have not been located at Truk."

So the *Sapporo Maru* was not one of the great warships of Truk. It was an ordinary small supply vessel – but, at 361 tons, one of the last of the larger vessels yet to be found there.

We searched with side-scan for several days, confirming known vessels in the general area, but as with all searches there were hours of frustrating steaming up and down in a systematic search pattern over the area thought to contain the site. The survey for the *Sapporo Maru* was planned to end on 13 February. On the last day on the very last run I saw a target. It was worth going back to for re-examination. On the return run we obtained a stunning image of a vessel lying upright on a sandy seabed with reefs all around. Incredible! Examination of the sonar target showed that we had a vessel with two masts, a central bridge "island," and a length of about 115 m (377 ft). Not only was the *Sapporo Maru* 113 m (371 ft) long, according to Bailey's book, but his published image corresponded almost exactly to the sonar image. There was no doubt we had found the *Sapporo Maru*.

We returned to our base at Moen, one of the islands in the lagoon, where Dan Bailey was staying. We told him that we were pretty sure we had found the last of the big missing ships of Truk. He was delighted and we planned to visit the site the next day. Diving on a new site is always exciting, even if one is an archaeologist, and this site was no exception. I swam around the bridge, looked in the holds, and saw the engine, while making the basic measurements and photographs to confirm that this was indeed the *Sapporo Maru*. One of our team found the ship's bell. Bill was particularly pleased because he had a site that no one had dived on before and it would be possible to use the site, once we made its location public, as a measure of the impact that sport diving or "eco-tourism" had on these sites. It was a unique and fascinating opportunity. Little did we realize how soon the impact would occur! While we worked, some people in the area had been interested in what we were doing. "What are you looking for?" was the usual question, but others generally kept their

Above **Corioli Souter, Bill Jeffery, and Glen Dillon, left to right, lower the 70-kg (154-lb) side-scan sonar fish carefully into the water, always a tricky operation. Working with big iron wrecks also posed a problem: note the nose of the fish has hit some major objects.**

Below **The side-scan trace of the *Sapporo Maru* lying on a sandy seabed between two reefs. Clearly visible are two masts, the forepeak, the bridge, and the engine room and funnel. Because the sonar is linked to a GPS (global positioning system) it is possible to measure the size of the vessel and to accurately plot its position.**

Right **Inside the wheelhouse of the *Sapporo Maru* on the first dive to the site. The wood of the ship's wheel has rotted away, leaving just the boss that can be seen at center right.**

Below right **A recent picture of the *Sapporo Maru*'s bell that was removed from the site less than 24 hours after its discovery.**

distance. I was told later that on the day we dived on the site a local dive boat passed us, but it neither stopped nor aroused any particular interest.

The next day we advised the Government that we had found a new site, and invited the Governor to dive on it. On the same day we arranged for a team to revisit the site to further record it with photographs. To our surprise, the team returned with news that the ship's bell was missing – not 24 hours after the discovery! We were stunned. Who could have done such a thing? It was only then that someone remembered the boat passing nonchalantly by while we were diving on the site. With modern GPS (Global Positioning System) devices they could have returned to the site easily, in late evening or early morning, and removed the bell. Imagine our chagrin, having spent so much time searching for the site, to have the bell stolen so quickly. Should we not have dived on the site? Was the work worth it, with such an iconic item stolen in such a short time? These are unanswerable questions. It shows however, the very real problems of managing sites such as Truk, a place visited by over 6,000 divers every year. There are anecdotal stories of other World War II souvenirs being taken from the lagoon, and artifacts said to be from Truk are sometimes sold on online auction sites such as Ebay. It was a long time after the discovery of the *Sapporo Maru* that I heard from Dan Bailey that the bell had been removed by a guide from a local dive shop. He recovered the bell to prevent it from being "stolen" by unscrupulous divers, and it is now apparently kept under lock and key by the dive shop. This is not really the way heritage should be managed. All we know is that if the wrecks of Truk Lagoon are going to survive for future generations, some serious management plans are needed – and quickly.

Exploring D-Day Landing Craft: Normandy, France

BRETT PHANEUF

D-Day Landings

Date 6 June 1944
Number of ships c 5,000
Number of landing craft over 3,000
Number of men over 150,000
Number of vehicles 30,000
Number of "DD" tanks 128

D-Day – 6 June 1944 – marked the long-anticipated Allied invasion of Nazi-held Europe. Operation Overlord had begun the day before with Operation Neptune, the most massive naval action in the history of warfare, aptly described by Cornelius Ryan in his moving work, *The Longest Day*: "They came, rank after relentless rank, ten lanes wide, twenty miles across, five thousand ships of every description."

In addition to the 5,000 ships were as many as 8,000 support aircraft, ranging from fighter planes to bombers, gliders, and paratroop transports. Essentially, anything that could float or fly was pressed into service and sent across the English Channel.

My involvement with this moment in history began in 1997 when I was in France with Robert Neyland, Head of the US Naval Historical Center Underwater Archaeology Branch, to collect sonar images of a 19th-century American shipwreck. A weather delay gave me time to tour the American D-Day landing sectors. Standing at Point du Hoc, or on Utah and Omaha Beaches, I found it impossible not to wonder what remains of the invasion fleet lay beneath the waves. I began planning for a survey of the area in collaboration with the Naval Historical Center.

Project Neptune 2K

Although more than 50 years of historical research had been conducted on the landings, and although modern navigation charts mark numerous wrecks and obstructions, there had been no archaeological investigation to correlate underwater remains with the historical record. Faced with the continued loss of the

Left **INA team members prepare to launch the *Oceaneering* remotely operated vehicle offshore of Omaha Beach, May 2001.**

Above **Side-scan sonar image of a "landing barge" in an exceptional state of preservation located off Utah.**

Below **Side-scan sonar image of a "DD" Sherman tank from the 741st Tank Battalion lost off Omaha Beach on D-Day. The tank sits upright on the seafloor with its front facing right. Its circular turret lies on the seafloor above the tank, likely dislodged by a fisherman's trawl.**

archaeological remains of Operation Neptune to erosion and the clearing of navigational hazards, the Institute of Nautical Archaeology (INA) at Texas A&M University, in cooperation with Naval Historical Center's Underwater Archaeology Branch, embarked upon an underwater archaeological reconnaissance: Project Neptune 2K.

After noting on French nautical charts the shipwrecks and other obstructions littering the seafloor, we began work in 2000 with a side-scan sonar and magnetometer survey off Utah Beach to the west and Omaha Beach to the east, with Point du Hoc between, utilizing a boat provided by INA director George Robb. Initially we eschewed consultation with local wreck divers as our intent was to compile a comprehensive archaeological map not only of shipwrecks, but also of artificial harbor-works, vehicles, artillery, ordnance, personal effects, and defensive obstacles and structures, without bias from persons who were actively disturbing them. These last vestiges of the largest invasion fleet ever assembled warrant the legal protection provided by the French government, but more exploration and interpretation are needed so that diving tourists can visit these sites with the same reverence they would show at the American Cemetery on the bluff nearby.

We incorporated into a master database and map the remains of landing craft, artillery, ships, ordnance, and any other equipment. Analysis of the data provided me with more than 800 targets that deserved inspection by a remotely operated vehicle – an expensive proposition. Fortuitously, the Discovery Channel and the BBC offered to fund the 2001 field season in exchange for exclusive rights to film our efforts for a documentary (*D-Day: Beneath the Waves*).

Of concern was the difficulty of crafting a coherent story for viewers; we could not investigate all potential targets on the seafloor in 2001, or 2002, or even during the next decade.

However, during the course of data analysis, we recognized near the eastern end of the Omaha Beach survey area several clusters of what I identified as tanks, most probably from the 741st Tank Battalion. Cursory research revealed that many of the personnel who served in the amphibious, or "DD (Duplex Drive)" Sherman tanks of that battalion were alive and willing to talk with us. The focus of our research and the film quickly became their harrowing ordeal when they were launched into the sea from landing craft-tanks (LCTs). Of the 32 amphibious tanks, only two managed the "swim" to the beach; three were taken directly to shore by LCT and the rest were lost at sea.

"DD" Amphibious Tanks

Shifting the focus of Project Neptune 2K to the loss of the 741st Tank Battalion not only allowed for the telling of a single, coherent story, but also for an exacting analysis of what was responsible for the failure of the "DD" tanks on D-Day. It was at this point that INA opted to embark on a separate program of research from that of the Naval Historical Center.

In May 2001 the INA team returned to Normandy. With the assistance of Oceaneering International we deployed a remotely operated vehicle (ROV) offshore of Omaha Beach to collect detailed photographs of the objects believed to be tanks from the 741st Tank Battalion. After nearly a month, all of the sonar anomalies

believed to be tanks had been identified, and further research in Britain at the Tank Museum in Bovington, as well as in the United States, was required. In Bovington, that research included my learning to drive a World War II vintage Sherman tank! I had driven M60A3 main battle tanks in the National Guard and jumped at the chance, especially since my instructor was the very person, now in his 80s, who had trained many of the servicemen from the UK and US Armies in Sherman tank operation for Operation Overlord.

"DD" (Duplex Drive) Sherman tanks were invented by a Hungarian-born engineer, Nicholas Straussler, working for the British Ministry of Defence. A veteran of the 741st Tank Battalion described one to me as a "large canvas bucket with a 35-ton iron bottom." A large rubberized canvas skirt around the tank, reinforced with metal hoops, could be raised by means of 36 rubber bladders attached to the tank and inflated by compressed air cylinders. The commander stood behind the turret and steered by means of a tiller attached to dual propellers that were driven by the rear track idler sprocket, so while the tank "swam" the tracks were turning. Once the driver, always inside, felt the tank touch bottom, the screen could be lowered and the tank was ready for action. From the shore, "DD" tanks looked like small rubber boats that, by design, would attract little enemy fire. Once ashore, they were to assist infantry and take out pillboxes. But it was not to be. The tanks were not seaworthy and foundered in the rough weather of D-Day.

After my trip to Bovington, I traveled to the National D-Day Memorial in Bedford, Virginia, to meet with survivors of the 741st Tank Battalion both to discuss my findings and to ask many questions. Immediately thereafter I returned to France to finalize fieldwork with a set of dives at selected sites to capture high-resolution images of several "DD" tanks for use in the Discovery Channel/BBC film.

Loss of the 741st Tank Battalion on D-Day

On the morning of 6 June 1944 the flotilla carrying the 741st and 743rd Tank Battalions arrived off Omaha Beach and prepared for their assault. Orders were to

launch at 5:30 in the morning about 5,500 m (6,000 yds) offshore, in order to arrive ten minutes before the infantry from the 1st and 29th Divisions. In perfect weather the "DD" Tanks could have made it.

The Naval Commander of the flotilla of 16 LCTs, in consultation with the Army commander of the two battalions, decided not to launch but instead to take the "DD" tanks directly to shore. Unfortunately, the commanding officers of the LCTs carrying the tanks, or the commanding officer of the 741st Tank Battalion, either never received the message, or ignored it; whether the Army or Navy ordered the launching of the tanks is still a point of contention. LCT600 launched the first tank and it swam only a short distance before succumbing to the high seas. During that launch the LCT lurched violently, ripping the flotation screens still onboard, and so carried its three remaining tanks directly to shore. However, the rest of the LCTs commenced launching and the tanks foundered one by one, some swimming only a short distance, others lasting for some time before sinking.

The tanks sank mainly because of weather conditions. Flotation skirts collapsed under the strain from the waves, and bilge pumps inside the tanks were too small to keep up with the influx of seawater. In addition, with a tide running at nearly 3 knots, the LCTs were being swept east along the coast, as were the tanks once they were in the water. To counteract this the crews steered a heading that was increasingly westward, which put the waves on the "beam" of their amphibious tanks, the weakest part of the flotation skirts. Canvas collapsed and the tanks sank from sight. Fortunately, the crews were equipped with life rafts and underwater breathing apparatus and most escaped drowning.

Two of the floating tanks made it to shore. Interviews with the families of their commanders revealed that both were avid boaters and fishermen who had turned their tanks' "sterns" into the waves to "surf" in on the swell. Once ashore they linked up with the three tanks carried directly in by LCT600, and with elements of the 743rd Tank Battalion, and served with distinction assisting in clearing German defenses and opening exits from the beach.

Above **Two "DD" Sherman tanks from the 741st Tank Battalion that made it to shore. Of 32 "DDs," only 5 reached the beach, two swimming and three taken directly ashore by the landing craft tank that carried them.**

Below **Tank crewman demonstrating the Advanced Tank Escape Apparatus. Because the ATEA could not actually fit through a Sherman hatch, the driver was instructed to "ride" a sinking tank to the seafloor, remove the ATEA, exit the tank, re-don the ATEA, and then make an ascent. Remarkably, several men of the 741st Tank Battalion accomplished this feat on D-Day!**

Further Reading

Past and future adventures of the Institute of Nautical Archaeology have been and will be described in the *INA Quarterly* (formerly the *INA Newsletter*), published by the Institute of Nautical Archaeology, P.O. Drawer HG, College Station, Texas 77841-5137, USA.

INTRODUCTION AND GENERAL SOURCES

Bass, G.F., *Archaeology Beneath the Sea* (New York, 1975)
——*Archaeology Under Water* (London & New York, 1966)
——(ed.), *A History of Seafaring Based on Underwater Archaeology* (London & New York, 1972)
——"A Plea for Historical Particularism in Nautical Archaeology," in R.A. Gould (ed.), *Shipwreck Anthropology* (Albuquerque, 1983), 91–104.
——(ed.), *Ships and Shipwrecks of the Americas* (London & New York, 1988)
Cousteau, J.-Y. with F. Dumas, *The Silent World* (London, 1953; New York, 1956)
Delgado, J.P. (ed.), *Encyclopaedia of Underwater and Maritime Archaeology* (London & New Haven, 1997)
Diolé, P., *4000 Years Under the Sea, Excursions in Underwater Archaeology* (London, 1954)
Franzén, A., *The Warship Vasa* (Stockholm, 1960)
Gianfrotta, P.A. & P. Pomey, *Archeologia subacquea, storia, tecniche, scoperte e relitti* (Milan, 1981)
Oeland, G., "The H.L. *Hunley*: Secret Weapon of the Confederacy," *National Geographic* 200.7 (July 2002), 82–101
Pomey, P. (ed.), *La navigation dans l'antiquité* (Aix-en-Provence, 1997)
Steffy, J.R., *Wooden Ship Building and the Interpretation of Shipwrecks* (College Station, 1994)
Throckmorton, P., *The Sea Remembers: Shipwrecks and Archaeology* (London, 1987; New York, 1991)
Uceli, G., *Le navi di Nemi* (Rome, 1950)
Wheeler, R.C., W.A. Kenyon, A.R. Woolworth & D.A. Birk, *Voices from the Rapids: An Underwater Search for Fur Trade Artifacts 1960–1973* (St. Paul, 1975)

ŞEYTAN DERESI

Bass, G.F., *Archaeology Beneath the Sea* (New York, 1975), 207–221
——"The Wreck at Sheytan Deresi," *Oceans* 10.1 (1977), 34–39
——"Sheytan Deresi: Preliminary Report," *International Journal of Nautical Archaeology* 5 (1976), 293–303

ULUBURUN

G.F. Bass, "A Bronze Age Shipwreck at Ulu Burun (Kaş): 1984 Campaign," *American Journal of Archaeology* 90 (1986), 269–96
——"Oldest Known Shipwreck Reveals Splendors of the Bronze Age," *National Geographic* 172.6 (December 1987), 692–733
——, C. Pulak, D. Collon, and J. Weinstein, "The Bronze Age Shipwreck at Ulu Burun: 1986 Campaign," *American Journal of Archaeology* 93 (1989), 1–29
C. Pulak, "The Bronze Age Shipwreck at Ulu Burun, Turkey: 1985 Campaign," *American Journal of Archaeology* 92 (1988), 1–37
——"The Uluburun Hull Remains," in H.E. Tzalas (ed.), *Tropis VII. Proceedings of the 7th International Symposium on Ship Construction in Antiquity (27–31 August, Pylos)* (Athens 2002), 615–36
——"Evidence from the Uluburun Shipwreck for Cypriot Trade with the Aegean and Beyond," in L. Bonfante and V. Karageorghis (eds.), *Italy and Cyprus in Antiquity, 1500–450 BCE* (Nicosia, Cyprus 2001), 13–60
——"The Cargo of Copper and Tin Ingots from the Late Bronze Age Shipwreck at Uluburun," in Ünsal Yalçın (ed.), *International Symposium 'Anatolian Metal I'*, (Der Anschnitt, Bochum, Beiheft 13, 2000), 137–57
——"The Uluburun Shipwreck: An Overview," *International Journal of Nautical Archaeology* 27 (1998), 188–224

CAPE GELIDONYA

Bass, G.F., *Cape Gelidonya: A Bronze Age Shipwreck*, Transactions of the American Philosophical Society 57 no. 8 (Philadelphia, 1967)
——*Archaeology Beneath the Sea* (New York, 1975), 1–59
——"Beneath the Wine Dark Sea: Nautical Archaeology and the Phoenicians of the *Odyssey*, in J. Coleman & C. Walz (eds.), *Greeks and Barbarians: Essays on the Interactions between Greeks and Non-Greeks in Antiquity and the Consequences for Eurocentrism* (Ithaca, 1997), 71–101
——"Sailing Between the Aegean and the Orient in the Second Millennium BC," in E.H. Cline & D. Harris-Cline (eds.), *The Aegean and the Orient in the Second Millennium: Proceedings of the 50th Anniversary Symposium, Cincinnati, 18-20 April 1997* (Liège & Austin, 1998), 183–91
——"The Hull and Anchor of the Cape Gelidonya Ship," in Betancourt, P.P. *et al* (eds.), *Meletemata* (Liège & Austin, 1999), 21–24
Throckmorton P., "Oldest Known Shipwreck Yields Bronze Age Cargo," *National Geographic* 121.5 (May 1962), 696–711
——*The Lost Ships: An Adventure in Underwater Archaeology* (Boston & Toronto, 1964)

PABUÇ BURNU

Casson, L., *Ships and Seamanship in the Ancient World* (Princeton, 1971)
Cook, R.M. & P. Dupont, *East Greek Pottery* (London, 1998)
Horden, P. & N. Purcell, *The Corrupting Sea: A Study of Mediterranean History* (Oxford, 2000)
Mark, S., "*Odyssey* 5.234-53 and Homeric Ship Construction: A Reappraisal," *American Journal of Archaeology* 95 (1991), 441-445
Pomey, P. (ed.), *La navigation dans l'antiquité* (Aix-en-Provence, 1997)
Roebuck, C., *Ionian Trade and Colonization* (New York, 1959)

TEKTAŞ BURNU

Bass, G.F., "Golden Age Treasures," *National Geographic* 201.3 (March 2002), 102–17
Carlson, D.N., "The Classical Greek Shipwreck at Tektaş Burnu, Turkey," *American Journal of Archaeology* 107 (2003), 581–600
Green, J., S. Matthews & T. Turanlı, "Underwater Archaeological Surveying Using PhotoModeler, VirtualMapper: Different Applications for Different Problems," *International Journal of Nautical Archaeology* 31 (2002), 283–92
Nowak, T.J., "A Preliminary Report on *Ophthalmoi* from the Tektaş Burnu Shipwreck," *International Journal of Nautical Archaeology* 30 (2001), 86–94
Trethewey, K., "Lead Anchor Stock Cores from Tektaş Burnu, Turkey," *International Journal of Nautical Archaeology* 30 (2001), 109–14

KYRENIA

Berthold, R.M., *Rhodes in the Hellenistic Age* (Ithaca & London, 1984)
Katzev, M.L., "Resurrecting the Oldest Known Greek Ship", *National Geographic* 137.6 (June 1970), 840–57
——and Katzev, S.W., "Last Harbor for the Oldest Ship", *National Geographic* 146.5 (November 1974), 618–25
Ormerod, H.A., *Piracy in the Ancient World* (Chicago, 1967)
Steffy, J.R, *Wooden Shipbuilding and the Interpretation of Shipwrecks* (College Station, 1994), 42–59

LA SECCA DI CAPISTELLO

Frey, D., "Deepwater Archaeology," *Sea Frontiers* 25 no.4 (1979), 194–203
——, F.D. Hentschel & D.H. Keith, "Deepwater Archaeology. The Capistello Wreck Excavation, Lipari, Aeolian Islands," *International Journal of Nautical Archaeology and Underwater Exploration* 7 (1978), 279–300
Keith, D.H. & D.A. Frey, "Saturation Diving in Nautical Archaeology," *Archaeology* 32 no. 4 (1979), 24–33

SERÇE LIMANI HELLENISTIC WRECK

C. Pulak & R. F. Townsend, "The Hellenistic Shipwreck at Serçe Limanı, Turkey: Preliminary Report," *American Journal of Archaeology* 91 (1987), 31–57

SEA OF GALILEE BOAT

Wachsmann, S. "The Galilee Boat: 2,000-Year-Old Hull Recovered Intact," *Biblical Archaeology Review* 14 no. 5 (1988), 18–33

——, et al., *The Excavation of an Ancient Boat in the Sea of Galilee (Lake Kinneret),* 'Atiqot 19, English Series (Jerusalem, 1990)

——*The Sea of Galilee Boat: An Extraordinary 2000 Year Old Discovery* (New York & London, 1995)

YASSIADA 7TH-CENTURY WRECK

Bass, G.F. & F.H. van Doorninck Jr (eds.), *Yassi Ada, vol. 1: A Seventh-Century Byzantine Shipwreck* (College Station, 1982)

Pevny, T., "Shipbuilding Traditions: Building the Yassıada Exhibit," *INA Quarterly* 24 no.3 (1997), 4–11

van Alfen, P.G., "New Light on the 7th-c. Yassı Ada Shipwreck: Capacities and Standard Sizes of LRA1 Amphoras," *Journal of Roman Archaeology* 9 (1996), 189–213

van Doorninck, F.H. Jr, "The Cargo Amphoras on the 7th Century Yassi Ada and 11th Century Serçe Limanı Shipwrecks: Two Examples of a Reuse of Byzantine Amphoras as Transport Jars," in V. Déroche & J.-M. Spieser (eds.), *Recherches sur la céramique byzantine,* Bulletin de Correspondance Hellénique Supplément 18 (Paris, 1989), 247–57

TANTURA LAGOON

Kahanov, Y., "The Byzantine Shipwreck (Tantura A) in the Tantura Lagoon, Israel: Hull Construction Report," in *Tropis VI. Sixth International Symposium on Ship Construction in Antiquity (Athens, 28–30 August 1996)* (Athens, 2001), 265–71

——"The Tantura B Shipwreck. Tantura Lagoon, Israel: Preliminary Hull Construction Report," in J. Litwin (ed.), *Down the River to the Sea,* Proceedings of the Eighth International Symposium on Boat and Ship Archaeology, Gdansk 1997 (Gdansk, 2000), 151–54

Royal, J. & Y. Kahanov, "An Arab Period Merchant Vessel at Tantura Lagoon, Israel," *International Journal of Nautical Archaeology* 29 (2000), 151–53

Wachsmann, S., "Technology Before its Time: A Byzantine Shipwreck from Tantura Lagoon," *The Explorers Journal* 74 no. 1 (1996), 19–23

——and K. Raveh, "A Concise Nautical History of Dor/Tantura," *International Journal of Nautical Archaeology* 13 (1984), 223–41

BOZBURUN

Hocker, F.M., "Cargo Stowage, Jettison and Wreck Formation Processes: Information on Middle Byzantine Commerce from the Ninth Century Bozburun Shipwreck," *Archeologia delle acque* I no. 2 (1999), 28–38

Treadgold, W., *The Byzantine Revival 780–842* (Stanford, California, 1988)

SERÇE LIMANI 11TH-CENTURY WRECK

Bass, G.F., "The Nature of the Serçe Limani Glass," *Journal of Glass Studies* 26 (1984), 64–9.

——, S.D. Matthews, J.R. Steffy, & F.H. van Doorninck Jr, *Serçe Limanı: An Eleventh-Century Shipwreck* (College Station, 2004)

Lledó, B., "Mold Siblings in the 11th-Century Cullet from Serçe Limanı," *Journal of Glass Studies* 39 (1997), 43–55

van Doorninck, F.H. Jr, "The Medieval Shipwreck at Serçe Limani: An Early 11th-Century Fatimid-Byzantine Commercial Voyage," *Graeco-Arabica* 4 (1991), 45–52

——"The Byzantine Ship at Serçe Limanı: An Example of Small-Scale Maritime Commerce with Fatimid Syria in the Early Eleventh Century," in R. Macrides (ed.), *Travel in the Byzantine World* (Aldershot and Burlington, 2002), 137–48

Steffy, J.R., *Wooden Ship Building and the Interpretation of Shipwrecks* (College Station, 1994), 85–91

ÇAMALTI BURNU

Günsenin, N., "From Ganos to Serçe Limani: Social and Economic Activities in the Propontis during Medieval Times, Illuminated by Recent Archaeological and Historical Discoveries," *The INA Quarterly* 26 no. 3 (1999), 18–23

——"L'épave de Çamaltı Burnu I (île de Marmara, Proconnèse): résultats des anneés 1998–2000," *Anatolia Antiqua* 9 (2001), 117–33

——"L'épave de Çamaltı Burnu I (île de Marmara, Proconnèse): résultats des anneés 2001–2002," *Anatolia Antiqua* 11 (2003), 361–76

——"Underwater Archaeological Research in the Sea of Marmara," in T. Akal, R.D. Ballard, & G.F. Bass (eds.), *The Application of Recent Advances in Underwater Detection and Survey Techniques to Underwater Archaeology* (Istanbul, 2004), 31–38

For the ongoing project please refer to Nergis Günsenin's website: www.nautarch.org

BLACK SEA DEEP-WATER PROJECT

Ballard, R.D. & W. Hively, *The Eternal Darkness: A Personal History of Deep-Sea Exploration* (Princeton, 2000)

——"Deep Black Sea," *National Geographic* 199.5 (May 2001), 52–69

——, et al., "Deepwater Archaeology of the Black Sea: The 2000 Season at Sinop, Turkey," *American Journal of Archaeology* 105 (2001), 607–23

De Jonge, P., "Being Bob Ballard," *National Geographic* 205.5 (May 2004), 112–29

Ward, C. & R.D. Ballard, "Black Sea Shipwreck Survey 2000," *International Journal of Nautical Archaeology* 33 (2004), 2–13

SHINAN WRECK

Green, J., "The Shinan Excavation, Korea: An Interim Report on the Hull Structure," *International Journal of Nautical Archaeology* 12 (1983), 293–301

——& Z.G. Kim, "The Shinan and Wando Sites, Korea: Further Information," *International Journal of Nautical Archaeology* 18 (1989), 33–41

Keith, D.H., "A Fourteenth-Century Cargo Makes Port at Last," *National Geographic* 156.2 (August 1979), 230–43

——"A Fourteenth Century Shipwreck at Sinan-gun," *Archaeology* 33 no. 2 (1980), 33–43

——& C.J. Buys, "New Light on Medieval Chinese Seagoing Ship Construction," *International Journal of Nautical Archaeology* 10 (1981), 119–32

ALMERE COG

Hocker, F.M., "Cogge en Coggeschip: Late Trends in Cog Development," in R. Reinders (ed.), *Bouwtraditie en Scheepstype* (Groningen, 1991), 25–32

——"Bottom-Based Shipbuilding in Northwestern Europe," in F.M. Hocker and C. Ward (eds.), *The Philosophy of Shipbuilding. Conceptual Approaches to the Study of Wooden Ships* (College Station, 2004), 65–93

——& K. Vlierman, *A Small Cog Wrecked on the Zuiderzee in the Early Fifteenth Century.* NISA Excavation Report 19/Flevobericht 408 (Lelystad, 1997)

KO SI CHANG

Green, J.N., "Maritime Archaeology in Southeast and East Asia," *Antiquity* 64 (1990), 347–63

——& R.Harper, "The Ko Si Chang Excavation Report 1983," *Bulletin of the Australian Institute for Maritime Archaeology* 7. 2 (1983), 9–37

——, R. Harper & V. Intakosi, "The Ko Si Chang One Shipwreck Excavation 1983–1985," *International Journal of Nautical Archaeology* 15 (1986), 105–22

——*The Maritime Archaeology of Shipwrecks and Ceramics in Southeast Asia and the Ko Si Chang Three Shipwreck Excavation,* Institute for Maritime Archaeology, Special Publication No. 4 (Fremantle, 1987)

——, R. Harper & S. Prishanchittara, *The Excavation of the Ko Kradat Wreck Site, Thailand 1979–1980*, Western Australian Museum Special Publication (Fremantle, 1981)

YASSIADA OTTOMAN WRECK

Beeching, J., *The Galleys at Lepanto* (New York, 1982)

Brummett, P., *Ottoman Seapower and Levantine Diplomacy in the Age of Discovery* (New York, 1994)

"SHIP IN A HAY FIELD", ZUIDERSEE

McLaughlin-Neyland, K. & R.S. Neyland, *Two Prams Wrecked on the Zuiderzee in the Late Eighteenth-Century*, Nederlands Instituut voor Scheeps- en onderwaterArcheologie Reports 15 and 16 (Lelystad, 1993)

Neyland, R.S., "The Preliminary Hull Analysis of Two Eighteenth-Century Dutch Prams", in J.C. Broadwater, (ed.), *Underwater Archaeology Proceedings from the Society for Historical Archaeology Conference, Richmond* (Richmond, Virginia, 1991), 111–4

—— & B. Schröder, *A Late Seventeenth Century Dutch Freighter Wrecked on the Zuiderzee*, Nederlands Instituut voor Scheeps- en onderwaterArcheologie Report 20 (Lelystad, 1996)

NOSSA SENHORA DOS MÁRTIRES

Afonso, S.L. (ed.), *Nossa Senhora dos Mártires: The Last Voyage* (Lisbon, 1998)

Castro, F., "The Remains of a Portuguese Indiaman at Tagus Mouth, Lisbon, Portugal (Nossa Senhora dos Mártires, 1606?)" in Alves, F. (ed.), *Proceedings of the International Symposium "Archaeology of Medieval and Modern Ships of Iberian-Atlantic Tradition", Lisbon, 1998* (Lisbon, 2001), 381–404

——"The Pepper Wreck", *Archaeology* (March/April 2003), 30–35

—— "The Pepper Wreck", *International Journal of Nautical Archaeology* 32 (2003), 6–23

——*The Pepper Wreck* (College Station, 2005)

——"Rigging the Pepper Wreck. Part I: Masts and Yards", *International Journal of Nautical Archaeology* 34 (2005), 112–124

MONTE CRISTI PIPE WRECK

De Roever, M., "The Fort Orange 'EB' Pipe Bowls: An Investigation of the Origin of American Objects in Dutch Seventeenth-Century Documents," in *New World Dutch Studies: Dutch Arts and Culture in Colonial America 1609–1776* (Albany Institute of History and Art, 1987)

Duco, D.H., "*De Kleipijp in de Zeentiende Eeuwse Nederlanden* (The Clay Pipe in Seventeenth-Century Netherlands)," in P. Davey (ed.), *The Archaeology of the Clay Tobacco Pipe V, Europe* (BAR International Series, 1981)

Hall, J.L., *A Seventeenth-Century Northern European Merchant Shipwreck in Monte Cristi Bay, Dominican Republic* (unpublished Ph.D. dissertation, Texas A&M University, 1996)

Lessman, A.W., *The Rhenish Stoneware From the Monte Cristi Shipwreck, Dominican Republic* (unpublished M.A. thesis, Texas A&M University, 1997)

LA BELLE

Arnold, J.B. III, "Magnetometer Survey of La Salle's Ship the *Belle*," *International Journal of Nautical Archaeology* 25 (1996), 243–49

——"The Texas Historical Commission's Underwater Archaeological Survey of 1995 and the Preliminary Report on the *Belle*, La Salle's Shipwreck of 1686," *Historical Archaeology* 30 (1996), 66–87

Bruseth, J.E., T. S. Turner, M.P. Kelsey, & R.B. Hutchison, *From A Watery Grave: The Discovery And Excavation Of La Salle's Shipwreck*, La Belle (College Station, Texas, 2005)

Weddle, Robert S., *The Wreck of the Belle, the Ruin of La Salle* (College Station, Texas, 2001)

PORT ROYAL

Donachie, M.J., *Household Ceramics at Port Royal, Jamaica, 1655–1692*, BAR International Series 1195 (Oxford, 2003)

Fox, G.L., *The Kaolin Clay Tobacco Pipe Collection from Port Royal, Jamaica.* BAR International Series 809 (Oxford, 1999)

Hamilton, D.L., "Simon Benning, Pewterer of Port Royal," in B.J. Little (ed.), *Text-Aided Archaeology* (Boca Raton, 1992), 39–53

——"The City Under the Sea," in *Science Year, 1986*, The World Book Science Annual (Chicago, 1986), 92–109

——"Port Royal Revisited," in C.R. Cummings (ed.), *Underwater Archaeology: The Proceedings of the Fourteenth Conference on Underwater Archaeology* (San Marino, California, 1986), 73–81

——"Preliminary Report on the Archaeological Investigations of the Submerged Remains of Port Royal, Jamaica, 1981–1982," *The International Journal of Nautical Archaeology and Underwater Exploration* 13 no. 1 (1984), 11–25

——and R. Woodward, "A Sunken 17th-Century City: Port Royal, Jamaica," *Archaeology* 37 no. 1 (1984), 38–45

Link, M.C., "Exploring the Drowned City of Port Royal," *National Geographic* 117.2 (1960), 151–182

Marx, R.F., *Pirate Port* (Cleveland, 1967)

——*Port Royal Rediscovered* (New York, 1973)

Pawson, M. & D. Buisseret, *Port Royal, Jamaica* (Kingston, Jamaica, 2000)

Smith, W.C., *The Final Analysis of Weights from Port Royal, Jamaica*, BAR International Series 675 (Oxford, 1997)

SANTO ANTONIO DE TANNA

Boxer, C. R. & C. de Azevedo, *Fort Jesus and the Portuguese in Mombasa* (London, 1960)

Kirkman, J.S., *Fort Jesus: A Portuguese Fortress on the East African Coast* (Oxford, 1974)

——*Men and Monuments on the East African Coast* (London, 1964)

——"A Portuguese Wreck off Mombasa," *International Journal of Nautical Archaeology* 1 (1972), 153–57

Piercy, R.C.M., "Mombasa Wreck Excavation Reports" *International Journal of Nautical Archaeology* 6 (1977), 331–47; 7 (1978), 301–19; 8 (1979), 303–09; 10 (1981), 109–18

Sassoon, H., "Ceramics from the Wreck of a Portuguese Ship at Mombasa," *Azania* 16 (1981), 98–130

GREAT BASSES REEF

Clarke, A.C., *The Treasure of the Great Reef* (rev. ed., New York, 1974)

Green, J.N., *The Australian-Sri-Lanka-Netherlands Galle Harbour Project 1992–1998*, Report of Maritime Archaeology, Western Australian Maritime Museum, No. 1 (Fremantle, 1998)

——and S. Devendra, "Interim Report on the Joint Sri Lanka–Australian Maritime Archaeology Training and Research Programme, 1992–3," *International Journal of Nautical Archaeology* 22 (1993), 331–43

SADANA ISLAND, EGYPT

Krahl, R. & J. Ayers (eds.), *Chinese Ceramics in the Topkapi Saray Museum, Istanbul III, Qing Dynasty Porcelains* (London, 1986)

Niebuhr, C., *Travels through Arabia, and Other Countries in the East, Performed by M. Niebuhr*, I & II, translated by R. Heron (Reading, 1994 reprint of 1792 edition)

Panzac, D., "International and Domestic Maritime Trade in the Ottoman Empire During the 18th Century," *International Journal of Middle East Studies* 24 (1992), 189–206

Pearson, M.N., Pious Passengers: The Haj in Earlier Times (New Delhi, 1994)

Raban, A., "The Shipwreck off Sharm-el-Sheikh," *Archaeology*, 24 no. 2 (1971), 146–55

Tuchscherer, M., "Production et commerce du café en Mer Rouge au XVIe siècle," in M. Tuchscherer (ed.), *Le Café avant l'ère des plantations coloniales: espaces, réseaux, sociétés (XVe-XVIIIe siécle)* (Cairo, 2001), 69–90

Ward, C., "The Sadana Island Shipwreck," in U. Baram & L. Carroll (eds.), *A Historical Archaeology of the Ottoman Empire* (New York 2000), 185–202

——"The Sadana Island Shipwreck: An Eighteenth-Century AD Merchantman off the Red Sea Coast of Egypt," *World Archaeology* 32 (2001), 371–85

CLYDESDALE PLANTATION VESSEL

Amer, C.F. & F.M. Hocker, "A Comparative Analysis of Three Sailing Merchant Vessels From the Carolina Coast," in W.C. Fleetwood, Jr, *Tidecraft: The Boats of South Carolina, Georgia and Northeastern Florida, 1550–1950* (Tybee Island, Georgia, 1995), 295–303

Footner, G.M., *Tidewater Triumph: The Development and World-Wide Success of the Chesapeake Bay Pilot Schooner* (Mystic Seaport Museum, 1998)

Hocker, F.M., "The Clydesdale Plantation Vessel Project: 1992 Field Report," *INA Quarterly* 19 no. 4 (1992), 12–16

Smith, J.F., *Slavery and Rice Culture in Low Country Georgia 1750–1860* (Knoxville, 1985)

DEFENCE

Allen, G., *Naval History in the Revolution*, 2 vols. (New York, 1962)

Leamon, J.S., *Revolution Downeast: The War For Independence in Maine* (Amherst, 1993)

Switzer, D.C., "Nautical Archaeology in Penobscot Bay: The Revolutionary War Privateer *Defence*," in C. Symonds (ed.), *Aspects of Naval History* (Annapolis, 1981), 90–101

——"The Excavation of the Privateer *Defence*," Symposium on the Archaeology of the Revolutionary War Period, *Northeast Historical Archaeology* 12 (1983), 43–50

——"Excavations of the Wreck of the Privateer *Defence*," in W. Swanson (ed.), *National Geographic Society Research Reports* 18 (1983), 719–31

——"The *Defence* Project," in M. Bound (ed.), *The Archaeology of the Warship* (Ostwestry, 1985), 183–91

——with B. Ford, *Underwater Dig: The Excavation of a Revolutionary War Privateer* (New York, 1982)

BETSY

Broadwater, J.D., "Secrets of a Yorktown Shipwreck," *National Geographic* 173.6 (June 1988), 804–23

——"Shipwreck in a Swimming Pool: An Assessment of the Methodology and Technology Utilized on the Yorktown Shipwreck Archaeological Project," in J.B. Arnold, III (ed.), *Historical Archaeology* 26 no. 4 (1992), 36–46

——"In the Shadow of Wooden Walls: Naval Transports During the American War of Independence," in M. Bound (ed.), *The Archaeology of Ships of War* (Oswestry, UK, 1995)

——, R.M. Adams, & M.A. Renner, "The Yorktown Shipwreck Archaeological Project; An Interim Report on the Excavation of Shipwreck 44YO88," *The International Journal of Nautical Archaeology and Underwater Exploration* 14 (1985), 301–14

Johnston, P.F., J.O. Sands, & J.R. Steffy, "The Cornwallis Cave Shipwreck, Yorktown, Virginia," *The International Journal of Nautical Archaeology and Underwater Exploration* 7 (1978), 205–26

Sands, J.O., *Yorktown's Captive Fleet* (Charlottesville, VA, 1983)

WRECK OF THE TEN SAIL

Leshikar, M.E., *The 1794 Wreck of the Ten Sail, Cayman Islands, British West Indies: A Historical Study and Archaeological Survey.* Ph.D. dissertation, Texas A&M University, 1993 (University Microfilms, Ann Arbor, Michigan)

Leshikar-Denton, M.E., *Our Islands' Past, Vol. 2, The Wreck of the Ten Sails* (Grand Cayman, 1994)

——"Caribbean, Cayman Islands, and Ten Sail," in J.P. Delgado (ed.), *Encyclopaedia of Underwater and Maritime Archaeology* (London, 1997), 86–9

——"Problems and Progress in the Caribbean," in C. Ruppé, & J. Barstad (eds.), *International Handbook of Underwater Archaeology* (New York, 2002), 279–98

Smith, R.C., *The Maritime Heritage of the Cayman Islands* (Gainesville, 2000)

CLEOPATRA'S BARGE

Crowninshield, F.B., *The Story of George Crowninshield's Yacht* Cleopatra's Barge *on a Voyage of Pleasure to the Western Islands and the Mediterranean 1816–1817* (Boston, 1913)

Ferguson, D.L., Cleopatra's Barge: *The Crowninshield Story* (Boston, 1976)

Johnston, P. F., "Preliminary Report on the 1998 Excavations of the 1824 Wreck of the Royal Hawaiian Yacht *Ha'aheo o Hawaii* (ex-*Cleopatra's Barge*)", in A.A. Askins and M.W. Russell (eds.), *Underwater Archaeology 1999* (Tucson: Society for Historical Archaeology, 1999), 107–114

HORSE FERRY

Crisman, K.J. & A.B. Cohn, *When Horses Walked on Water: Horse-Powered Ferries in Nineteenth-Century America* (Washington and London, 1998)

Shomette, D., "Heyday of the Horse Ferry," *National Geographic* 176, no. 4 (October, 1989), 548–556

HEROINE

Bates, A.L., *The Western Rivers Steamboat Cyclopedium* (Leonia, NJ, 1968)

Hunter, L.C., *Steamboats on Western Rivers, An Economic and Technological History* (New York, 1969)

Kane, A.I., *The Western River Steamboat* (College Station, 2004)

DENBIGH

Arnold, J. B., T.J. Oertling & A.W. Hall, "The Denbigh Project: Initial Observations on a Civil War Blockade-Runner and its Wreck-Site," *International Journal of Nautical Archaeology* 28 (1999), 126–44

——"The Denbigh Project: Excavation of a Civil War Blockade-Runner," *International Journal of Nautical Archaeology* 30 (2001), 231–49

Griffiths, D., "Marine Engineering Development in the 19th Century," in R. Gardiner (ed.), The Advent of Steam: The Merchant Steamship Before 1900 (London, 1993)

Watson, W., *The Civil War Adventures of a Blockade Runner* (College Station, 2001)

Wise, S., *Lifeline of the Confederacy: Blockade Running during the Civil War* (Columbia, SC, 1988)

LAKE CHAMPLAIN SAILING CANAL BOATS

Cohn, A.B., *Lake Champlain's Sailing Canal Boat: An Illustrated Journey From Burlington Bay to the Hudson River* (Lake Champlain Maritime Museum, 2003)

——& M.M. True, "The Wreck of the General Butler and the Mystery of Lake Champlain's Sailing Canal Boats," *Vermont History* 60 no. 1 (1992), 29–45

TITANIC

Ballard, R.D., *The Discovery of the Titanic* (Toronto, 1987)

Lord, W., *A Night to Remember* (New York, 1955)

Lynch, D & K, Marschall, *Ghosts of the Abyss: A Journey into the Heart of the Titanic* (Toronto, 2003)

Wels, S., *Titanic: Legacy of the World's Greatest Ocean Liner* (Alexandria, Virginia, 1997)

Winocour, J. (ed.), *The Story of the Titanic as Told by its Survivors* (New York, 1960)

TRUK LAGOON

Bailey, D.E., *World War II Wrecks of the Truk Lagoon* (Redding, California, 2000)

D-DAY LANDINGS

Harris, G., *Cross Channel Attack* (1951)

Hunnicutt, R.P., *Sherman: History of the American Medium Tank* (1994)

Lewis, A., *Omaha Beach, A Flawed Victory* (2001)

Messenger, C., *The D-Day Atlas: Anatomy of the Normandy Campaign* (London & New York, 2004)

Morison, S.E., *History of the United States Naval Operations in World War II, volume XI: The Invasion of France and Germany, 1944-1945* (Boston, 1957)

Ryan, C., *The Longest Day: June 6, 1944* (New York, 1959)

Winser, J., *The D-Day Ships – Neptune* (Kendal, England, 1994)

Acknowledgments and Sponsors

When great discoveries are made, archaeologists bask in the limelight. But equally important are those who pay for the archaeologists' research. Without the generous but modest Directors of INA, little in this book could have occurred. Those on the Board who contributed substantially and annually, a few for only one or two years, but most for decades, are:

Oren E. Atkins, Oŷuz Aydemir, John H. Baird, Joe Ballew, George F. Bass, Harry W. Bass Jr, Richard D. Bass, Duncan Boeckman, Edward O. Boshell Jr, Elizabeth L. Bruni, Allan Campbell, John Cassils, Charles Collins, Gregory M. Cook, John Brown Cook, Marian Miner Cook, Harlan Crow, William C. Culp, Frank Darden, Lucy Darden, Thomas F. Darden, John De Lapa, Claude Duthuit, Harrison Eiteljorg II, Danielle J. Feeney, Donald G. Geddes III, Sumner Gerard, Nixon Griffis, Harry C. Kahn II, Selçuk Kolay, David C. Langworthy, Norma Langworthy, Francine LeFrak-Friedberg, Samuel J. Le Frak, Frederick R. Mayer, Charles McWhirter, Alex G. Nason, George E. Robb Jr, W.F. Searle Jr, Lynn Baird Shaw, J. Richard Steffy, William T. Sturgis, Frederick H. van Doorninck Jr, Peter M. Way, Garry A. Weber, Elizabeth A. Whitehead, Martin A. Wilcox, and George O. Yamini.

Because he was the first to make a pledge of financial support, when INA was more dream than reality, I dedicate this book to Jack W. Kelley and to his fellow Tulsa, Oklahoma, businessmen who joined him on the Board of Directors: John A. Brock, Ronnie Chamness, Robert E. Lorton, L. Francis Rooney, Ray H. Siegfried II, T. Hastings Siegfried, Richard A. Williford, and Lew O. Ward from nearby Enid.

INA Associate Directors, who also contribute annually, have included Raynette Boshell, Nicholas Griffis, Robin P. Hartmann, Faith D. Hentschel, Susan Katzev, William C. Klein, George Lodge, Thomas McCasland Jr, Dana F. McGinnis, Michael Plank, Molly Reily, Betsey Boshell Todd, Casidy Ward, William Ward, and Robyn Woodward.

Those who have endowed professorships or fellowships in INA or the affiliated Texas A&M University Nautical Archaeology Program include the Abell-Hanger Foundation, John H. Baird, Marian Miner Cook, Donald G. Geddes III, Frederick Mayer, Meadows Foundation, Ray H. Siegfried II, Mary Ausplund Tooze, and George O. Yamini.

And there are those whose generous patronage for specific or general purposes has meant so much to the Institute over the years: Archaeological Institute of America, Fred B. Aurin, Edward Bader, Toni & Maria Pia Bassani, Baroline & Richard Bienia, Mimi & Gerald Branower, Ron Bural, Joy Campanaro, Frederick Campbell, Stanley Chase, J.E.R. Chilton, Peter Clark, Anna & Oliver Colburn, Charles W. Consolvo, Donna & Bob Dales, P.S. de Beaumont, Maurice Duca, Bruce Dunlevie, Cynthia & James Eiseman, Roger H. Gesswein Jr, Griffis Foundation, Theodor Halpern, Chatten Hayes, Michael Hitchcock, Institute for Aegean Prehistory, Jean B. James, Erik Jonsson, the Joukowsky Family, Norma & Rubin Kershaw, Richard MacDonald, Hillary Magowan, Mark Mathesen, Roy Matthews, Anna Maguerite McCann, John Merwin, Drew Morris, Marjorie & Isaac A. Morris, Nason Foundation, National Endowment for the Humanities, Ernestine O'Connell, Jenniffer & David Perlman, Alice & Howard Rankin, Leon Riebman, Sanford Robertson, Margaret Rogers, Mary & Richard Rosenberg, Robert Rubenstein, Billings Ruddock, L.J. Skaggs and Mary C. Skaggs Foundation, Peter Skinner, Patricia Stephens, Ellie & John Stern, Stephen Susman, Hazel & Ronald Vandehey, Shelby White & Leon Levy, James Wikert, the Northwest Friends of INA in Portland, Oregon, anonymous donors, and all INA members.

MAJOR PROJECT SPONSORS:
Abbreviations: NEH: National Endowment for the Humanities; NGS: National Geographic Society; NSF: National Science Foundation; TAMU: Texas A&M University

ŞEYTAN DERESI, TURKEY: INA; NGS; SCM Corporation; Alcoa Foundation; Triopian Foundation; F. Alex Nason; Harrison Eiteljorg, Sr

ULUBURUN, TURKEY: INA; NEH; NGS; NSF; TAMU; Institute for Aegean Prehistory; Shell; Cressi-sub

CAPE GELIDONYA, TURKEY: University of Pennsylvania Museum; American Philosophical Society; Nixon Griffis; John Huston of the Council of Underwater Archaeology; Lucius N. Littauer Foundation; British Academy and the Craven Fund; US Divers Co.; La Spirotechnique; Wellcome Foundation; British School at Athens; Bauer Kompressoren; Nikon Company; Polaroid Corporation; INA; TAMU

PABUÇ BURNU, TURKEY: INA; NGS; TAMU; Smothers-Bruni Foundation; Eugene McDermott Foundation; Claude Duthuit; Wellesley College

TEKTAŞ BURNU, TURKEY: INA; TAMU; NGS; NEH; Turkish Airlines

KYRENIA, CYPRUS: Cyprus Department of Antiquities; Oberlin College; University Museum of the University of Pennsylvania; Cook Foundation; National Geographic Society; Cyprus Mines Corporation; National Endowment for the Humanities; UNESCO; Dietrich Foundation; Ford Foundation; Houghton-Carpenter Foundation; Louise Taft Semple Foundation; INA; HIPNT; and generous individual donors

LA SECCA DI CAPISTELLO, ITALY: Sub Sea Oil Services of Milan; INA; TAMU

SERÇE LIMANI HELLENISTIC WRECK, TURKEY: INA; NGS; TAMU

SEA OF GALILEE BOAT, ISRAEL: Model built at TAMU under graduate assistantship funded by the Meadows Foundation

YASSIADA 7TH-CENTURY WRECK, TURKEY: University of Pennsylvania Museum; NGS; Catherwood Foundation; American Philosophical Society; Littauer Foundation through Colgate University; Bauer Kompressoren of Munich; Main Line Divers Club of Philadelphia; Corning Museum of Glass; Nixon Griffis; Ruth and James Magill; Bodrum Museum of Underwater Archaeology; INA; TAMU; NSF; William van Alen

TANTURA LAGOON, ISRAEL: NGS; L.J. Skaggs & Mary C. Skaggs Foundation; Mr & Mrs Harry Kahn II; INA; TAMU College of Liberal Arts; and numerous other supporters

BOZBURUN, TURKEY: INA; NEH; TAMU; Smothers Foundation; Türk Hava Yoları (Turkish Airlines); Efes Brewing; MARES Diving Equipment; Paradise Scuba; Feyyaz Subay & Fey Diving; Mary & Richard Rosenberg; Hazel & Ron Vandehey; Cem Boyner; Jon Faucher; John DeLapa; Danielle Feeney; George Robb; the Muhtar and people of Selimiye; and numerous others, including INA members who contributed to the 1998 annual appeal

SERÇE LIMANI 11TH-CENTURY WRECK, TURKEY: NEH; INA; NGS; TAMU; NSF; Corning Glass Works Foundation; F. Alex Nason; Ashland Oil Company

ÇAMALTI BURNU, TURKEY: Istanbul University Research Fund; Turkish Ministry of Culture; Turkish Foundation of Underwater Archaeology (TINA); French Institute of Anatolian Studies (IFEA); the Turkish Army; NGS; INA; and many generous individuals

BLACK SEA DEEP-WATER PROJECT
NSF; NGS; Florida State University; INA; IFE

SHINAN WRECK, KOREA: South Korean Cultural Property Preservation Bureau; South Korean Navy; National Maritime Museum at Mokpo; and NGS for Donald Keith's visits to the site

ALMERE COG, ZUIDERSEE, NETHERLANDS: Museum voor Scheepsarcheologie; Ketelhaven International Association for the Exchange of Students for Technical Experience; INA; TAMU

KO SI CHANG, THAILAND: Western Australian Museum; Australian Research Council

YASSIADA OTTOMAN WRECK, TURKEY: INA; TAMU; Bodrum Museum

"SHIP IN A HAY FIELD, ZUIDERSEE, NETHERLANDS: Nederlands Instituut voor Scheeps- en OnderwaterArcheologie (Netherlands Institute for Ship and Underwater Archaeology); TAMU

NOSSA SENHORA DOS MÁRTIRES, PORTUGAL: Instituto Portugues de Arqueologia; and the Portuguese Navy and MARCASACAIS for docking facilities

MONTE CRISTI PIPE WRECK, DOMINICAN REPUBLIC: RPM Nautical Foundation; Ronald Halbert; Neil Blaine Fisher; Don Pedro Borrell Bentz; Marvin Omar Hall; Malinda Mary Hall; Francis Soto Tejeda; Earthwatch; INA; TAMU

LA BELLE, TEXAS, USA: The survey was sponsored by the Texas Historical Commission, Trull Foundation, Kathryn O'Connor Foundation, and Texas Department of Transportation's Intermodal Surface Transportation Efficiency Act program; with equipment donations by Trimble Navigation, Inc. and Compaq Computer Corporation. Conservation is sponsored by the Texas Historical Commission; TAMU; Baldor Electric; Dow Chemical Company; Dow Corning Corporation; Dynacon, Inc.; Fibergrate Composite Structures, Inc.; Fuji NDT Systems; Huntsman Chemicals; Mallinckrodt-Baker, Inc.; INA; and donations of equipment and supplies by over 250 other generous firms and individuals

PORT ROYAL, JAMAICA: TAMU; INA; Jamaica Defense Force; Kaiser Aluminum Corporation; Port Royal Brotherhood

SANTO ANTONIO DE TANNA, KENYA: NGS; INA; Charles Consolvo; Harry Kahn; National Museums of Kenya; Kenya Navy; Gulbenkian Foundation; Western Australian Maritime Museum; elements of the Royal Navy, Royal Air Force, and British Army particularly the Royal Engineers Diving Unit; Kenya Port Authority; Bamburi Cement Co.; Hamo Sassoon; DiveCon; Portuguese Navy; TAMU; British School in Eastern Africa; East African Marine Engineering Ltd; Mombasa Club Ltd; Frederick Mayer; Conway Plough; the Hinawy Family; Fort Jesus Museum; the people of Mombasa and generous individuals who gave donations or gifts in kind.

GREAT BASSES REEF, SRI LANKA: Western Australian Museum; Australian Research Council

SADANA ISLAND, EGYPT: Amoco Foundation; Billings Ruddock; NGS; INA; John & Donnie Brock Foundation; Harry & Joan Kahn; George & Marilyn Lodge; Richard & Mary Rosenberg; Danielle Feency. And the generous assistance of the Supreme Council of Antiquities of Egypt, the American Research Center in Egypt, and many individuals and organizations described on http://www.adventurecorps.com/sadana/inasponsors.html

CLYDESDALE PLANTATION VESSEL, SOUTH CAROLINA, USA: INA; South Carolina Institute of Archeology and Anthropology; Rusty Fleetwood and the Coastal Heritage Society, Savannah; 24th Infantry Division (Mechanized) Museum, Ft. Stewart, Georgia; Judy Wood and the US Army Corps of Engineers, Savannah District; Craig and Stanley Lester

DEFENCE, PENOBSCOT BAY, MAINE, USA: INA; TAMU; NGS; Maine Bicentennial Commission; Maine State Museum; Maine Maritime Academy; Maine Historic Preservation Commission; Earthwatch

BETSY, YORKTOWN, VIRGINIA, USA: Yorktown Shipwreck Archaeological Project; Commonwealth of Virginia; County of York; East Carolina University Maritime Studies Program; NGS; INA; NEH; TAMU Nautical Archaeology Program; US Dept. of the Interior; HCRS Maritime Grants Program; Yorktown Maritime Heritage Foundation; Amoco Foundation; Max and Victoria Dreyfus Foundation; Norfolk Foundation; Virginia Institute of Marine Science; The College of William and Mary

WRECK OF THE TEN SAIL, CAYMAN ISLANDS: TAMU College of Liberal Arts dissertation award; Cayman Islands National Museum; and equipment and services donated by INA, Atlantis Research Submersibles, Morritts Tortuga Club, Tortuga Divers, Keith Moorehead of NGS, and the yacht Platinum

CLEOPATRA'S BARGE, KAUAI, USA: Ship Plans Fund; National Museum of American History; Smithsonian Research Opportunities Fund; Salem Marine Society, Salem, MA; and, in Hawaii, The Princeville Corporation and Hotel, Princeville; Bay Island Watersports, Princeville; Save Our Seas and Bali Hai Realty, Inc., Hanalei; Sunrise Diving Adventures, Kapa'a; Ship Stores Gallery of Kapa'a

HORSE FERRY, LAKE CHAMPLAIN, USA: Lake Champlain Maritime Museum; Vermont Division for Historic Preservation; TAMU; INA; Ray Siegfried II; John & Ellie Stern; Harry Kahn

HEROINE, RED RIVER, OKLAHOMA, USA: Oklahoma Historical Society; TAMU; Oklahoma Department of Transportation; INA; Harry Kahn; Carrington Weems; and a "Creative and Scholarly Activities" grant provided by the TAMU Office of the Vice President for Research

DENBIGH, GALVESTON, TEXAS, USA: Albert & Ethel Herzstein Charitable Foundation of Houston; Anchorage Foundation of New Braunfels; Communities Foundation of Texas; Brown Foundation, Houston; Ed Rachal Foundation of Corpus Christi; Hillcrest Foundation of Dallas, founded by Mrs. W.W. Caruth, Sr.; Horlock Foundation, Houston; Houston Endowment, Inc.; Strake Foundation of Houston; Summerfield G. Roberts Foundation of Dallas; Summerlee Foundation of Dallas; TAMU-Galveston; Joseph Ballard Archeology Fund of the Texas Historical Foundation of Austin; Trull Foundation of Palacios

LAKE CHAMPLAIN SAILING CANAL BOATS, USA: City of Burlington, Vermont; Freeman Foundation; Champlain Basin Program; Lake Champlain Maritime Museum; Lintilhac Foundation; Lois & J. Warren McClure; INA; TAMU; University of Vermont; Vermont Division for Historic Preservation; Waterfront Diving Center

TITANIC, ATLANTIC OCEAN: National Oceanic and Atmospheric Administration

TRUK LAGOON, PACIFIC OCEAN: Western Australian Museum; Australian Research Council; Prospero Productions

D-DAY LANDINGS, NORMANDY, FRANCE: US Naval Historical Center Underwater Archaeology Branch; Discovery Channel; British Broadcasting Corporation; Oceaneering International; INA; TAMU

Of course we are all most grateful to those national and state governments who permitted our research in their waters, and to the local museums that curate and display our finds for the public.

Sources of Illustrations

a: above; b: below; c: center; l: left; r: right

The following abbreviations are used to identify sources: CP – Courtney Platt; DAF – Donald A. Frey; IFE/IAO – Institute for Exploration, Mystic, CT/Institute for Archaeological Oceanography, URI/GSO; INA – Institute of Nautical Archaeology; JDB – John D. Broadwater; JG – Jeremy Green; LCMMC – Lake Champlain Maritime Museum Collection; ML – ML Design © Thames & Hudson Ltd, London; MSM – Maine State Museum; NAP – Nautical Archaeological Program, TAMU; NISA – Netherlands Institute for Ship- and Underwater Archaeology; PB – Peter Bull Art Studio © Thames & Hudson Ltd, London; PT – Peter Throckmorton; R/V *AMK* – Courtesy of R/V *Akademik Mstislav Keldysh*; S/NMAH – Courtesy of the Smithsonian/National Museum of American History – Transportation; SWK – Susan Womer Katzev

1 DAF; 2–3 Alexander Mustard; 5c DAF; 5b SWK; 6a DAF; 6c H. Edward Kim/National Geographic; 6b José Pessoa (CNANS archives); 7a Elizabeth Greene; 7c S/NMAH; 7b INA; 10–11a JDB; 11b Robin Piercy; 12 PT; 13al DAF; 13br Davis Meltzer; 14 PT; 15 DAF; 16al Waldemar Illing; 16–17b DAF; 17a Charles R. Nicklin, Jr; 18–19a University of Pennsylvania Museum; 18bl Tony Boegeman; 18–19b DAF; 20 Robin Piercy; 21a JDB; 21br JDB; 22 JDB; 23bl Friends of *Hunley*; 23br Friends of *Hunley*; 24 Tufan Turanlı; 25c Library of Congress, Washington D.C.; 25b US Navy, NOAA *Monitor* Collection; 26l Xu hai bin; 26-27a Larry LePage; 26-27b Dennis Denton; 28 DAF; 30a DAF; 30b ML; 31cl JDB; 31b JDB; 32a INA; 32b Robin Piercy; 33a John Cassils; 33c John Cassils; 34bl DAF; 34–35a INA; 35bl INA; 36 Cemal Pulak and Wendy Van-Duivenvoorde; 37a DAF; 37b DAF; 38al DAF; 38–39a Shih-Han Samuel Lin; 39b DAF; 40l DAF; 40r DAF; 41a DAF; 41b DAF; 42a DAF; 42c DAF; 42b DAF; 43a DAF; 43b DAF; 44a PB after Cemal Pulak; 44b DAF; 45 DAF; 46a DAF; 46b Egypt Exploration Society; 47a DAF; 47b DAF; 48–49 PT; 49r Herb Greer; 50a Herb Greer; 50b PT; 51cl DAF; 51ac DAF; 51ar DAF; 51c DAF; 51cr DAF; 51br DAF; 52–53a PT; 52b DAF; 53ar from *The Tomb of Huy* by Nina de Garis Davis & Alan H. Gardiner, Egypt Exploration Society, 1926; 54l DAF; 54–55 DAF; 55r DAF; 56 DAF; 58a John Veltri; 58b ML; 59 DAF; 60a Sheila Matthews; 60cr DAF; 60b DAF; 61 Sheila Matthews; 62l Sheila Matthews; 62r Volkan Kaya; 63a PB after Mark Polzer; 63b British Museum, London; 64–65b CP; 65a British Museum, London; 65br CP; 66a CP; 66–67b CP; 67ar CP; 67br DAF; 68a DAF; 68c DAF; 69al DAF; 69ar CP; 69bl PB after Robert La Pointe; 69br CP; 70–71a JG and Sheila Matthews; 70b INA; 71ar Donald Demers; 72–73 Bates Littlehales; 73ar Michael L. Katzev; 74al Michael L. Katzev; 74ar SWK; 74–75b SWK; 75ac SWK; 75ar SWK; 76a SWK; 76b SWK; 77ar SWK; 77b Richard Schlecht; 78al Ira Block; 78ar SWK; 78–79b Yiannis Vichos, HIPNT; 80 Donald H. Keith; 81a Donald H. Keith; 81b DAF; 82–83 INA; 83r DAF; 84 DAF; 85al DAF; 85bl DAF; 85r DAF; 86 DAF; 88a DAF; 88b ML; 89 Shelley Wachsmann; 90a William H. Charlton Jr; 90b William H. Charlton Jr; 91a Danny Syon; 91bl Jim Lyle; 91br Jim Lyle; 92ar Robert

Goodman; 92–93b Charles R. Nicklin, Jr; 93br University of Pennsylvania Museum; 94al Robert Goodman; 94ar DAF; 94cl DAF; 94bl Donald M. Rosencrantz; 95 DAF; 96al DAF; 96–97b Bobbe Baker; 97al Oğuz Hamza; 97ar Bodrum Museum of Underwater Archaeology; 98bl Shelley Wachsmann; 98ar Shelley Wachsmann; 98–99b Shelley Wachsmann; 99ar Arik Baltinester; 100–101 DAF; 101cr DAF; 101br DAF; 102 INA; 103 INA; 104a INA; 104bl DAF; 104bc DAF; 105a DAF; 105b DAF; 106–107 Donald H. Keith; 107br Jonathan Blair; 108–109 Jonathan Blair; 109ar DAF; 110 DAF; 111 DAF; 112a DAF; 112b DAF; 113a Cemal Pulak; 113b DAF; 114a PB after J. Richard Steffy; 114b DAF; 115al DAF; 115ar DAF; 115cr DAF; 115b DAF; 116al DAF; 116ar DAF; 116cr DAF; 117a DAF; 117b DAF; 118–119 Engin Aygün; 119r Engin Aygün; 120 Recep Dönmez; 121 Recep Dönmez; 122a Nergis Günsenin; 122b Recep Dönmez; 123a Recep Dönmez; 123c Nergis Gunsenin; 123b Ufuk Kocobaş; 124–125 Cheryl Ward; 125bl IFE/IAO; 125br IFE/IAO; 126a IFE/IAO; 126b Dave Wright; 127a Aurora Photos, Photo David McLain; 127b IFE/IAO; 128 JG, Department of Maritime Archaeology, WA Maritime Museum; 130a DAF; 130b ML; 131 H. Edward Kim/National Geographic; 132–133 H. Edward Kim/National Geographic; 133ar British Library, London; 133br H. Edward Kim/National Geographic; 134l NISA/ROB; 134r NISA/ROB; 135a NISA/ROB; 135b NISA/ROB; 136bl Brian Richards; 136ar Brian Richards; 137al Brian Richards; 137ar Brian Richards; 137br Private Collection; 138–139 DAF; 139ar INA; 140 DAF; 141al DAF; 141ar PB after Jay Rosloff; 141b Cemal Pulak; 142 JG; 144a INA; 144b ML; 145 Robert S. Neyland; 146a Robert S. Neyland; 146b Robert S. Neyland; 147 Robert S. Neyland; 148bl Pinto, Maria Helena Mendes, Biombos Namban, Lisbon: Museu Nacional de Arte Antiga, 1993; 148ar Memoria das Armadas, Biblioteca da Academia das Ciências de Lisboa; 149a Guilherme Garcia (CNANS archives); 149b Pedro Gonçalves (CNANS archives); 150 Pedro Gonçalves (CNANS archives); 151a José Pessoa (CNANS archives); 151cr Pedro Gonçalves (CNANS archives); 151br PB after Filipe Castro; 152l Jerome Lynn Hall; 152–153 Jerome Lynn Hall; 153bl Jerome Lynn Hall; 153ar Tinken Museum of Art, San Diego, CA; 154al Courtesy of PIMA Archives; 154cl Jillian Nelson; 154bl Pedro Borrell Bentz; 155a Larry Sanders; 155b Len Tantillo; 156 Center for American History, The University of Texas at Austin; 157a NAP; 157c Clif Bosler; 157b Texas Historical Commission; 158al NAP; 158b Texas Historical Commission; 159 Texas Historical Commission; 160a NAP; 160c NAP; 160bl NAP; 160–161b NAP; 161a NAP; 162a NAP; 162b NAP; 163al NAP; 163ar NAP; 163br Denis Lee; 164ar Science Year, The World Book Science Annual 1982; 164b Dennis Denton; 165ar INA; 165b INA; 166al Oliver Cox; 166ar Luis Marden; 166bl INA; 167a Broadside, London, 1692; 167b W.D. Vaughn; 168al INA; 168ar INA; 168bl INA; 168br INA; 169 INA; 170al INA; 170–171a INA; 170bl INA; 171cl INA; 171bl INA; 172–173 Noel Jones; 173a From *Descripçam da Fortaleza de Sofala, e das mais da Índia com uma Rellaçam das Religiões todas q há no mesmo Estado, pelo Cosmógrafo Mor António de Mariz Carneiro*, 1639; 174 Hamo Sassoon; 175a Noel Jones; 175b Robert K. Vincent; 176a Robert K. Vincent; 176b Hamo Sassoon; 177ac Robert K. Vincent; 177ar Robert K. Vincent; 177br Robert K. Vincent; 178a JG; 178–179b Netia Piercy; 179a PB after Caroline Sassoon; 180 Udo Kefrig; 182a Philip Voss; 182b ML; 183 Patrick Baker, Department of Maritime Archaeology, WA Maritime Museum; 184–185 Patrick Baker, Department of

Maritime Archaeology, WA Maritime Museum; 185a Patrick Baker, Department of Maritime Archaeology, WA Maritime Museum; 186–187b Netia Piercy; 187a Lyman Labry; 188al Meredith Kato; 188bl Netia Piercy; 188br Meredith Kato; 189a Meredith Kato; 189br Alan Flanigan; 190b Netia Piercy; 190–191a Alan Flanigan; 191a From *Travels through Arabia, and Other Countries in the East*, Niebuhr, C.,1792; 191br Howard Wellman; 192 Fred Hocker; 193 Fred Hocker; 194 Courtesy of the Mariner's Museum, Newport News, VA; 195 Philip Voss; 196al Roger Smith; 196ar David Switzer; 196-197b PB after Peter Hentschel; 197cl David Switzer; 197cr MSM; 197br David Switzer; 198al MSM; 198ar MSM; 198cl MSM; 198bl MSM; 199al David Switzer; 199cr MSM; 200–201 Courtesy of the Mariner's Museum, Newport News, VA; 201bl National Portrait Gallery, London; 202a National Maritime Museum, London; 202b Bates Littlehales; 203a JDB, courtesy Virginia Department of Historic Resources; 203b Bates Littlehales; 204bl Bates Littlehales; 204–205a JDB, courtesy Virginia Department of Historic Resources; 205ar JDB, courtesy Virginia Department of Historic Resources; 205cr Roy Anderson; 206 Margaret Leshikar-Denton; 207ar from *One Hundred Silhouette Portraits from the Collection of Francis Wellesley*, Oxford University Press, 1912; 207bl Royal Gazette XVI, no. 4, 18–25 January 1794, Jamaica, from the Public Record Office, Kew, London; 207br Collection Jean Boudriot, France; 208bl Margaret Leshikar-Denton; 208br Indiana University SRD; 208-209a Dennis Denton; 209ar Mike Guderian; 209br Photo courtesy of Lennon Christian, Cayman Islands Government Information Services; 210 R/V*AMK*; 212a Amy Borgens; 212b ML; 213l Peabody Essex Museum; 213r Photo Courtesy Peabody Essex Museum M8255; 214a Courtesy of the Bernice Pauahi Bishop Museum; 214b S/NMAH; 215a Painting by Richard W. Rogers, S/NMAH; 215cr S/NMAH; 215br S/NMAH; 216al S/NMAH; 216ar Photo by Conservation Research Laboratory, TAMU; 216br S/NMAH; 217a S/NMAH; 217b S/NMAH; 218cr John Butler; 218–219b Vermont Division for Historic Preservation; 219ar John Butler; 219c Kevin Crisman; 220bl Amon Carter Museum, Fort Worth, Texas; 220br Kevin Crisman; 220–221a Carrie Sowden; 221ar Carrie Sowden; 221br Steven Wilson; 222 Private Collection; 223a Brett Phaneuf/Barto Arnold; 223b Andy Hall; 224cr Andy Hall; 224b Andy Hall; 225a Andy Hall; 225bc Helen Dewolf/Barto Arnold; 225br Barto Arnold; 226 Kevin Crisman; 227al LCMMC; 227ac LCMMC; 227ar LCMMC; 227br LCMMC; 228al Pierre LaRocque, LCMMC; 228ar LCMMC; 228bl Kevin Crisman; 229ar Nick Lavecchia, LCMMC; 229bl Eric Bessette, LCMMC; 230–231b Courtesy of the Mariner's Museum, Newport News, VA; 231a R/V*AMK*; 232al Jeremy Weirich; 232ar R/V*AMK*; 233a Sergei Gyduk, courtesy Anatoly Sagalevitch; 233b R/V*AMK*; 234l R/V*AMK*; 234r Produced by Yuri Rzhanov for the National Oceanic and Atmospheric Administration and the University of New Hampshire's Center for Coastal Ocean Mapping; 235l R/V*AMK*; 235r George F. Bass; 236al R/V*AMK*; 236ac R/V*AMK*; 236bl Courtesy of National Oceanic and Atmospheric Administration; 237ar R/V*AMK*; 237bl Jeremy Weirich; 238l US National Archives and Records Administration; 238–239 US National Archives and Records Administration; 239ar JG; 240ar JG; 240–241b JG; 241a JG; 241br Brian Beltz; 242 INA; 243a INA; 243b INA; 244al Courtesy of the BBC and Discovery Channel; 244br Tank Museum, Bovington; 245a Photo © Robert Capa Magnum Photos; 246br Tank Museum, Bovington

Index

Page numbers in *italic* refer to illustrations and in **bold** to main entries